Collins

Cambridge IGCSE®
Business Studies

TEACHER'S GUIDE

Also for Cambridge O Level and Cambridge IGCSE® (9-1)

Denry Machin, James Beere,
Andrew Dean, Mark Gardiner

William Collins' dream of knowledge for all began with the publication of his first book in 1819.

A self-educated mill worker, he not only enriched millions of lives, but also founded a flourishing publishing house. Today, staying true to this spirit, Collins books are packed with inspiration, innovation and practical expertise. They place you at the centre of a world of possibility and give you exactly what you need to explore it.

Collins. Freedom to teach.

Published by Collins
An imprint of HarperCollins*Publishers*
The News Building
1 London Bridge Street
London
SE1 9GF

Browse the complete Collins catalogue at
www.collins.co.uk

© HarperCollins*Publishers* Limited 2018

10 9 8 7 6 5 4 3 2 1

ISBN 978-0-00-825806-1

All rights reserved. No part of this publication may be reproduced, stored in a retrieval system, or transmitted in any form by any means, electronic, mechanical, photocopying, recording or otherwise, without the prior written permission of the Publisher or a licence permitting restricted copying in the United Kingdom issued by the Copyright Licensing Agency Ltd., Barnard's Inn, 86 Fetter Lane, London, EC4A 1EN.

British Library Cataloguing in Publication Data

A catalogue record for this publication is available from the British Library.

Commissioning editor: Rachael Harrison
In-house editor: Lara McMurray
Authors: Denry Machin, James Beere, Andrew Dean, Mark Gardiner, Donna Marie Jestin
Development editors: Alison Silver, Viv Church
Copyeditor: Caroline Low
Proofreader: Karen Williams
Permissions researcher: Rachel Thorne
Cover illustrator: Maria Herbert-Liew
Cover designer: Kevin Robbins
Illustrator: Jouve India Private Ltd
Production controller: Tina Paul
Printed and bound by: CPI
® IGCSE is a registered trademark

The publishers wish to thank Cambridge Assessment International Education for permission to reproduce questions from past IGCSE® Business Studies papers. Cambridge Assessment International Education bears no responsibility for the example answers to questions taken from its past papers, which are contained in this publication. All exam-style questions and sample answers were written by the author(s). In examination, the way marks would be awarded to answers like these may be different.

We are grateful to the following for permission to reproduce copyright material: 3.4.1 Activity sheet, The Kit Kat slogan, © Nestlé. Reproduced with permission; Data in Case Study 3 from *Tanzania Annual tourist arrivals*, The World Bank, 2012, https://data.worldbank.org, © The World Bank; and Figure in Case Study 3 based on data from Tanzania economic indicators, Trading Economics, https://tradingeconomics.com/tanzania/indicators. Reproduced with permission.

MIX
Paper from
responsible sources
FSC™ C007454

This book is produced from independently certified FSC paper to ensure responsible forest management.

For more information visit:
www.harpercollins.co.uk/green

Contents

Downloads of editable learning episodes, worksheets, practical notes and answers are available at www.collins.co.uk/CambridgeInternationalDownloads.

Introduction	v
1 UNDERSTANDING BUSINESS ACTIVITY	**8**
Introduction	8
1.1 Business activity	**9**
1.1.1 The purpose and nature of business activity	9
1.2 Classification of businesses	**16**
1.2.1 Business activity in terms of primary, secondary and tertiary sectors	16
1.2.2 Private sector and public sector	20
1.3 Enterprise, business growth and size	**24**
1.3.1 Enterprise and entrepreneurship	24
1.3.2 The methods and problems of measuring business size	33
1.3.3 Why some businesses grow and others remain small	39
1.3.4 Why some (new or established) businesses fail	44
1.4 Types of business organisation	**48**
1.4.1 Main features of different forms of business organisation	48
1.5 Business objectives and stakeholder objectives	**58**
1.5.1 Business objectives and their importance	58
1.5.2 The role of stakeholder groups involved in business activity	63
1.5.3 Objectives of private and public sector enterprises	68
Key terms revision	72
2 PEOPLE IN BUSINESS	**73**
Introduction	73
2.1 Motivating employees	**74**
2.1.1 The importance of a well-motivated workforce	74
2.1.2 Methods of motivation	79
2.2 Organisation and management	**83**
2.2.1 Organisational charts	83
2.2.2 Role of management	86
2.2.3 Leadership styles	90
2.2.4 Trade unions	93
2.3 Recruitment, selection and training of employees	**96**
2.3.1 Recruiting and selecting employees	96
2.3.2 The importance of training and methods of training	100
2.3.3 Reducing the workforce	103
2.3.4 Legal controls over employment and their impact	107
2.4 Internal and external communication	**111**
2.4.1 Achieving effective communication	111
2.4.2 Communication barriers	114
Key terms revision	117
3 MARKETING	**118**
Introduction	118
3.1 Marketing, competition and the customer	**119**
3.1.1 The role of marketing	119
3.1.2 Market changes	122
3.1.3 Niche marketing and mass marketing	125
3.1.4 Market segmentation	128
3.2 Market research	**131**
3.2.1 The role and methods of market research	131
3.2.2 Presentation and use of market research results	135
3.3 Marketing mix	**139**
3.3.1 Product	139
3.3.2 Price	143
3.3.3 Place – distribution channels	146
3.3.4 Promotion	150
3.3.5 Technology and the marketing mix	155
3.4 Marketing strategy	**158**
3.4.1 Appropriate marketing strategies	158
3.4.2 Legal controls related to marketing	162
3.4.3 Entering foreign markets	165
Key terms revision	168

4	**Operations Management**	**169**
	Introduction	169
4.1	**Production of goods and services**	**170**
	4.1.1 The meaning of production	170
	4.1.2 The main methods of production	175
	4.1.3 How technology has changed production methods	179
4.2	**Costs, scale of production and break-even analysis**	**183**
	4.2.1 Identify and classify costs	183
	4.2.2 Economies and diseconomies of scale	187
	4.2.3 Break-even analysis	192
4.3	**Achieving quality production**	**199**
	4.3.1 The importance of quality and how to achieve quality production	199
4.4	**Location decisions**	**203**
	4.4.1 Factors influencing location and relocation decisions	203
	Key terms revision	207
5	**FINANCIAL INFORMATION AND DECISIONS**	**208**
	Introduction	208
5.1	**Business finance: needs and sources**	**209**
	5.1.1 The need for business finance	209
	5.1.2 The main sources of finance	214
5.2	**Cash flow forecasting and working capital**	**220**
	5.2.1 The importance of cash and of cash flow forecasting	220
	5.2.2 Working capital and liquidity	225
5.3	**Income statements**	**229**
	5.3.1 What profit is and why it is important	229
	5.3.2 Income statements	238
5.4	**Statement of financial position**	**245**
	5.4.1 The main elements of a statement of financial position	245
	5.4.2 Interpreting a statement of financial position	252
5.5	**Analysis of accounts**	**256**
	5.5.1 Profitability and financial performance	256
	5.5.4 Why and how accounts are used	260
	Key terms revision	265
6	**EXTERNAL INFLUENCES ON BUSINESS ACTIVITY**	**266**
	Introduction	266
6.1	**Economic issues**	**267**
	6.1.1 Business cycle	267
	6.1.2 How government control over the economy affects business activity and how businesses may respond	270
6.2	**Environmental and ethical issues**	**275**
	6.2.1 Environmental concerns and ethical issues as both opportunities and constraints for businesses	275
6.3	**Business and the international economy**	**279**
	6.3.1 The importance of globalisation	279
	6.3.2 The importance and growth of multinational companies (MNCs)	284
	6.3.3 The impact of exchange rate changes	288
	Key terms revision	291
Scheme of work		**292**

Available online:
- MS Word versions of the above contents
- Activity sheets
- Sample answers to exam sections
- Levels of response and sample answers
- An additional bank of case studies with accompanying questions.

Introduction

As we declare on the opening page of the Student's Book, Business Studies is an amazing subject.

The joy of teaching Business Studies is that examples, case studies and real world illustrations are everywhere. The challenge, though, is that many of the topics are abstract and require students to grasp concepts of which they have little prior knowledge. Moreover, Business Studies has its own vocabulary and a unique and sometimes confusing terminology; in the international context especially, teaching Business Studies shares many similarities with teaching students another language.

We have designed this Teacher's Guide to help.

Downloadable material

Printable, editable resources in MS Word format are available as digital downloads at www.collins.co.uk/CambridgeInternationalDownloads so that you can tailor your lessons and activities. The content has been arranged in folders by section and then by topic, with all the materials you need so that you can quickly and easily prepare for your lessons.

Lesson plans

Every topic in the Student's Book has an associated 'lesson plan' within this Teacher's Guide that includes:

- a set of **aims** (linked to the Student's Book)
- related **key terms**
- a list of **resources** needed for the lesson
- suggested **starter** activities
- a series of **main lesson** ideas
- suggested use of the Student's Book **Case Study** and **Skills Activity** features
- at least one **key activity** (with associated Activity sheets and Activity sheet teacher notes)
- suggested **plenary** activities.

Activity sheets

The Activity sheets form the heart of this Teacher's Guide. They have been carefully designed to scaffold learning, to make topics practical, real and relevant and, above all, to make lessons engaging. Examples of activities include:

- a **categorisation exercise** on motivation theory
- a trade union **role-play exercise**
- a **pair-work crossword** on reducing the size of the workforce
- a **memory game** on types of internal and external communication
- a communication **listening activity**
- a **dominoes activity** on the meaning of production
- a **gapped reading activity** on how technology has changed production methods
- a **ranking exercise** on factors influencing location and relocation
- a **snakes and ladders game** requiring knowledge on entering markets abroad.

Every activity is designed to ensure that students not only develop their knowledge but also develop the relevant examination skills of application, analysis and evaluation. Activity sheet teacher notes are provided for each activity. They identify which skills are addressed, give an overview of the content, offer timing guidance and give detailed instructions on the procedure.

The activity instructions are presented as easy-to-follow, step-by-step guidelines. There are **Teacher tips** that offer useful advice or alternative approaches and **Extension tasks** that can be used for differentiation.

Each task has also been designed with the needs of learners of **English as an Additional Language (EAL)** or **English as a Second Language (ESL)** in mind. As experienced international schoolteachers, we know how important it is to make resources accessible to all students. Many of the activities are based on techniques and tools adapted from EAL teaching strategies, and all are informed by many years of adapting resources for the international market.

Each activity is also tried and tested. We have run these activities within our own classes, asked for student feedback and adjusted accordingly. If students did not like (or did not respond well to) an activity, we altered it and asked for students' feedback again. You can be confident, therefore, that these activities work, that students will enjoy them and that – above all – students will learn from them.

Answers

In addition to the activities, this Teacher's Guide also acts as a companion to the Student's Book. For each Student's Book topic, we provide detailed answers to Knowledge Check and Exam Practice questions, as well as guidance on possible Skills Activity outcomes.

Additional resources

You will also find included printed in this Teacher's Guide:

- **Key terms revision** for each section of the Student's Book that you can use to check students' knowledge and vocabulary
- an exemplar **Scheme of work**.

Case studies

There are several case studies in each chapter of the Student's Book. These have been written to be as up-to-date as possible, as well as engaging and inspiring for students on the course. You may wish to expand upon the content in the book by researching further details of the case study online and creating activity sheets built around these.

The case studies in the Student's Book can be used in different ways in the classroom: you may wish to set them as independent reading, either prior to the start of subject teaching or as homework. The case studies can be read alongside teaching of the content and relevant questions asked to gauge understanding.

Some general questions you may ask include:

- What is the key issue in this case study?
- What are the key facts in this case study?
- What internal/external influences acted on the business in this case study?
- What impact do you think the decision/event in the case study would have had upon both internal and external stakeholders of the business?
- What advantages/disadvantages do you think the decision/event in the case study would have had for the business?
- Do you agree with the outcome of the case study? Justify your answer.
- What theory/method is the case study demonstrating?
- Can you think of any similar examples to the case study?

We hope you enjoy using this Teacher's Guide as much as we enjoyed writing it. We designed it to save you time, to make planning and preparation easier, and to help you help your students learn – it is our sincere hope that it achieves those aims.

Denry Machin, James Beere, Andrew Dean and Mark Gardiner

1 Understanding business activity

Introduction

Many students will have some existing knowledge of business activity and the various forms it takes around the world. Although many students will have experienced opportunity costs, seen specialisation and engaged with different types of businesses, they may not have developed detailed knowledge of these concepts. The topics in Section 1 may appear to some students fairly straightforward, yet students will be expected to apply these concepts to businesses of different sizes and sectors.

The activities in this section allow students to understand the key concepts before challenging them to analyse and evaluate them. The activities include:

- a multiple-choice activity on needs and wants
- a linking activity on opportunity costs and specialisation
- voting on the method of adding value
- sorting businesses into sectors
- a case study on the public and private sector
- designing an entrepreneur using their skills and attributes
- a matching activity on the parts of the business plan
- a case study on business size
- paired mini case studies on business growth
- a voting task on business failure
- a business ownership case study
- a case study that explores business objectives
- paired discussions on stakeholder conflict.

To introduce students to the concepts they will study and to help gauge prior student knowledge, a useful starter activity might be:

> Arrange students into small groups of around 3–5. Each group will need a sheet of A3 paper and some pens.
>
> Propose the following statement to the students: 'Businesses all aim to make large profits.'
>
> Ask students to discuss this statement in their groups and write down points they may use for either side of the argument. Students may identify some of the key ideas such as profit and revenue and may discuss whether sectors, business sizes or ages, or ownership types affects this.
>
> Students may need some additional ideas to help them. For example, ask students to consider whether business ownership plays a part in this statement being correct or not.
>
> This activity will engage the students in many of the section's topics.

The business activity topic is ideal for allowing students to learn the basic ideas of business studies, as well as some of the key terms they will use throughout the course. Those students with prior understanding will be able to build and link these ideas.

Use the Skills builder at the end of Section 1 to help students develop their application skills and their understanding of why different businesses have differing aims, ownership types and measures of size.

1.1 Business activity

1.1.1 THE PURPOSE AND NATURE OF BUSINESS ACTIVITY

Aims (1.1.1)

Knowledge	Resources
By the end of this section, students will understand: • the concepts of needs and wants, scarcity and opportunity cost • the importance of specialisation • the purpose of business activity • the concept of adding value and how added value can be increased.	• Student's Book pages 8–16 • Activity sheets 1.1.1A, 1.1.1B and 1.1.1C • A range of products such as a football, trainer (training shoe) and toy car • Access to ICT (if possible)

Key business terms

added value; capital; division of labour; enterprise; factors of production; land; needs; opportunity costs; scarcity; specialisation; wants

Lesson ideas

You should aim to cover the materials in 1.1.1 in three one-hour lessons, plus, as appropriate, homework assignments. Homework tasks could be answering the Knowledge check questions (pages 13 and 16 of the Student's Book) or end of section assessments. To achieve the Aims for this topic, we recommend doing some of the following activities over the course of the lessons.

Starter suggestions

Lesson 1 Discussion: Ask the class: 'What resources are needed to make the following products: Nike footballs, cars, diamond rings and houses?' Allow students a few minutes to discuss these products in small groups, then collate the answers on the board. To highlight which of the resources is expensive, ask: 'Why do certain products, such as diamond rings and sports cars, cost so much money?'

Lesson 2 Brainstorming: Ask the class to work in pairs to identify reasons why high-profile footballers such as Wayne Rooney, or movie stars such as Chris Hemsworth, get paid such large amounts of money. Ask students to focus on the skills needed in those professions and lead into a discussion about specialisation and its importance. Ask students to think of businesses, individuals and countries that specialise in a product or service.

Lesson 3 Discussion: Ask students to work in pairs to list the reasons why businesses exist. You may want to suggest a range of businesses to stimulate discussion of reasons other than 'money', including examples of small local businesses, social enterprises and charities.

Main lesson activities

Need versus want: Ask students to discuss the difference between a need and a want. Students will need to know this for Activity 1.1.1A. Discuss their suggestions as a class and write key points on the board.

Student activity: Ask students to complete Activity 1.1.1A, a sorting task that will help them understand the difference between a need and a want. In the second part of the activity, students identify scarce resources.

Discussion: Ask students to work in pairs to identify three things they would want if they had the choice. These should be goods or services. Then ask them to choose only one of these items. Use this to discuss opportunity costs and their impact on everyday decisions.

Ask students to identify a business that specialises in making shoes. They should explain how this business manages to produce so many shoes. Encourage them to discuss the skills of the workforce.

Discussion and note-taking (whole class): Talk students through opportunity costs and specialisation using pages 10–13 of the Student's Book, asking them to take notes as relevant.

Student activity: Ask students to complete Activity 1.1.1B, a linking exercise that will help cement their knowledge of opportunity costs and specialisation.

Discussion: Ask students to discuss in pairs ways in which businesses can add value. They may wish to read pages 15–16 of the Student's Book to help with this. Collate their ideas on the board, with examples, so they can all see the ways of adding value to use in Activity 1.1.1C.

Student activity: Do Activity 1.1.1C with the class. In this activity, students show their understanding of the different ways a business can add value by taking part in a voting game.

Skills activity: Students work in small groups or pairs to complete the Skills activity on page 15 of the Student's Book: they examine the benefits to a business of adding value.

Knowledge check: Ask students to answer the Knowledge check questions on page 16 of the Student's Book (optional).

Tip: This could be given as a homework exercise.

Plenary suggestions

Discussion: Ask individual students around the class to give an example of a need or a want. The rest of the class have to decide which one it is. Then ask individual students to name resources that are scarce. These may include oil, time, skilled labour, money, metals, and so on.

Hot seat: Ask students to work in groups to brainstorm reasons why businesses might face opportunity costs on a daily basis. Then place a chair at the front of the room (the hot seat), and ask a student to come and sit on it. Give the student one of the different levels of specialisation (employees, businesses, regions, countries); they have to name as many benefits/drawbacks of specialisation at that level as they can. Repeat with other students in the hot seat.

Adding value: Give students examples of different products or services – you may wish to use props to support this activity. Ask individual students to say how the business that makes each product/provides each service adds value. Then ask another student to say whether they agree or disagree with this answer.

Answers to Student's Book activities

Skills activities: possible outcomes

Skills activity 1 (page 9)

Students are likely to give a wide range of wants and needs, which may include:

- Needs: food, water, shelter, education.
- Wants: mobile phone, games consoles, cars, toys.

Students should identify that needs and wants will be different in various countries, depending on wealth and standard of living. They may comment on people in certain countries lacking necessities such as water, food and shelter, and having very few of the items that they may want, such as computers. They may also mention that in wealthier countries, such as the USA, many people have many of the items they want.

Final question: What do you notice about wants and needs around the world?

Students should identify that needs and wants vary depending on the wealth of the country and that, within each country, there is variation between people.

Skills activity 2 (page 11)

Students may identify these government-funded businesses or industries: education, health care, armed forces, transport, utilities such as gas and water, and so on.

- Student responses will depend on the country. General ideas may include: money is hard to account for as the businesses do not have to answer to private investors or shareholders; this gives them more freedom.
- Give the following example to students to get them started: keeps people in work, keeps production high, available no matter how old you are (answer: health care).

Skills activity 3 (page 15)

The benefits of adding value might include: increase in revenue; increased profit; increase in market share; higher prices; easy to differentiate the business from its competitors; makes the business unique; helps the business stay ahead of competition.

- Students are likely to choose to order the benefits in different ways. The focus should be on their justification of the order.
- Students might suggest: By selling at a higher price, the business will increase revenue/profit as long as the customer continues to buy it. This means that the business must work hard in marketing themselves and their products.

Extension: Answers might include clothing, food or real estate.

Knowledge check (page 13)

Audi now has a global reputation for comfort and quality. Its range of cars can cost up to $500 000 and is only targeted at the richest customers. Its products include the Audi R8 and Audi RS, two very exclusive cars with only a few thousand of each being made

1. **Define** the term scarcity.

   Scarcity is the shortage of a resource.

   Examples include: oil, wheat or land.

2. **Explain** the opportunity costs to Audi of producing the R8 and RS cars.

   The next best alternative will have been missed.

   Instead of spending large amounts of money on these two models, Audi could have increased spending on marketing and developing new models. Other potential opportunity costs: less money spent on employee wages; fewer employee benefits; less focus given to other models of car.

3. **Explain** how specialisation benefits an employee of Audi.

   Definition: A person, business, region or country focuses on producing one good or service. The employee will be specialised in a certain skill, which may gain them certain benefits.

   Benefits may include: extra pay; can focus on a certain task; can become very skilled at that task and may be offered more jobs.

4. Do you believe that specialisation will benefit Audi when making their cars? **Justify** your answer.

   Examples of benefits: Increased sales revenue; skilled labour, can focus on one particular product and do it well; employees can focus on their particular tasks; improved quality; more efficient use of time and resources; less waste.

   Examples of drawbacks: The lack of diversity may damage the business long term if they become old-fashioned or unpopular; larger costs for Audi because of high wages, specialist machines and resources; low employee morale as they become bored.

   (Students need to cover both sides of the argument, and provide discussion of benefits and drawbacks, as well as justification of the student's position.)

Knowledge check (page 16)

1. **Define** the term added value.

   Creating a product that is worth more than the cost of making it; output is worth more than inputs.

   For example, a car is sold for more than the cost of the inputs.

2. **Explain** two ways in which a business can add value.

   Any two from: design; marketing; quality and efficiency; convenience.

   For example, a business such as Apple adds value by placing its logo on its products. The business's reputation means that customers now associate the logo with high-quality innovative products that allows Apple to add value.

   The design of a product can add value if it is distinct or has a uniqueness that differentiates it from competitors. If the design attracts customers, it will add value.

Additional quality allows businesses to add value as the product is better than competitors.

Also, if the product is sold in a convenient place, the price is likely to be higher, for example in train station convenience stores.

3 **Explain** why businesses can have different purposes.

Purposes include: profit; improving society; helping a specific cause; creating new products; education; creating a brand or listening to stakeholders.

Explanation: businesses with different products often differ in their purpose. For example, Nike's purpose is sales, as opposed to a business that sells medicine and is trying to reduce a medical condition or illness.

1.1.1 The purpose and nature of business activity: Activity A

Activity type

Sorting task

Time

30 minutes

Content

Needs, wants and scarcity

Key terms

need; scarcity; want

Skills practised

AO1: Knowledge and understanding	✓
AO2: Application	✓
AO3: Analysis	
AO4: Evaluation	

Preparation

Make one copy of Activity sheet 1.1.1A for each student in the class.

Aims

To understand the difference between wants and needs, and how these are affected by scarcity (1.1.1)

Procedure

1. Tell students that they are going to work in small groups to complete a sorting task, in which they have to identify which statements represent needs and which represent wants. Students need to decide based on the item in relation to the person in each statement.
2. Divide the class into groups of three to four and give a copy of Activity sheet 1.1.1A to each student.
3. Explain that the students need to work as a team to categorise the statements. They read the statement, decide whether it is a need (N) or a want (W) and write the correct letter in the box.
4. Give students about 10 minutes to do this. Then take feedback from different groups for each statement, asking them to explain their choice of category to the class.
5. Students then complete the second part of the activity sheet. In their groups, students have five to six minutes to make a list of five resources which they think are scarce. The aim of this activity is for them to come up with five resources that other groups do not think of.
6. Ask groups to feed back and award one point for every resource that no other group has. For example, many groups may have oil on their list, whereas not many groups may think of capital. You will have to make judgements as to whether the resources are scarce or not.

Teacher tip: Group students so that there is a mix of abilities in each group, so more able students can support the less able ones in terms of subject knowledge and language.

Variation: Adapt the list of needs and wants to those of a specific business or a person in the class.

Extension: Students answer the exam-style question at the bottom of the activity sheet.

Suggested answers to Activity sheet 1.1.1A

Needs and wants: 1 W, 2 N, 3 W, 4 W, 5 N, 6 N, 7 W, 8 N, 9 N, 10 N

Scarce resources: *Examples include:* coal, oil, gas, land, trees

Extension question: The key ideas to mention in this question are: choice of uses for the scarce resource means that its value increases, lack of supply and time/cost needed to make the product.

Example answers: Petrol: The time taken and resources needed to create petrol from oil result in a high price. Petrol is also used by millions of people and businesses and is seen as a necessity.

Diamond rings: Diamonds are very scarce and are therefore rare. This increases their price as not everyone can have one.

1.1.1 The purpose and nature of business activity: Activity B

Activity type

Matching game

Time

20 minutes

Content

Opportunity costs

Key terms

choice; opportunity cost; resources; specialisation

Aims

To understand and explain examples of opportunity costs and specialisation (1.1.1)

Skills practised

AO1: Knowledge and understanding	✓
AO2: Application	✓
AO3: Analysis	
AO4: Evaluation	

Preparation

Make one copy of Activity sheet 1.1.1B for each group of two to three students in the class.

Procedure

1 Tell students that they are going to play a matching game, in which they will have to match business decisions with the correct examples of opportunity costs.

2 Divide students into groups of two or three and give a copy of Activity sheet 1.1.1B to each group.

3 Ask students to work together to match the business situations with the correct opportunity costs.

4 Discuss the answers with students. Nominate individual groups/students to justify their choices.

5 Students then complete the task on specialisation: For each scenario, they should discuss and decide on an advantage and a disadvantage that is specific to the content. They should be ready to explain their reasons in the feedback session.

Teacher tip: When students are offering their suggestions, ask other students whether they agree or disagree. This peer observation will maintain the focus of the class and will help stimulate discussion and debate.

Variation: Cut out the different business decisions and opportunity costs. Divide the class into two groups. Give one business decision to each student/pair in the first group and one opportunity cost to each student/pair in the second group. Students walk around the classroom to find a student/pair from the other group. They read aloud what is on their pieces of paper and decide if their statements match. If not, they continue until they have found the matching statement.

Extension: Ask students to develop their understanding of opportunity costs by identifying a business that has made/makes a choice every day. Ask students how these choices may impact on the business.

> **Suggested answers to Activity sheet 1.1.1B**
>
> **Opportunity costs:** 1g, 2d, 3e, 4f, 5a, 6b, 7c, 8h
>
> **Specialisation:** *Example answers:*
>
> 1 Advantage: Can charge a higher wage for his/her skills. Disadvantage: The cakes and pastries may become unpopular and he/she may lose his/her job.
>
> 2 Advantage: Large market to sell to. Disadvantage: Another method of transport or competitor could enter the market.
>
> 3 Advantage: Large amounts are sold abroad as they are in demand globally, raising income for Jamaica. Disadvantage: If another country starts to grow bananas, Jamaica could lose its income.
>
> 4 Advantage: Reputation is created allowing higher prices to be charged. Disadvantage: If people have less money (for example, in a recession), they may not buy expensive cars so the region loses their business.

1.1.1 The purpose and nature of business activity: Activity C

Activity type

Voting game

Time

10–15 minutes

Content

Adding value

Key term

adding value

Aims

To show understanding of ways in which businesses add value (1.1.1)

Skills practised

AO1: Knowledge and understanding	✓
AO2: Application	✓
AO3: Analysis	✓
AO4: Evaluation	

Preparation

Make one photocopy of the voting cards on Activity sheet 1.1.1C for each student in the class. Either cut these out or ask students to do this. Prepare a list of businesses, ranging from local small businesses to large multinational companies from around the world. You may also wish to use specific products such as Nike trainers, Microsoft software, and so on.

Procedure

1. Tell students that they are going to take part in a voting game. You will name examples of businesses/products and students must decide how they think each business/product adds value. They hold up the appropriate voting card to indicate their choice.

2. Give a set of voting cards from Activity sheet 1.1.1C to each student in the class. Ask students to cut these out if you have not already done so.

3. Start the activity by naming a business or product. If students think that the business uses more than one method of adding value, they should pick the method that they think the business uses the most or that is the most important to the business.

4. You could use the examples of businesses (Nokia, Samsung and Apple) from the case study features (pages 11 and 15 of the Student's Book) to start the activity. These may help students to understand the activity.

5. Generate discussion with students, asking them to justify their choices. Call on students who have voted differently to generate a debate.

Teacher tip: When students are offering their suggestions, ask other students whether they agree or disagree. This peer observation will maintain the focus of the class and will help stimulate discussion and debate.

Variation: Photocopy the voting cards on to A3 paper and place one card in each corner of the classroom. For each business/product you name, students must go and stand next to the method of adding value they think the business uses. Ask students to justify why they have chosen that method.

Extension: Ask students to order the voting cards, from easiest for the business to achieve to most difficult, or from most to least used.

1.2 Classification of businesses

1.2.1 BUSINESS ACTIVITY IN TERMS OF PRIMARY, SECONDARY AND TERTIARY SECTORS

Aims (1.2.1)

Knowledge	Resources
By the end of this section, students will understand: • the basis of business classifications, using examples to illustrate the classifications. • the reasons for the changing importance of business classification, for example, in more and less industrialised countries.	• Student's Book pages 17–19 • Activity sheet 1.2.1 • A range of different products • Local examples of all three sectors: printed information, websites or a field trip • Access to ICT for research tasks • Video clips of businesses operating in the different sectors

Key business terms

primary sector; secondary sector; tertiary sector

Lesson ideas

You should aim to cover the materials in 1.2.1 in a single one-hour lesson, plus, as appropriate, a homework assignment. The homework could be answering the knowledge check questions or end of section assessments. To achieve the Aims for this topic, we recommend doing some of the following activities over the course of the lesson.

Starter suggestions

Discussion using props: Bring into class a range of different products (or ask students to bring them in). Ask students to describe the production process of each product, including the raw materials needed at the start. Focus on the process that the raw materials go through from the start (for example, mining) to the end product that is sold to customers.

Class discussion: Using example products or industries, ask students what factors or resources are needed to make and then to sell the product. For example, petrol needs an oil field, an oil refinery and petrol stations. In order to produce and sell petrol, a country would need oil fields, enough land to build large oil refineries, a workforce with the skills for this industry and areas with petrol stations. Use this activity to help students understand that not all countries have each sector.

Main lesson activities

Discussion and note-taking (whole class): Talk students through the three sectors, with examples of businesses in each sector, using pages 17–18 of the Student's Book.

Case study: Using the Coca-Cola example on page 19 of the Student's Book, ask students to suggest reasons why Coca-Cola wanted to own all parts of the production process. Then ask them to think about the added value to the product as it passes through each sector.

Student activity: Ask students to complete Activity 1.2.1, a sorting task designed to help them understand which types of business operate in each sector.

Skills activity: Ask students to carry out the Skills activity on page 19 of the Student's Book. They research changes in the employment structure in a country of their choice. They then produce a short statement on the research they have found and discuss their findings in small groups.

Extension: Ask students to evaluate the likely impact for a country if it focuses on one sector in particular.

Ideas should include: If a country focuses on one area, it can become vulnerable to changes in demand. If the area it focuses on becomes unwanted, the country may lose income and suffer job losses. However, the country may become specialised in this area and produce large quantities. This is good for the country as it may increase its income and create jobs.

The impact will depend on the product and how diverse it is. It may also depend on whether other countries focus on the same sector or industry, which is riskier for the country.

All three sectors: Ask students to focus on one industry and to find a business in each sector that operates in or supplies this industry. For example, three businesses involved in the car industry are: a steel plant, a car factory and a sales showroom.

Tip: This could be given as a homework exercise.

Knowledge check: Ask students to answer the Knowledge check questions on page 19 of the Student's Book.

Tip: This could be given as a homework exercise.

Plenary suggestions

Linking game: Name a primary sector business, for example an iron mine. Ask a student to suggest a secondary sector business that uses this raw material, for example, a factory that makes iron pins. A third student then completes the process by suggesting an appropriate tertiary sector business, for example the pins are used to make trains, which are then sold.

Continue the activity to involve all the students in the class. After the first teacher-led example, students should think of their own examples of primary, secondary and tertiary businesses.

Video clips: Show short video clips of businesses operating in different sectors, for example, machinery being used, a product being made, and so on. Ask students to identify the sector represented in each clip.

Answers to Student's Book activities

Skills activity (page 19): possible outcomes

To help students focus their research, ask them to find:

- general information about the economy of their chosen country (population, GDP, main products exported)
- the different sectors that operate in that country
- examples of businesses in each sector – these should vary in size and how long they have been in business
- the businesses that are the main employers in the country and the sector that they operate in
- evidence to back up the information provided (graphs, tables, and so on.)
- how the sectors have changed in size in the past 10–15 years and the reasons for this.

Offer support to students who need it by providing suitable websites or guiding them to use search terms such as 'sector changes in [country name]', 'primary sector changes in [country name]' when searching online.

Students should be able to outline their chosen country's structure, showing clear knowledge of each sector, giving examples and using figures as evidence. Ask more able students to interpret these figures for the rest of the class.

Students should then produce a statement that explains why their chosen country operates mainly in a certain sector. The reason may include: availability/lack of resources, availability/lack of labour, availability of oil or gas, location, demand in the country or abroad, and so on.

Discuss changes in the balance of sectors within a country and the reasons for these changes, such as changes in the resources available, improvements in the education system, and so on.

Knowledge check (page 19)

1. **Define** the term primary sector.

    The primary sector extracts raw materials from the land or sea ready to be used by other industries.

    Any relevant example, such as: oil, coal, steel.

2. **Identify** two businesses that operate in the tertiary sector.

    Any two examples, such as: restaurant, shop, accountancy firm, bank, and so on.

3. **Explain** two key differences between the primary and secondary sectors.

    The primary sector extracts raw materials, whereas the secondary sector takes the raw material and turns it into a semi-finished or finished product.

    A secondary sector business can be in any country, regardless of the resources available there, whereas the primary sector needs specific resources to be available.

    Examples such as: Trees are cut down by the primary sector and they are then made into wooden panels by the secondary sector to be sold as fencing.

    Coal can only be mined in countries where it is available, but can be used in the secondary sector by businesses in any country.

1.2.1 Business activity in terms of primary, secondary and tertiary sectors: Activity

Activity type
Sorting task

Time
20 minutes

Content
Business activity sectors

Key terms
sectors: primary, secondary and tertiary

Aims
To understand the business activity sectors (1.2.1)

Skills practised

AO1: Knowledge and understanding	✓
AO2: Application	✓
AO3: Analysis	
AO4: Evaluation	

Preparation
Make one copy of Activity Sheet 1.2.1 for each student in the class.

Procedure
1. Tell students that they will be sorting businesses according to the sectors they operate in.
2. Hand out Activity sheet 1.2.1 and ask students to complete the activity individually.
3. Students then work with a partner to make sure they agree on their answers.
4. Choose pairs to feed back their answers and discuss them as a class.
5. Ask students to suggest further examples of businesses in each sector and add them to the table on the activity sheet.

Teacher tip: Use mixed ability pairs for the checking stage. Allowing students to check their work with a partner will help less able students to feel more confident when feeding back to the class. More able students will extend their learning by 'teaching' their partner.

Extension: Ask students to produce a three-stage (primary, secondary, tertiary) process with a gap in it. They then pair up with another student, and each has to identify which sectors are represented in the process and which sector is missing. For example, a student writes that a car is made in a car plant and sold in a car showroom. Their partner identifies the secondary and tertiary sectors here, and the missing primary sector activity (mining iron to make the steel for the car).

Answers to Activity 1.2.1
Primary: oil rig, coal mine, farm

Secondary: steel factory, bottling factory, car factory, leather factory

Tertiary: restaurant, clothes shop, bookshop, accountancy firm

1.2.2 Private sector and public sector

Aims (1.2.2)

Skills

By the end of this section, students will be able to:

- classify business enterprises between private sector and public sector in a mixed economy.

Resources

- Student's Book pages 20–23
- Activity sheet 1.2.2
- Access to ICT for research tasks
- Materials and images to produce a classroom display

Key business terms

market economy; mixed economy; nationalisation; private sector; public limited company; public sector; shareholder

Lesson ideas

You should aim to cover the materials in 1.2.2 in a single one-hour lesson, plus, as appropriate, a homework assignment. The homework could be answering the Knowledge check questions or end of section assessments. To achieve the Aims for this topic, we recommend doing some of the following activities over the course of the lesson.

Starter suggestions

Definitions: Briefly define the differences between a private sector and a public sector organisation in preparation for the next starter suggestion.

Contrast: Using two example businesses, one from the public sector and one from the private sector, ask students to list the differences and similarities. Choose two businesses that are very different, for example the military, hospital or other government-run organisation and a large multinational business. Students should work in pairs to note down their ideas. Ask the class for feedback, noting their responses on the board.

Main lesson activities

Discussion and note-taking (whole class): Discuss with students the key concepts of the public and private sector, using pages 20–23 of the Student's Book to help with this. Ask students to make notes.

Discussion: Ask students why they think the government might intervene in a market. You could use examples from the local area that students can relate to. Ask students to read page 20 of the Student's Book in order to understand the different types of market.

Student activity: Ask students to complete Activity 1.2.2. Students answer questions on the public and private sectors and market conditions based on a case study.

Skills activity: Build on the starter activity by asking students to complete the Skills activity on page 23 of the Student's Book. Students research local private sector and public sector businesses and a social enterprise in order to identify how the aims and objectives differ. They then produce a classroom display.

Tip: This could be given as a homework exercise.

Knowledge check: Ask students to answer the Knowledge check questions on page 23 of the Student's Book.

Tip: This could be given as a homework exercise.

Plenary suggestions

Hot seat: Ask a volunteer to come to the front of the class. Give the student a category depending on their ability. *For less able students:* give a broad category such as private or public sector. *For more able students*: give a specific industry within a sector, for example the airline industry within the private sector. Ask the student to give as many examples of businesses as they can to demonstrate their understanding of which sector businesses belong to.

Guess the sector: Describe a sector and ask students to guess which one you are talking about. For example, words such as *profit*, *shareholders* and *individuals* would suggest the private sector, whereas *government*, *funding* and *society-based aims* would suggest the public sector.

Answers to Student's Book activities

Skills activity (page 23): possible outcomes

- Students should state the similarities and differences between their two chosen businesses. For example: *Similarities:* Both businesses aim to make a profit, meet customer needs and have employees. *Differences:* Private sector aims: growth, profit, market share and reputation. Public sector aims: to cater for all people, customer service and efficient service.
- Remind students that social enterprises aim to achieve social projects or have aims and objectives based on improving an aspect of society.

    Some students may recognise that a social enterprise is still trying to make a profit, but that it reinvests this into the business and/or social project it supports.
- When creating the class display, encourage students to organise their findings so that it is easy to find information. They should identify the key points to use in their display and use photos and graphs/charts to illustrate it.

Knowledge check (page 23)

1 **Explain** why Ali is operating in the private sector.

   Ali is a private owner of a business with no government intervention. The business aims to make a profit and expand.

2 **Identify** two differences between the public and private sector.

   Any two of the following: The private sector is made up of businesses that are owned by private individuals and shareholders, but not the government. The private sector is purely funded by these private individuals, and receives no long-term funding from the government. The public sector is funded and run by the government. It is often businesses that offer a product or service to the public that a private individual would not want to provide, as it does not make profit.

3 **Explain** two benefits of Ali's business becoming a PLC.

   Any two benefits from: Raises extra money for the business through selling shares, which allows the business the capital to expand the business or spend it on marketing.

   Brings new ideas from shareholders; helps cash flow; helps increase the global reputation of the business.

4 **Explain** why a government may nationalise an industry or business.

   To save jobs: rather than pay to support the unemployed, the government may choose to take over the industry/business. The government may also feel it can run the industry/business more efficiently, therefore increasing the output of the country.

   Other reasons may include: to reduce prices for customers; to increase government revenue.

1.2.2 Private sector and public sector: Activity

Activity type

Case study

Time

30 minutes

Content

Public and private sectors

Key terms

market economy; mixed economy; private sector; public sector

Aims

To understand the two sectors: private and public (1.2.2)

Skills practised

AO1: Knowledge and understanding	✓
AO2: Application	✓
AO3: Analysis	✓
AO4: Evaluation	✓

Preparation

Make one copy of Activity sheet 1.2.2 for each student in the class.

Procedure

1 Tell students that they will be reading a case study and answering a series of questions based on the case study.

2 Give each student a copy of Activity sheet 1.2.2.

3 You can provide differentiation by asking students of different abilities to answer all or just some of the questions.

4 Split the class into pairs to answer the questions and ask them to focus on their exam technique. Remind students of the importance of application in allowing them to analyse and evaluate.

5 Provide support for learners who may have difficulty with key words in the case study, such as 'grant' and 'obesity'.

6 When students have completed the questions, discuss answers as a whole class.

7 If time allows, ask students to do the extension activity below.

Teacher tips: This activity creates an opportunity for teaching students how to apply their knowledge. Ask students to peer assess each other's answers, with a particular focus on application.

You could also use this activity as a formal assessment of this topic.

Variation: When organising pairs for this activity, put a less able student with a more able student. Split Questions 1 and 3 into two parts: the less able student answers the first part of the question and the more able student justifies the answer. They both agree on the answer to write down for the whole question.

Extension: Ask students to write their own questions and share these with a partner. They can also identify the key characteristics of both the public and private sector.

Answers to Activity 1.2.2

Part 1

1 Is Primal's business public or private sector? Justify your answer.

Private sector. It is owned by Primal only. It is profit-driven. There is no government intervention or funding on a day-to-day basis.

Students cannot use the grant as evidence that the business is public sector.

2 What percentage of the business does the government own?

   0%

   Students may state that the grant is government shares, but it is not.

3 Is Primal's second year aim common for a business in this sector? Justify your answer.

   Yes – private businesses often look to expand and grow.

   Students may state that not all businesses would set this aim, as they may want to consolidate on the first year or they may set a target of less than 10%.

Part 2

Public	Private
Government-funded	Profit-driven
Run in order to benefit society	Shareholders
Large employer	No government funding
Funded by taxes	Very common – most businesses are private

1.3 Enterprise, business growth and size

1.3.1 ENTERPRISE AND ENTREPRENEURSHIP

Aims (1.3.1)

Knowledge	Resources
By the end of this section, students will understand: • the characteristics of successful entrepreneurs • the contents of a business plan and how business plans assist entrepreneurs • why and how governments support business start-ups, for example, grants, training schemes.	• Student's Book pages 24–29 • Activity sheets 1.3.1A, 1.3.1B, 1.3.1C and 1.3.1D • Websites/resource materials with information about government support for businesses

Key business terms

business plan; corporation tax; enterprise; entrepreneur; grant; gross domestic product (GDP); loan; mentor; stakeholder; start-up; tax relief; training

Lesson ideas

You should aim to cover the materials in 1.3.1 in two one-hour lessons, plus, as appropriate, homework assignments. The homework could be the completion of the Knowledge check questions (page 29 of the Student's Book) or end of section assessments. This topic lends itself to lots of research, using either ICT or other sources, to investigate local government support for businesses. To achieve the Aims for this topic, we recommend doing some of the following activities over the course of the lessons.

Starter suggestions

Imagine: Give students the blank outline of a person on Activity sheet 1.3.1A. Ask students to note down the characteristics of an entrepreneur round the outline. Encourage them to think about the skills and attributes of a successful entrepreneur, such as being committed to hard work, organised and a good communicator. Students may want to use pages 24–25 of the Student's Book to help them.

Ask the class for feedback, noting their responses on the board. Encourage students to justify their answers. Ask more able students to justify other students' answers or to disagree, with their own opinions.

Discuss: Alternatively, ask students the same question orally, and collect their answers on the board. Then split the class into small groups and ask each group to agree on which skill they think is the most important. Facilitate a class discussion/debate, with each group presenting and justifying their ideas.

Main lesson activities

Skills activity: Ask students to complete the Skills activity on page 26 of the Student's Book. They describe their favourite entrepreneur and compare themselves and their classmates to the characteristics they have identified.

Tip: For homework, you could ask students to research entrepreneurs of their own choice and produce a report or presentation outlining their characteristics.

Discussion and note-taking (whole class): Ask the class what they think goes into a business plan. Note their ideas on the board and then ask them to read pages 26–27 of the Student's Book. Go through each part of the business plan, outlining the benefits of each particular part to an entrepreneur. Ask students to make notes as appropriate.

Student activity: Ask students to complete Activity 1.3.1B, which requires them to match extracts from a business plan with the correct headings from the plan.

Knowledge check: Ask students to answer the Knowledge check questions on page 29 of the Student's Book.

Tip: This could be given as a homework exercise.

Skills activity: Ask students to complete the Skills activity on page 27 of the Student's Book. Follow this with Activity sheet 1.3.1C, which supports this. Students work in pairs to identify the benefits and drawbacks of a business plan to a business and to an entrepreneur. They then make an overall judgement on how useful a business plan is.

Discussion and note-taking (whole class): Make sure that students have read and understood pages 27–29 of the Student's Book on how governments support entrepreneurs and businesses. You could then test their knowledge using a key terms test to include: advice, grants, loans, tax relief, training and mentors.

Research: Ask students to carry out research into the different methods governments use to support businesses. Ask them to try to find real-life examples of each method of government support. You might want students to focus on one particular country or area. Then ask students to discuss in groups the benefits and drawbacks of the different types of support.

Student activity: Ask students to read the case study in Activity 1.3.1D and to answer the questions on the activity sheet.

Tip: This could be given as a homework exercise.

Plenary suggestions

Snowball: Name a government support method, for example 'grants'. Ask students to give a benefit **or** a drawback **or** a reason why governments offer this. Continue around the class until students cannot think of any more benefits/drawbacks/reasons for this method. Then name another method for students to respond to.

Answers to Student's Book activities

Skills activity (page 26): possible outcomes

Students should choose an entrepreneur whom they are interested in and they should have a good understanding of the entrepreneur's business and products.

For the second question, emphasise to students that the ability to identify their weaknesses is a positive and very important skill. Encourage them to explain how they intend to reduce the impact of their weaknesses. These may include: poor timekeeping, motivation, communication, attitude, commitment or teamwork.

The final question is best suited to a class discussion based on the first two questions. Students can suggest any of the characteristics as long as they can justify why it is the most important one.

Skills activity (page 27): possible outcomes

Students might include the following in their arguments for and against using a business plan:

For: helps planning; reduces costs; helps motive employees; can be used to judge the success of the business.

Against: opportunity costs in time; becomes out of date quickly; if it is poorly written, this can cause problems in the long term.

When identifying the key points for and against having a business plan, students should show a good understanding of a business plan and its contents. They should be able to give both the advantages and the disadvantages of a business plan. Make the link to a possible exam question if possible.

The key aspect of this activity is for students to justify their choice. Encourage more able students to help and support the less able students to improve their evaluation skills.

Skills activity (page 29): possible outcomes

Students' discussions might include:

- A grant will provide the business with money, but it may not be enough. The business may waste the grant if the business owner does not have a good understanding of what to spend it on, or choose the best options.

- Other methods such as training or mentors help the owner improve their own skills and make it more likely that they will make the correct decisions and solve problems.
- Loans and tax relief allow the business to have a better cash flow and so allow it to grow.
- Giving the business owners knowledge and access to help and advice, as well as money, is key for long-term success.

Extension: This question tests students' knowledge of the forms of support a government may offer. Being able to discuss each one will be very useful for the exam. Encourage more able students to offer alternative ideas on how governments can support businesses and to evaluate these ideas.

Students may come up with a variety of ideas. The focus here should be on their justification, not the answer.

The final question asks students to evaluate whether governments should have to provide support to start-up companies. Students may argue for or against this. Again, focus on their justification. They may argue that businesses need some support in the short term but not in the long term. However, they should arrive at the judgement that many businesses, especially small ones, do need support.

Knowledge check (page 29)

1 **Identify** two attributes that you would expect a successful entrepreneur to have.

Any two from the Student's Book, including: risk seeking; focused and determined; organised; team player; committed; resourceful; creative; hard working; intelligent; business knowledge; innovative; enthusiastic; good communicator.

2 **Identify** two parts of a business plan.

Any two from: business summary; business details; market research, marketing; day-to-day running of the business; finance.

A brief description of what is included in each part.

3 **Explain** two reasons why a start-up business should use a business plan.

Example answers: Finances: planning the finances helps the business to plan for possible future cash flow shortages and allows them to seek sources of finance.

Employment: the business can decide who it needs to employ and when to do this.

Marketing budget: the business can plan and deliver their marketing strategy based on a realistic budget.

4 **Outline** two forms of support a government can offer a business.

Any two from: grants; training; loans; advice; mentors; tax relief.

Student discusses each form and clearly explains how it supports a business.

Refer to the Student's Book pages 28–29 for definitions and details.

1.3.1 Enterprise and entrepreneurship: Activity A

Activity type

Outline of a person

Content

Entrepreneur skills and characteristics

Key terms

enterprise; entrepreneur

Time

10 minutes

Skills practised

AO1: Knowledge and understanding	✓
AO2: Application	
AO3: Analysis	
AO4: Evaluation	

Preparation

Make one copy of Activity sheet 1.3.1A for each student in the class.

Aims

To understand the different skills and characteristics of an entrepreneur (1.3.1)

Procedure

1. Give each student a copy of Activity sheet 1.3.1A and explain that the outline image represents an entrepreneur.
2. Ask students to write notes round the image about the different skills, attributes and characteristics of a successful entrepreneur.
3. Encourage more able students to write their ideas next to the appropriate part of the body. For example, they could write 'Good communicator' next to the mouth.
4. Take feedback from students and create a definitive list of characteristics on the board.

Teacher tip: The more able students are likely to think of more ideas. Encourage them to start ordering the characteristics and skills in order of importance, possibly from the start of the task.

Variation: This activity lends itself to differentiation, as students of different abilities will be able to think of a varying range of skills and characteristics.

Extension: Ask students to highlight the skills, attributes and characteristics that they think are the most important to an entrepreneur. If time allows, ask students to include some ideas of possible weaknesses that are common among entrepreneurs who wish to set up their own business.

Possible answers to Activity 1.3.1A

Students' answers might include:

Good timekeeper; Good communicator; Organised (good at time management); Problem solver; Motivator; Creative; Risk seeking; Intelligent; Committed; Focused; Determined; Inspirational; Hard working; Honest; Innovative; Team player; Resourceful; Excellent business knowledge; Enthusiastic.

1.3.1 Enterprise and entrepreneurship: Activity B

Activity type

Matching activity

Content

The parts of a business plan

Key term

business plan

Time

10 minutes

Aims

To understand the different parts of a business plan (1.3.1)

Skills practised

AO1: Knowledge and understanding	✓
AO2: Application	✓
AO3: Analysis	
AO4: Evaluation	

Preparation

Make one copy of Activity Sheet 1.3.1B for each student in the class.

Procedure

1. Ask students to read the information about the business plan on pages 26–27 of the Student's Book.
2. Give each student a copy of Activity sheet 1.3.1B.
3. Ask students to read the extracts from a business plan and to draw lines to match these with the correct section of the plan. Students could work in pairs or small groups to do this.
4. Ask for feedback, ensuring students justify their choices.

Teacher tip: Some of the less able students may not be able to apply the content to the section headings. Allow them to use the Student's Book to support them with this activity.

Variation: Cut out the headings and extracts from the activity sheet and mix them up before giving each pair or small group a set. As well as matching up the extracts with the headings, students should also put them in the order they would appear in the business plan. They can then stick the correctly ordered headings and extracts into their notebooks.

Extension: Encourage more able students to identify the most important parts of the business plan and to justify their choices.

Answers to Activity 1.3.1B

Business summary: F

Business details: B

Market research: A

Marketing: C

Day-to-day running of the business: E

Finance: D

1.3.1 Enterprise and entrepreneurship: Activity C

Activity type

Pair work discussion

Content

Identifying the benefits and drawbacks of a business plan

Key terms

business; business plan; entrepreneur

Time

25 minutes

Aims

To understand how useful a business plan is; to understand the limitations of a business plan (1.3.1)

Skills practised

AO1: Knowledge and understanding	✓
AO2: Application	
AO3: Analysis	✓
AO4: Evaluation	✓

Preparation

Make one copy of Activity sheet 1.3.1C for each student in the class.

Procedure

1. Tell students that they are going to work in pairs to identify the benefits and limitations of a business plan to a business and to an entrepreneur. They will then make a judgement on how useful a business plan is overall.
2. Split the class into pairs and give each student a copy of Activity sheet 1.3.1C.
3. Students discuss the benefits and limitations with their partner, first from the point of view of a business and then from the point of view of an entrepreneur. They need to think of three benefits and three limitations for each and write them in the table.
4. Using the benefits and limitations that they have identified, students then discuss how useful a business plan is overall and write their judgement and justification in the last box in the table.
5. Take feedback from different pairs and decide as a whole class how useful a business plan is.

Teacher tip: This activity can be used to highlight exam skills: weighing up arguments for and against, and coming to an overall judgement with justification.

Variations: Divide the class so some students focus on the benefits and others on the limitations. Then reorganise the groups, so that a student who has worked on the benefits is paired with a student who has worked on the limitations. Students share their points with their partner and fill in the gaps in their table, before reaching a judgement together.

This activity can also be used to prepare for an exam-style question to give students the opportunity to practise structuring their writing. For example: To what extent should an entrepreneur use a business plan when starting up? Justify your answer.

Extension: Ask students to use their points to write a complete answer to an exam-style question.

Answers to Activity 1.3.1C

Business plan	Benefits	Limitations
Note down the benefits and limitations of a business plan to a **business**.	1 Gives targets and aims for employees.	1 It can become out of date very quickly as the environment changes.
	2 Useful for investors and other lenders, such as a bank, to see how the business is likely to perform.	2 The business plan may not contain accurate information. For example, it may have inflated its projected sales or the value of its assets.
	3 The business can measure its progress against the financial aims it set in the plan.	3 The business plan can give unrealistic targets for employees and owners, increasing pressure on the business.
Note down the benefits and limitations of a business plan to an **entrepreneur**.	1 It gives the entrepreneur aims and objectives to measure their own performance against.	1 Some entrepreneurs may feel it restricts day-to-day running as the business evolves.
	2 It can highlight areas the entrepreneur is weak at and needs to develop.	2 It doesn't take into account changes to the economy that the entrepreneur may struggle to adapt to.
	3 The plan helps attract employees, who can see what the business is trying to achieve.	3 The plan can give too much confidence to the entrepreneur, who might think the plan covers all aspects of business.
Conclusion: Give an overall judgement on how useful the business plan is. Justify your answer.	A business plan is very useful to most businesses and entrepreneurs. However, it cannot be relied on in the long term as the business and the environment will change. It is a vital tool for business owners who lack experience and it can help businesses in the short term; it should not be depended on as it may include inflated finances or unreliable market research.	

1.3.1 Enterprise and entrepreneurship: Activity D

Activity type

Case study

Content

The different ways in which a government supports businesses

Why a government supports businesses

Key term

government support

Time

35 minutes

Aims

To understand the different ways in which a government supports businesses; to explain why a government supports businesses (1.3.1)

Skills practised

AO1: Knowledge and understanding	✓
AO2: Application	✓
AO3: Analysis	
AO4: Evaluation	✓

Preparation

Make one copy of Activity sheet 1.3.1D for each student in the class.

Procedure

1. Tell students that they will be reading a case study about how governments support businesses and answering questions based on the case study.
2. Give a copy of Activity sheet 1.3.1D to each student.
3. Ask students to read the case study first and highlight key terms and key content. It is very useful for students to develop the exam technique of highlighting the key ideas and any numerical evidence that they can use to justify their answers.
4. If any students find the language of the case study difficult, you could give them the key words to highlight.
5. Ask students to read and answer the questions in their exercise books or notebooks.
6. You could ask more able students to skip Questions 1–2 and start on Question 3.
7. Discuss the answers to the questions with the class. Focus on the exam skills (Application, and so on) that are required to answer these questions. Make sure that students use evidence from the case study to support their answers. Encourage students to explain why they agree or disagree with the statement in Question 5, using as many relevant key terms as possible.

Teacher tip: Encourage students to use the questions to help start their answers. For example, when answering Question 4: 'A business plan will help Paolo because …'

Encourage students to use words that demonstrate analysis, such as 'however' and 'depends'.

Variation: Students may wish to read the case study out loud or go through it in pairs. You may wish to allocate questions to small groups or tell students which questions to answer, based on their ability.

Extension: Ask students to write their own questions based on the case study, which they can swap for other students to answer.

Suggested answers to Activity 1.3.1D

1. Identify two characteristics of a successful entrepreneur.

    Any two from: risk taker; focused and determined; organised; creative; hardworking; innovative; good communicator; multi-skilled.

2. Identify two ways in which the government has supported Paolo and his new business.

    Providing a mentor and government-funded finance training.

3. Using one of the methods of support you identified in Question 2 explain how this will help Paolo's business to be successful in the future.

    Any one method from:

    Mentor: Advice from someone who has experience will help Paolo make the right decisions for his business. The mentor is someone he can go to for answers or advice.

    Training: This fills in an important gap in Paolo's skills, allowing him to understand how to manage his own finances. This will reduce mistakes and allow him to see how the business is performing.

4. Explain how a business plan could have helped Paolo make his new business a success.

    The business plan will help Paolo keep on track with his aims and objectives. It will allow any employees Paolo employs to know what the business is trying to achieve. The plan will help Paolo attract investment to the business. It will provide a benchmark to measure how well he has done based on his predictions.

5. 'The government should support businesses.' To what extent do you agree with this statement? Justify your answer.

    For: Businesses are the key to a country's economy and so need to be supported. They provide jobs and income for the government.

    Against: It is not the government's job to support all businesses. When a business goes bankrupt, this allows other businesses to do well or start up. A private owner is keeping the profits and so doesn't need support.

    Conclusion: It is good for the government to offer support, especially for small start-up businesses. However, as businesses get larger, they don't need as much support. Without grants and mentors, for example, small business owners would struggle and it is important for the government to support them with these forms of help.

    Students should offer valid points for and against, and reach an appropriate and balanced judgement based on the case study.

1.3.2 The methods and problems of measuring business size

Aims (1.3.2)

Knowledge

By the end of this section, students will understand:

- the methods used for measuring business size, for example, number of people employed, value of output, capital employed
- the limitations of methods of measuring business size.

Resources

- Student's Book pages 30–32
- Activity sheets 1.3.2A and 1.3.2B
- Access to ICT for research tasks
- Video clip of a large business (for example, from a news website such as Sky News, ESPN)

Key terms

capital employed; market share; output

Lesson ideas

You should aim to cover the materials in 1.3.2 in a single one-hour lesson, plus, as appropriate, a homework assignment. The homework could be answering the Knowledge check questions (page 32 of the Student's Book) or end of section assessments. To achieve the Aims for this topic, we recommend doing some of the following activities over the course of the lesson.

Starter suggestions

Discussion: Ask students to name local or national businesses of different sizes. Ask them to identify the ways in which they vary in size: number of employees, number of outlets, and so on.

Prove it!: Give students an example of a very large business, for example, Microsoft or Samsung. Ask them to prove to you that this is one of the largest businesses in the world. Encourage them to mention the number of employees, capital employed and value of output.

Main lesson activities

Discussion and note-taking (whole class): Use pages 30–32 of the Student's Book to go over the different methods used to measure the size of a business, including the benefits and drawbacks of each method. Ask students to take notes as appropriate.

Student activity: Ask students to complete Activity 1.3.2A. This case study allows students to recognise the types of data that are used for the different methods of measuring the size of a business.

Video clip: Show students a video clip of a large business. Ask them to identify the different methods that could be used to measure its size. The clip should represent the business in detail so students can identify the ways in which it can be measured.

Discussion: Give students examples of two local businesses to compare. Local examples will make it easier for students to understand. Choose two businesses with different levels of output, number of outlets, employees, and so on. Ask students to suggest the limitations of some of the methods used to measure business size in the context of these two businesses. Remind them that profit is not a measure of size.

You could use the case study feature on page 30 to highlight the fact that the number of outlets does not necessarily mean a business is bigger, and that you cannot use one method on its own.

Student activity: Ask students to complete Activity 1.3.2B. This exercise looks at the limitations of each measure and highlights the need for a range of measures to be used for each business.

Emphasise that some businesses employ very few people but generate large amounts of revenue, for example, firms of accountants or lawyers.

Skills activity: Ask students to complete the Skills activity on page 32 of the Student's Book. Students choose a private or public sector business from their country and use their research skills to look at the different ways of measuring the business's size.

Tip: This could be given as a homework exercise.

Knowledge check: Ask students to answer the Knowledge check questions on page 32 of the Student's Book.

Plenary suggestions

Hot seat: Ask a volunteer to come to the front of the class and do one of the following:

- Ask the student to name as many methods of measuring a business as they can.
- *For more able students:* Give the student a method of measuring business size. The student has to name as many limitations of the method as they can.

List and explain: Ask one student to name a method of measuring a business; the next student has to give a limitation of that method; the next student gives an example of a business that suits this method of measuring size. Continue around the class until all methods have been covered.

Answers to Student's Book activities

Skills activity (page 32): possible outcomes

Students should demonstrate excellent research skills and good understanding of the business they have chosen. They should identify appropriate methods of measuring the size of the business and support these with evidence. They should be able to identify one key method that best suits the business.

Students could present their findings as a poster, report or presentation. This should contain clear evidence of the business's size in the form of graphs, charts, tables, and so on.

Students should recommend using more than one method. Many students may suggest sales revenue as a key measure. However, this may not correlate with outlets as one large outlet or office may provide a large revenue, whereas a business with many outlets may only have a small revenue.

Knowledge check (page 32)

1 **Identify** two ways in which a business's size can be measured.

   Any two from: capital employed; market share; number of outlets; number of employees; value of the business; value of output.

2 **Explain** why a business should use a variety of methods to measure its size.

   Using a variety of methods gives a wider view of the business and its size. Some of the methods have limitations that do not really show the true size of the business. For example, the number of outlets can be very small but the value of output could be very high. This is often the case for accountancy or law firms.

3 **Identify** two limitations of using the number of employees as a way of measuring the size of a business.

   Possible answers: Some businesses have a small number of employees who generate large amounts of value for the business. This is often the case in businesses such as accountancy firms, law firms or other service businesses. There are businesses that employ huge numbers of people that produce very little output.

1.3.2 The methods and problems of measuring business size: Activity A

Activity type

Case study

Content

Measuring a business size

Time

15 minutes

Key terms

business size; employees; market share; outlets; turnover; value

Aims

To identify the methods used to measure business size (1.3.2)

Skills practised

AO1: Knowledge and understanding	✓
AO2: Application	✓
AO3: Analysis	
AO4: Evaluation	

Preparation

Make one copy of Activity sheet 1.3.2A for each student in the class.

Procedure

1 Give each student a copy of Activity sheet 1.3.2A and read through the case study together.

2 Students are given five methods that can be used to measure the size of a business.

3 Ask students to list the methods they can use to measure the size of Dean's Doughnuts based on the information in the case study. They then identify the evidence for each method given in the case study and write it in the table. Give them five minutes to do this.

4 Finish the activity by taking feedback from students.

Teacher tip: Encourage students to identify any numbers or statistics that they could use as application in their answers, for example, revenue or number of employees.

Variation: During the feedback session, allow students to give their own examples from their research activities.

Extension: If time allows, ask students to identify the benefits and limitations of each method as it applies to Dean's Doughnuts. They could create a table in their exercise books or notebooks to do this. (See the suggested answer below for format.)

Answers to Activity 1.3.2A

Method	Evidence from case study
1 Market share	20% of South American market
2 Value of the business	$12 million
3 Number of outlets	25 outlets
4 Number of employees	220 employees
5 Turnover	$2.3 million per year

Remind students that profit is not an indicator of a business's size.

Extension

Method	Benefits	Limitations
1 Market share	Shows how the business compares to others in South America.	The percentage doesn't show value of turnover or potential value of the business.
2 Value of the business	This is useful as it shows a true value of what the business is worth to its competitors.	This may not take into account how good employees are, or other assets the business may have.
3 Number of outlets	This gives a good idea of how well spread the business is.	It doesn't say how many people use each outlet, or what value the outlets create.
4 Number of employees	This shows how many people the business employs and can be compared to competitors.	Other businesses may employ thousands of people, so this figure needs to be compared to competitors.
5 Turnover	This gives a general indicator of how big the business is in comparison to others.	This figure needs to be compared to previous years and to competitors.

Students may want to suggest using a variety or all of these methods to give the best picture of business size. Students may also suggest using past figures to show growth and size, as well as other businesses' information to give a comparison.

1.3.2 The methods and problems of measuring business size: Activity B

Activity type

Small group discussion

Content

Business size

Key terms

business size; employees; market share; outlets; turnover; value

Time

20 minutes

Aims

To describe the limitations of the different methods of measuring business size (1.3.2)

Skills practised

AO1: Knowledge and understanding	
AO2: Application	
AO3: Analysis	✓
AO4: Evaluation	✓

Preparation

Make one copy of Activity sheet 1.3.2B for each student in the class.

Procedure

1. Divide the class into small groups or pairs and explain that in this activity, students will identify the limitations of the methods for measuring a business's size.
2. Give each student a copy of Activity sheet 1.3.2B.
3. Students discuss the limitations of each method and write three limitations of each method in the second column of the table. Discuss their responses as a whole class.
4. Students then discuss and agree on the main limitation of each method and write it in the third column of the table. Discuss their responses as a whole class and come to a class consensus on the main limitation of each method.

Teacher tip: You could ask more able students to support other students by working in pairs. This will help less able students to understand the limitations and give more able students the opportunity to explain key concepts.

Variation: Organise the activity as a whole-class discussion instead of in small groups.

Extension: Repeat the activity for the benefits of each method. You could organise this as a debate, which will give more able students the chance to lead the exercise.

Answers to Activity sheet 1.3.2B

Here are some of the limitations for each method; they are supplemented in the Student's Book. The main limitations may be different for each group. Encourage students to justify their decision.

Market share: Doesn't show a value of sales, just a percentage. You cannot use this to compare businesses in different industries.

Number of outlets: This doesn't show how much money each outlet makes or if the business is even selling products in these outlets. Some businesses have one large office as opposed to small outlets.

Capital employed: This doesn't show the value of assets such as employees, the website or brand name. Some businesses have very few assets or investments but are worth large amounts of money, for example, Google.

Number of employees: Labour-intensive businesses need lots of employees but have a relatively low output/revenue. This needs to be compared with other businesses in the industry.

Value of the business: This is only what another business would pay for the business. It may be influenced by the potential value in the future, assets such as employees and what a business might pay to eliminate a competitor.

Value of output: Some businesses have very high revenues but large costs.

1.3.3 Why some businesses grow and others remain small

Aims

Knowledge

By the end of this section, students will understand:

- why the owners of a business may want to expand it
- different ways in which businesses can grow
- problems that are linked to business growth and how these might be overcome
- why some businesses remain small.

Resources

- Student's Book pages 33–37
- Activity sheets 1.3.3A and 1.3.3B
- Access to ICT for research tasks
- Guest speaker: invite a local business owner to come and speak to students

Key business terms

efficiency; external growth; inorganic growth; internal growth; merger; organic growth; takeover

Lesson ideas

You should aim to cover the materials in 1.3.3 in two one-hour lessons, plus, as appropriate, a homework assignment. The homework could be the completion of the Knowledge check questions or end of section assessments. To achieve the Aims for this topic, we recommend doing some of the following activities over the course of the lessons.

Starter suggestions

Discussion: Ask students to imagine that they run their own health food business (or a business in any sector; the business should be small and only operate in one location or outlet).

Ask: 'Why might you want to expand your business? What would you like the business to be doing in five years' time? Do you want to operate in just one country or globally?'

Mention some large businesses that students will be familiar with as examples of how businesses can grow. You could also ask students to suggest ways in which they would expand their business.

Link the business: Name a large business that students know. Ask them to identify problems the business might face if it grew even larger. It is best to use an example of a business that has experienced problems, for example, Tesco's move into the USA with its 'Fresh and Easy' outlets, or Apple trying to sell its products all around the world.

Main lesson activities

Discussion and note-taking (whole class): Ask students why businesses might want to grow. Students should identify four or five key reasons. Write these on the board or ask students to note them down. Use the case studies on pages 34 and 35 of the Student's Book to support this activity. For example, use the case study on page 34 to explain to students the idea of extra revenue or resources as a reason for expansion.

Go through pages 33–35 of the Student's Book and ask students to take notes as necessary.

Student activity: Ask students to complete Activity 1.3.3A. Students identify the type of growth for each of five case study businesses.

Discussion: Hold a class discussion on the problems linked with growth that some businesses experience. You could use the following words to start a discussion: money, employees, competitors, product quality, culture clashes, ability of the owner, and so on.

Ask students why each of these factors could harm growth. Ask more able students to evaluate each factor and choose the one that is the biggest issue a business may face. Encourage students to give examples of real businesses where possible.

Research activity: Ask students to research a real-life example of a business which has grown. They could start with their local high street or shopping centre, and use the internet, newspapers and magazines. Students should identify why the business wanted to grow, how it achieved growth and if there have been any problems.

Tip: This could be given as homework.

Skills activity: Ask students to complete the Skills activity on page 35 of the Student's Book. Students create a 'help leaflet' for businesses that want to grow.

Tip: This could be given as homework.

Student activity: Ask students to complete Activity 1.3.3B, an evaluation activity in which students suggest possible solutions to issues linked with growth.

Guest speaker: If possible, invite a local business owner to come and speak to students about their business. They can talk about their business, whether/how it has grown and whether they wish to grow or not.

Pair-work: Ask students to work in pairs and suggest reasons why a business might decide to remain small. They may be able to use local businesses as examples.

Knowledge check: Ask students to answer the Knowledge check questions on page 37 of the Student's Book.

Plenary suggestions

Role play: Ask students to work in small groups to produce a role play outlining a problem a business may face when growing. The rest of the class have to guess what problems the role play demonstrates.

Case study: Give students an example of a business that has struggled or failed when growing; it could be a small local business or a large multinational. Ask them to give suggestions for why the business failed. Encourage them to identify one key reason for the failure.

Video clip: Show a video clip of a merger or takeover in the news. Ask students to use their knowledge from this topic to identify the reason behind the growth, potential problems that the business has or may face, and ideas on how these can be overcome.

Answers to Student's Book activities

Skills activities: possible outcomes

Skills activity (page 34)

Possible reasons for expansion: it is a successful business with proven sales; reputation is good; a new product range could help increase sales and profit.

Possible reasons against expansion: the business is going to open a new factory, which may increase costs and cause diseconomies of scale; the new factory will be in Egypt which Sammi knows nothing about; communication between the two sites could be poor; Sammi may not have the ability to run a larger business.

Skills activity (page 35)

Ask students to produce the leaflet using word processing or design software.

They should include: why a business may want to grow, the problems it may face and the key factors in making it a success. For example, they may consider money, employees, location, product and competitors.

Dangers of growth could include: diseconomies of scale, production problems; loss of reputation; increased costs; clash of cultures; low employee morale; communication problems.

Tips could include (in addition to those listed on pages 36–37 of the Student's Book): businesses could use mentors to help gain advice; use a business plan to help solve problems before they arise; cash flow and profit and loss planning may help; government help may also be available to the businesses.

Students may suggest organic growth as the best method for businesses to grow.

Skills activity (page 37)

Students can use a variety of points in their answers as long as they justify them.

Ideas may include: Many businesses are different and no two have the exact same culture or ideas. This makes it hard to guarantee success. Many takeovers do fail because of a clash of culture and ethos. Students may also suggest other reasons why business takeovers fail, for example, long-term funding, drop in demand for the product or service, poor managers or employees or poor understanding of the new market/country. However, not all takeovers do fail, and many have been huge successes.

Students should use examples to support their ideas.

Knowledge check (page 37)

1 **Identify** two reasons why a business might want to grow.

   Any two from: increase revenue; increase profit; increase market share; improve reputation; spread risk over more than one country.

2 **Explain** why larger businesses often choose external growth.

   It is quicker and allows them to grow bigger than organic. It is often more cost-effective to buy an existing business that has customers, employees, and so on, in place. Larger businesses have the funds to buy out an existing business, whereas smaller businesses often have to grow more slowly and using cheaper options. Split costs allow both businesses to reduce debt or borrowing. Sharing the risk between two firms makes it easier to justify decisions. The two businesses can share resources such as employees, office space and assets.

3 **Consider** why some businesses choose not to grow.

   Some owners are happy with the business as it is and fear growth will take up more of their time, reduce their control, reduce quality and ruin their business. The owner may also not have the drive or desire to grow the business, or may lack the skills needed to do so. The business may be operating at its maximum already and cannot grow. It may not be able to afford the extra cost of expanding. It may already be enjoying economies of scale, and any growth could cause an increase in its costs.

4 **Identify** one problem with a business expanding.

   Any one from: communication breaks down; drop in quality; extra costs; morale of employees may drop; inability to cope with larger orders; a clash of cultures between new and old employees.

1.3.3 Why some businesses grow and others remain small: Activity A

Activity type
Mini case studies

Content
Business growth

Time
20 minutes

Key terms
external growth; inorganic growth; internal growth; merger; organic growth; takeover

Aims
To understand the different ways in which a business can grow (1.3.3)

Skills practised

AO1: Knowledge and understanding	✓
AO2: Application	✓
AO3: Analysis	
AO4: Evaluation	

Preparation
Make one copy of Activity sheet 1.3.3A for each student in the class.

Procedure

1. Before students start this activity, make sure they understand the two main ways in which businesses can grow, covered on pages 34–35 of the Student's Book, and that they understand the difference between a takeover and a merger.
2. Give a copy of Activity sheet 1.3.3A to each student. Explain that they are going to read a series of mini case studies and identify the type of growth represented in each one.
3. Students work in pairs to read the case studies and decide together on the type of growth.
4. You could ask each pair to take turns to read out a case study, the listening partner has to identify the type of growth.
5. Students write the type of growth for each case study in the table and then join another pair to compare and discuss their answers.
6. Ask for feedback and clear up any misunderstandings. Make sure that students use the correct business terms.

Teacher tip: Encourage students to highlight key information in the case studies, for example, the business type and information about how well the business is performing financially.

Variation: Give students examples of the growth of real businesses and ask them to identify the type of growth.

Extension: Ask students to write their own mini case studies to share with other students. If they have internet access and/or information sources about local businesses, they could base these case studies on real businesses.

Answers to Activity 1.3.3A

1. Internal/organic
2. External/inorganic: takeover
3. External/inorganic: merger
4. External/inorganic: merger
5. External/inorganic: takeover; internal/organic

1.3.3 Why some businesses grow and others remain small: Activity B

Activity type

Mini case studies

Content

The problems associated with business growth

Time

20 minutes

Key terms

external growth; inorganic growth; internal growth; merger; organic growth; takeover

Aims

To understand the problems that are linked to business growth and how these might be overcome (1.3.3)

Skills practised

AO1: Knowledge and understanding	
AO2: Application	✓
AO3: Analysis	✓
AO4: Evaluation	✓

Preparation

Make one copy of Activity sheet 1.3.3B for each student in the class.

Procedure

1. Tell students they will read a set of mini case studies about businesses that have experienced problems as they have grown. Their task is to suggest the most appropriate solution(s) for these businesses.
2. Divide the class into pairs or small groups, and give each student a copy of Activity sheet 1.3.3B.
3. Ask students to read each scenario and identify the problem the business is facing. Ask them to decide how this problem could be overcome. They write their suggestions in the boxes.
4. Ask the class for feedback. Discuss each solution and aim to reach a class consensus.

Teacher tip: Mind map ways of solving problems linked with growth (such as a bank loan, employ new employees, train employees, set new objectives) and write these on the board for students to refer to.

Variation: Organise this as a whole-class activity, with the class offering suggestions of how they would solve the issues. Discuss and evaluate the suggestions.

Extension: Ask students to evaluate the likely effect of each solution. Will it definitely solve the problem? Will it solve the problem in the long term?

Suggested answers to Activity 1.3.3B

1. Appointing new managers may bring new ideas and ethos, which may increase employee motivation.

   Incentives for employees may help increase motivation and create a focus on performance.

   Communication: employees could have a new communication forum to discuss their problems. This may make them feel they are being listened to.

2. Setting realistic targets will help employees feel they are achieving and working well.

   Incentives for employees may help them work harder and produce more.

3. Training: both Fran and her employees could have some training to improve performance.

   Communication: a new communication system could help improve efficiency and reduce problems.

   New managers may be able to help the business run more effectively.

4. Training: Employees may need some additional skills or practice in order to improve.

   Employee incentives: these may help boost confidence and performance.

1.3.4 Why some (new or established) businesses fail

Aims (1.3.4)

Knowledge

By the end of this section, students will understand:

- the causes of business failure, for example, lack of management skills, changes in the business environment, liquidity problems
- why new businesses are at a greater risk of failing.

Resources

- Student's Book pages 38–40
- Activity sheets 1.3.4A and 1.3.4B
- Photos of local shops that have closed
- Guest speaker (local businessperson) or video clip about a failed business in the news
- Access to ICT for research tasks

Key terms

business environment; management

Lesson ideas

You should aim to cover the materials in 1.3.4 in a single one-hour lesson, plus, as appropriate, a homework assignment. The homework could be the completion of the Knowledge check questions or end of section assessments. To achieve the Aims for this topic, we recommend doing some of the following activities over the course of the lesson.

Starter suggestions

Setting the scene: Give students this scenario: They have started up their own business, for example, a restaurant or clothes shop. Ask them: 'What issues would you face? Why are you more likely to fail than an established business?' Encourage students to apply the scenario of their business to what they know about this industry, using real-life businesses and competitors as examples.

Contrast: If there is a local business that has recently failed, use this as an example by comparing it to a larger, more well-known business that is successful. You could show photos of local shops that have closed to students as a visual stimulus for this activity. Ask students to suggest why one business failed and the other did not.

Main lesson activities

Discussion and note-taking (whole class): Ask the class why they think some businesses fail. Use pages 38–40 of the Student's Book to expand on all of the reasons, as well as the case study on page 40. Ask students to take notes as appropriate.

Variation: Give each student a set of the cards from Activity sheet 1.3.4A. Read out the description of each reason for business failure on pages 38–40 of the Student's Book, but without giving the heading. Students hold up the card with the reason they think you are describing. Note that students will use these cards again to complete Activity 1.3.4B.

Research task: If the class has access to ICT, they could look into a large business that is well established and successful. They should try to find out when the business started, its history and any specific achievements or problems the business has faced. They should try to identify why the business has become such a success. Ask them to focus on how the business overcame potential problems.

Pairwork activity: Ask students: 'Why are new businesses at greater risk of failing?' Ask them to work in pairs to note down three reasons why they think new businesses are at greater risk of failure than more established businesses. Then ask them to give their reasons and justify them to the class, using the reasons from pages 38–40 of the Student's Book.

Guest speaker/video clip: If possible, invite a guest speaker to come in and talk about their business successes and failures. Alternatively, show a video clip taken from a current affairs website about a business that has failed recently.

Student activity: Ask students to complete Activity sheet 1.3.4B. This activity involves students identifying the main cause of failure for a number of case study businesses.

Skills activity: Use the Skills activity on page 40 of the Student's Book to test students' understanding at this point. Students create a poster with their top three tips for a new business owner.

Knowledge check: Ask students to answer the Knowledge check questions from page 40 of the Student's Book.

Research task: Ask students to research a business that has failed. This is most likely to be a small local business, but could possibly be a larger national business. Ask them to produce a presentation or report giving the reasons why the business failed.

Tip: This could be given as homework.

Plenary suggestions

Class vote: Ask students to use the cards from Activity sheet 1.3.4A to vote on which factor they think has caused the most businesses to fail.

Alternatively, ask students to vote on the factor that has caused failure in different situations. For example:

- A local restaurant opens up near large chains such as McDonald's. Why might this business fail?
- A DVD rental shop or bookstore closes after 23 years. What could have caused this?

Answers to Student's Book activities

Skills activity (page 40): possible outcomes

This poster should be well researched and contain an up-to-date and relevant set of tips for businesses. It should include dangers such as lack of communication, quality dropping and employee morale.

Suggestions may include training, benefits for employees and adapting to changes.

Students should try to include graphs or other numerical evidence to show how many businesses have closed down, or the reasons for the closures.

Students should produce an A4 poster, either on a computer or on paper that clearly shows their top three tips for success. The three points need to be accurate but can vary between students. More able students may put them in order and explain why they have chosen that order.

Students should include images of businesses that have failed, such as closed businesses and for sale signs, as well as images of businesses that have been very successful.

The poster could also include some images of businesses closing which are relevant to their three key tips. For example, a picture of a small clothes shop next to a larger well-known store could represent lack of brand image.

Knowledge check (page 40)

1 **Identify** two reasons why a start-up business may fail.

   Any two from: lack of long-term funding; liquidity or cash flow issues; no reputation; the economy; market conditions; large competitors; lack of management skills; initial errors.

2 **Explain** why poor management decisions can cause a business to fail.

   A poor decision may cause the business to overspend, so the business has less money to spend. This may reduce the working capital of the business so it cannot pay its bills. Poor management may also mean the business misses out on opportunities, does not hire the correct employees or secure the correct source of finance. The business may decide to sell the wrong product in a market that wants something else. The business may use an incorrect pricing method, it may underestimate costs or enter the wrong market.

3 **Explain** why start-up businesses are more likely to fail than established businesses.

Start-ups lack: reputation, customer base, brand loyalty, market share and are vulnerable to larger, more established competitors. In contrast, established businesses have all of these. Small start-up businesses are more likely to have a smaller budget, which may not be enough to keep going long term and therefore they could suffer from poor liquidity.

1.3.4 Why some (new or established) businesses fail: Activities A and B

Activity type

Voting activity

Content

Why businesses fail

Key business term

business failure

Time

20 minutes

Aims

To understand why businesses fail and why new businesses are more likely to fail (1.3.4)

Skills practised

AO1: Knowledge and understanding	✓
AO2: Application	✓
AO3: Analysis	✓
AO4: Evaluation	

Preparation

Make one copy of the voting cards from Activity sheet 1.3.4A for each pair of students and cut them out (or ask students to do this). Make one copy of Activity sheet 1.3.4B for each student in the class.

Procedure

1. Tell students that they will identify the main reason for failure of a number of case study businesses.
2. Divide the class into pairs. Give each pair of students a set of cards from Activity sheet 1.3.4A.
3. Read the scenarios out and allow students to talk briefly with their partner before voting on which factor they think is the main reason for each business failing. Record the majority opinion for each scenario on the board and ask students to justify their decisions using evidence from the case study.
4. Give each student a copy of Activity sheet 1.3.4B and ask them to record the main reason for failure, together with a brief justification using evidence from the case study.
5. Then ask students to write their own scenario in the space at the bottom of the activity sheet to share with other pairs and the class.

Teacher tip: You could ask students to complete the activity individually, and then mark their partner's attempt. This will help them understand what the examiner expects of them.

Variation: Ask students to read and complete the activity sheet in pairs, and hold the class vote after they have done this.

Extension: Ask students: 'Which factor is the most common in causing new businesses to fail?' Hand out the cards from Activity sheet 1.3.4A and ask students to work in pairs to order them from most common to least common. Then ask students to think of a real-life example of a business that has failed for each reason and to write this on the card. Ask for feedback and encourage students to explain their choice of the most common reason.

Suggested answers to Activity 1.3.4

1. The economy; Market conditions
2. Lack of long-term funding; Initial errors; No reputation
3. Larger competitors; No reputation/brand loyalty
4. Lack of long term funding; Lack of management skills
5. Lack of management skills; No reputation
6. Answers will depend on students' scenarios

1.4 Types of business organisation

1.4.1 MAIN FEATURES OF DIFFERENT FORMS OF BUSINESS ORGANISATION

Aims (1.4.1)

Knowledge

By the end of this section, students will:

- understand the key features of sole traders, partnerships, private and public limited companies, franchises and joint ventures
- understand the differences between unincorporated businesses and limited companies
- understand the concepts of risk, ownership and limited liability
- be able to recommend and justify a suitable form of business organisation to owners/management in a given situation
- understand business organisations in the public sector, for example, public corporations.

Resources

- Student's Book pages 41–54
- Activity sheets 1.4.1A, 1.4.1B, 1.4.1C and 1.4.1D

Key business terms

company; control; deed of partnership; franchise; joint venture; limited liability; partnership; private limited company; private sector; public corporations; public limited company; public sector; risk; shares; separate legal entities; sole trader; unlimited liability

Lesson ideas

You should aim to cover the materials in 1.4.1 over four one-hour lessons, plus, as appropriate, homework assignments. The homework could be the completion of the Knowledge check questions or end of section assessments. To achieve the Aims for this topic, we recommend doing some of the following activities over the course of the lessons.

Starter suggestion

Business owners: Ask students if any of their parents/carers or other relatives own their own business or are self-employed. Ask students to explain some of the difficulties and benefits their parents/carers experience in owning their own business. Make a list of some of the key issues on the board.

Tip: Be careful to clear up any student misunderstandings, such as confusing owning a business and owning/running a company.

Main lesson ideas

Discussion and note-taking (whole class): Talk students through the key features of the different types of business organisation, including the advantages and disadvantage of each type. Instruct students to take notes as relevant.

Class discussion: Present students with a selection of business scenarios, using the examples on pages 41–54 of the Student's Book as a starting point. Ask students to recommend a suitable form of business organisation for each one. Encourage them to justify their answers using the key headings on pages 53–54 of the Student's Book.

Student activity: Ask students to complete Activity 1.4.1A. Students read a case study about a sole trader and answer questions to help reinforce their understanding of this concept. Two versions of the activity sheet have been provided to allow for differentiation.

Student activity: Ask students to complete Activity 1.4.1B, a role play activity in which students must find a suitable partner for their business and then draw up a deed of partnership.

Skills activity: Ask students to carry out the Skills activity on page 44 of the Student's Book. Students research a famous business partnership (examples include Marks & Spencer, Hewlett-Packard) and create a presentation about it.

Discussion and note-taking: Explain the key concepts of private and public limited companies: issuing shares to raise capital and shareholder protection (limited liability). Ask students to make notes as necessary. It is important to emphasise the difference between a public limited company and a private limited company. The following table can be used as an easy way for students to remember:

Private/Public	Limited	Company
Who buys the shares – privately selected or the public selects?	Limited liability for shareholders	Can sell shares to raise finance. This means that they have to release financial information.

Private or public limited company?

Write/Display the following statements on the board:
- Limited liability
- Needs £50 000 worth of share capital
- Can employ specialist directors
- Can sell shares via a stock exchange
- Has to release financial information
- Can employ specialist directors
- Easier to control
- Chooses who to sell shares to
- Financial information is available on request
- Must pay corporation tax.

Ask students to work in pairs to decide whether each statement refers to a private or public limited company or to both. They should then decide whether each statement is an advantage or a disadvantage. Take feedback from students, asking them to justify their responses.

Knowledge check: Ask students to answer the Knowledge check questions on page 49 of the Student's Book.

Skills activity: Ask students to carry out the Skills activity on page 51 of the Student's Book, in which they research and evaluate franchise opportunities in their area/country. Good examples for students to research include: Subway, McDonalds, Toni and Guy, TumbleTots.

Student activity: Ask students to carry out Activity 1.4.1C, a role-play activity in which students take on the roles of stakeholders in a proposed joint venture.

Student activity: After talking students through the differences between private sector and public sector organisations, ask them to read the short case study in Activity 1.4.1D and answer the questions.

Knowledge check: Ask students to answer the Knowledge check questions on page 54 of the Student's Book.

Tip: This could be completed as a homework task.

Plenary suggestion

Spider diagram: Ask students to create a spider diagram to include all of the key features of the following organisations: sole trader, partnership, private limited company, public limited company, franchise, joint venture, public sector organisation. This can be done individually or as pairs, depending on the ability of the group. Students can then feed back so you can create a class spider diagram on the board. Students can use this to add to their own diagrams if they missed any important information.

Tip: Allow sufficient time for students to do this (up to 20 minutes). Encourage them to look over their notes and use the Student's Book.

Answers to Student's Book activities

Skills activities: possible outcomes

Skills activity (page 44)

Students' presentations may cover the following points:

- A business that started as a partnership (for example, Warner Brothers).
- Why did they become a partnership? Reasons could include: access to more funds (than if they went into business on their own); more expertise (perhaps the partners had slightly different roles in developing their business); more access to capital (than if they started on their own); to keep control of the business and not have to answer to shareholders.
- Where are they now? It is unlikely that the business will still be a partnership now. Reasons for the change should include: access to more capital to grow the business, having to remain competitive in the type of market (students should mention a floatation or a move into becoming a company); the original partners may have passed the business on to other people to allow for continuity.

Skills activity (page 51)

Students' evaluations should cover the following points:

- what a franchise arrangement is (key terms: franchisee; franchisor; royalties; agreement; start-up fee; brand)
- an explanation of the franchise researched: who it is with; what the business does; the benefits of entering this franchise
- what the franchisor offers and what they expect as part of the agreement, including help provided and length of agreement
- what the franchisor expects in return: amount of the initial fee; how much the yearly royalties are; any additional fees
- whether this is a better business opportunity than setting up independently, including a justification of this decision.

You may prefer students to present their findings as a PowerPoint presentation rather than a role-play scenario.

Knowledge check (page 49)

1 **Define** the term sole trader.

   A sole trader is an unincorporated business that is owned by one person.

2 **Identify** and **explain** two advantages of being a partnership rather than a sole trader.

   Any two advantages and any two from the suggested explanations:

   Partnerships have more expertise available to them. This could allow the business to run more efficiently or offer more services/products, helping the business appeal to a wider market.

   There is less financial risk: liability is shared between all of the partners (with the exception of a silent partner).

   There is greater access to capital: a partnership can have more than one owner, so it can attract more investment from multiple owners and from new partners.

   There is more continuity: if one of the owners leaves the business, the partnership can continue to operate.

3 **Define** the term unlimited liability.

   The owners of a business are personally liable/responsible for the business's debts.

   Also accept: Owners can lose personal possessions if the business is unable to pay its debts.

4 **Explain** one reason why Chahel and Pavel might want to draw up a deed of partnership.

   A deed of partnership is a legally binding document, so it can be used to settle disputes between partners.

5 **Explain** one advantage and one disadvantage of being a public limited company rather than a private limited company.

Any one advantage and any one disadvantage, plus any one explanation per answer:

Advantage: Public limited companies sell shares on the stock exchange. This allows them to raise more finance.

Easy to expand as a public limited company, as they can raise more finance.

Public limited companies can benefit from managerial economies of scale, which allow the business to have managerial expertise.

Disadvantage: Anyone can buy a share in a public limited company. This can mean the business can be taken over.

As a public limited company has more shareholders, decision making can take longer and the existing shareholders could lose control.

6 Chahel has recently considered forming a private limited company. Do you think this is the best form of ownership for his business? **Justify** your answer.

Private limited companies have limited liability, meaning if the company struggles with debt the owners only lose what they have invested and not personal possessions.

As Chahel is going into business with his brother, a private limited business would be possible as shares can be sold to family members and friends.

This could be the best form of business as if any conflict occurred and a brother wanted to leave the business he would only lose the amount invested, unlike with a partnership; this could mean that more security for Chahel and Pavel.

A business is also more likely to grow through a private limited company than a partnership. This means the brothers could look to expand. However, if additional shareholders enter the business it could mean that the brothers may have to give up some control.

Knowledge check (page 54)

1 **Define** the term franchisor.

An existing business that will allow new business to trade under its name.

2 **Explain** two benefits to a franchisee of entering a franchise arrangement.

Any two benefits, plus any one explanation per benefit:

Easier to obtain finance. As franchisees are viewed as less risky, they are easier to set up than an independent business.

Established customer base. This reduces the risk of failure and will not require an expensive advertising campaign.

Systems are often provided. This allows the business to run more efficiently and does not require expensive accounting and stock control systems to be implemented.

Can sell established products. This makes a franchise arrangement less risky and more likely to succeed.

3 **Explain** two disadvantages to a franchisor of entering a franchise arrangement.

The franchisee will keep most of the profit. This means less profit is made by the franchisor than if the business was not owned by a franchisee.

A poor franchisee can do a bad job. This can have a negative impact on the franchisor's reputation.

4 **Explain** the differences between public and private sector organisations in terms of their:

a) ownership

b) objectives.

a) Private sector businesses are owned by private individuals such as sole traders, partners or shareholders, whereas public sector organisations are owned by the government.

b) Private sector business exist to make a profit/money, whereas a public sector organisation exists to provide a service or to provide good value for taxpayers' money.

5 **Define** the term joint venture.

An agreement between two businesses to work together on a project.

6 Explain two benefits to Safesave PLC of forming a joint venture with a Chinese business in order to help their expansion.

Any two benefits, plus any two explanations per benefit:

Risks are shared by both organisations. This is important, as Safesave is entering a new market with very little knowledge of the customers' tastes.

Expertise can be offered by both organisations. This is important, as a Chinese business has knowledge of the market and can provide advice about customers' needs and wants.

Capital can be provided by both organisations. This is important, as the UK-based business is moving location abroad, which will require a lot of finance to pay for items such as premises, new product lines and advertising.

1.4.1 Main features of different forms of business organisation: Activity A

Activity type

Case study

Content

Sole traders

Key terms

sole trader; unlimited liability

Time

30 minutes

Aims

To understand the key features of sole traders, including the advantages and disadvantages (1.4.1)

Skills practised

AO1: Knowledge and understanding	✓
AO2: Application	✓
AO3: Analysis	✓
AO4: Evaluation	

Preparation

Two versions of the activity sheet have been provided for differentiation. Version 2 can be used for lower ability or EAL students. Make one copy of Activity sheet 1.4.1A (either version 1 or version 2, depending on students' ability/language level) for each student in the class.

Procedure

1 Tell students that they are going to read a case study about a sole trader called Ben, and answer some questions about it.
2 Give each student a copy of Activity sheet 1.4.1A (either version 1 or version 2) and ask them to read the case study.
3 Ask students to answer the questions. Encourage them to read page 42 of the Student's Book for additional help.
4 Students should then be prepared to feed back their answers as part of the plenary activity.

Teacher tip: Students could complete the activity as a 'think, pair, share' task.

Activity 1.4.1 A: Suggested answers

Version 1

1 A sole trader is a business owner who is not legally separate from their business that they own and run themselves.
2 Unlimited liability means that a sole trader is personally responsible for any debts run up by the business.
3 As a sole trader, unlimited liability could affect Ben because he is personally responsible for any debts run up by the business. This means his home or other assets may be at risk if the business runs into trouble.
4 *Advantages*: total control of the business by the owner, cheap and easy to set up (there are fewer forms to fill in and it's easier to set up than other forms of business), all the profits are kept by the owner, business records are private therefore the competition can't see what you are earning and so on.

Disadvantages: unlimited liability (personal possessions are at risk if the business goes into debt, income is based solely on the number of hours worked, injury and/or sickness can prevent work and subsequently income and so on.

5 Answers are subjective, accept any answer that is valid.

Version 2

1 Answers from fill in the gap are in bold.

A sole trader is a **person** who **owns** and runs a **business** on his or her own.

Unlimited liability means that the sole **trader** has to **pay** for all of the **debts** of the business.

Questions 2 and 3 should be similar to the answers provided in version 1.

1.4.1 Main features of different forms of business organisation: Activity B

Activity type
Information matching game

Time
45 minutes

Content
Partnership and the role of the deed of partnership

Key terms
deed of partnership; partnership

Aims
To understand the key features of a partnership and the role of the deed of partnership (1.4.1)

Skills practised

AO1: Knowledge and understanding	✓
AO2: Application	✓
AO3: Analysis	
AO4: Evaluation	

Preparation
Make copies of Activity sheet 1.4.1B so that, when you have cut out the information cards, there are enough cards for one per student. Depending on the size of the class, more than one of each card may be used.

Procedure

1. Tell students that you are going to give them a role card with details of their profession, skills, available finance and what they are looking for in a partner. They need to find a person with whom to form a partnership.
2. Shuffle the cards, then give one card to each student.
3. Allow students a few minutes to read through the information on their card and to decide on the kind of person they would like to form a partnership with.
4. Ask students to move around the classroom, asking and answering questions about each other's profession, skills, and so on, in order to find a suitable business partner. (Groups of three partners are also acceptable; partnerships of any more should be at your discretion.)
5. When students have formed their partnerships, ask them to work together to create a table of the advantages and disadvantages of being a partnership instead of a sole trader. Students can use the Student's Book (page 43) for help.
6. Students negotiate the terms of their partnership and draw up a deed of partnership (legal document) for their partnership, using the bullet points on page 43 of the Student's Book to help them.

Teacher tip: Make sure that during step 4 of the activity, students ask and answer questions verbally, rather than show each other their cards.

Teacher tip: Allow students to form partnerships of more than two people, but make sure that the students choose appropriate business partners. Students may also choose to form partnerships with people of a different profession, for example Architect and Tradesperson.

Variation: You may choose to leave out the 'silent partner' cards depending on the ability profile of the class.

1.4.1 Main features of different forms of business organisation: Activity C

Activity type
Role play/group work

Time
1 hour

Content
The effects of a joint venture on a business's stakeholders

Key terms
joint venture; stakeholder

Skills practised

AO1: Knowledge and understanding	✓
AO2: Application	✓
AO3: Analysis	✓
AO4: Evaluation	✓

Preparation
Make one copy of Activity sheet 1.4.1C for each group of six students in the class. Cut out the stakeholder cards and the scenario.

Aims
To understand the consequences of a joint venture on a business's main stakeholders (1.4.1)

Procedure

1 Ask students to imagine that they are the stakeholders of a European company that wants to form a joint venture with a Chinese company. Tell them that they will be working in groups and taking on the roles of the stakeholders. They will each take on the role of one stakeholder and will need to consider the implications of the joint venture for that stakeholder.

2 Divide the class into groups of six. Give a copy of the scenario to each group and give a different stakeholder card to each member of the group. Designate one individual per group to read the scenario aloud to the group. Each group member should then read through their stakeholder card.

3 Students will need to think about the impacts of a joint venture on their allocated stakeholder and discuss them with the group. Allow the group 10 minutes to do this.

4 Ask students to prepare their thoughts on how the joint venture will affect each stakeholder on poster paper using a concept map or spider diagram. The concept map should include: positive impacts of the merger and negative impacts of the merger in the short term and the long term (using the points to consider as a framework). Students should try to rank the impacts in order of importance.

5 Each group should then use the information from their concept maps to evaluate whether they think the joint venture is a good thing, considering the consequences for all of the stakeholders involved.

6 Ask students to present their concept map or spider diagram to the rest of the class. Each stakeholder should present their own contribution.

Teacher tip: Give students clear timings for each of their tasks to avoid discussion drifting off topic. You could collect the stakeholder cards from the students after the designated time limit has been reached.

Extension: Ask the students to write a report advising SweetTaste PLC on the potential takeover. Students should consider:

- short-term benefits and potential problems for the **important** stakeholder groups
- long-term benefits and potential problems for the **important** stakeholder groups
- a judgement on whether they think **they** should go ahead with the merger. They should use the impacts on the **most important** stakeholder group to justify their decision.

1.4.1 Main features of different forms of business organisation: Activity D

Activity type

Case study

Time

45 minutes

Content

The difference between public sector and private sector organisations

Key terms

funding; objective; ownership; private sector; public sector

Aims

To understand the role of the public sector within the economy (1.4.1)

Skills practised

AO1: Knowledge and understanding	✓
AO2: Application	✓
AO3: Analysis	✓
AO4: Evaluation	✓

Preparation

Make one copy of Activity sheet 1.4.1D for each student in the class.

Procedure

1. Tell students that they are going to read a short case study about the health system in the UK. They will then answer some questions to demonstrate their understanding of the differences between private and public sector organisations.
2. Give each student a copy of Activity sheet 1.4.1D and ask them to work individually or in pairs to answer the questions.
3. Ensure that students understand the difference between private and public sector organisations and explain difficult terminology used in the case study, such as privatising.
4. Students can peer assess the activity using the suggested answers or you can assess their work.

Teacher tip: Ensure that students justify their answers to Question 3.

Variation: This activity could be carried out in pairs, instead of individually. You could assess students' understanding by asking them to give a presentation at the end of the session, rather than a piece of written work.

Suggested answers to Activity 1.4.1D

1.

	Private sector organisations	Public sector organisations
Ownership	Owned by private individuals (people like me and you) These can be sole traders, partners (including silent partners) and shareholders	Owned by the government on behalf of the taxpaying public
Funding	Funded through a combination of capital (from banks and share issue) and revenue (money paid by customers to receive their service)	Funded by taxpayers' money
Objective	To make a profit (why else would an individual want to go into business?)	NOT to make a profit, but to provide a service that provides taxpayers with the best value for money

2

Owners: The owners will now be private individuals (shareholders) who will want to make the health system profit making. They will therefore have to make considerable changes to the way the organisation is run, either by increasing the income (from customers) or cutting the costs (as a service provider, the main costs are employees).

Employees: Employees could be split into management/health employees. Management is often replaced when a takeover of a business occurs. This might mean that managers lose their jobs. Terms and conditions of the health employees might change. As the owners are now profit-orientated, it may mean that some employees are made redundant; others might have to change/increase their working hours or accept a pay cut. However, if the health system does become profitable, then employees may receive some of the profit as bonuses or profit sharing. In addition, employees may benefit from a number of other incentives that are more commonly associated with the private sector, such as fringe benefits and better working conditions. Furthermore, doctors and nurses will be able to choose which hospital to work for on the basis of pay; this may mean that the hospitals that pay the highest will have the best health employees.

Customers: As the health system is now profit-making, customers will have to pay for their health care. However, this should mean they receive a better service. As customers will now have to pay, they will have a choice of health care providers, which will lead to increased competition in the market. This may mean that people with more money will be able to pay for the best health care (and have more chance of receiving the top medical treatment) and those with less money (will receive poorer medical treatment, which could risk their lives!).

3 Whether the privatisation would be a good thing depends on a number of factors. Students should make a judgement either way and may use some of the following in their justification.

- Will it mean better health care for everyone or just those who can afford it? What impact will this have on society?
- What is more important with health care: value for money or receiving the best treatment?
- Would it save people money? Many people pay taxes that contribute to funding the health service, yet lead healthy lives and rarely need to use it. How would it affect these people?
- Ultimately, students should make their choice by considering the following question: Is everyone entitled to a certain standard of health care or just those who can afford it?

1.5 Business objectives and stakeholder objectives

1.5.1 BUSINESS OBJECTIVES AND THEIR IMPORTANCE

Aims (1.5.1)

Knowledge	Resources
By the end of this section, students will: • understand the need for business objectives and the importance of them • be able to outline different business objectives, for example, survival, growth, profit and market share • understand the objectives of social enterprises.	• Student's Book pages 55–58 • Activity sheets 1.5.1A and 1.5.1B • Access to ICT for research tasks (websites of businesses and social enterprises that display their aims and objectives on their website)

Key business terms

aims; objectives; SMART objectives; social enterprise

Lesson ideas

You should aim to cover the materials in 1.5.1 in a single one-hour lesson, plus, as appropriate, a homework assignment. The homework could be the completion of the Knowledge check questions or end of section assessments. To achieve the Aims for this topic, we recommend doing some of the following activities over the course of the lesson.

Starter suggestions

Contrast: Ask each student to set some objectives for the next two to three years of their life. These may include results in forthcoming exams, university, employment or other personal goals. Then ask them to reflect on these objectives: what would happen if they didn't set aims and objectives? How would this affect their future plans?

Explain that businesses, as well as individuals, need to set objectives in order to achieve their goals.

Main lesson activities

Discussion and note-taking (whole class): Follow up the starter activity by asking the class what aims and objectives are. Explain the difference between these two terms and use Student's Book pages 55–56 to cover why businesses need aims and objectives. Then explain the objectives listed on page 57, explaining which types of business each objective might be appropriate for. Ask students to make notes as necessary.

Student activity: Ask students to complete Activity 1.5.1A in pairs. Students decide on an appropriate objective for each of the businesses in the scenarios and justify their choice.

SMART objectives: Make sure that students understand what a SMART objective is and why it is helpful to set SMART objectives (page 56 of the Student's Book). Ask them to choose one of the objectives they set in Activity 1.5.1A and make it into a SMART objective for that business.

Research activity: Ask students to research a business of their choice, identifying its aims and objectives. Direct students to larger businesses that often display their aims and objectives on their website and in published documents. Students can then write a short report on their findings, which makes links between the objectives and the business's activity and progress over the years.

Tip: This activity could be set as a homework task.

Student activity: Make sure that students understand the differences between the aims and objectives of a social enterprise and those of other types of business (page 58 of the Student's Book). Then ask students to complete Activity 1.5.1B, a case study about the aims and objectives of Divine Chocolate. Students answer the exam-style questions based on the case study.

Skills activity: Ask students to do the Skills activity on page 58 of the Student's Book. Students research a social enterprise and answer questions about its aims and objectives. They then produce a written report on the social enterprise. You could display students' reports around the room; students walk around and read each other's reports.

Knowledge check: Ask students to answer the Knowledge check questions on page 58 of the Student's Book.

Tip: This activity could be set as a homework task.

Plenary suggestions

Class vote: Give students an example business and ask the class to vote on which objective this business is most likely to set itself. You could give a variety of businesses, including local, national and global, large and small, in different sectors and varying in popularity. Select one student to justify the choice of objective for each business or to argue against this choice.

Poster: Ask students to produce a poster outlining the main aims and objectives for a business of their choice. Encourage them to use a real business and to make sure their aims and objectives are appropriate for this business.

Imagine: Ask students to imagine that they have started up their own business (in their own choice of industry). What aims and objectives would they set themselves? How would these differ from the aims and objectives of established businesses in that industry?

Answers to Student's Book activities

Skills activity (page 58): possible outcomes

Students should choose a social enterprise rather than another type of business, such as a private limited company or sole trader.

Students should identify clear objectives for the social enterprise, which they may have obtained from the website or a phone interview.

They should mention the reasons why it is important for the social enterprise to set objectives (targets, all stakeholders know what they are working towards, measure of success).

They should identify what the social enterprise gives back to its community; this may be money, facilities or resources.

The report should have a conclusion that evaluates whether the social enterprise is achieving its aims and objectives.

Knowledge check (page 58)

1 **Identify** two ways in which a social enterprise is different from a private limited company such as your local shop.

   A social enterprise aims to make a profit but to then use this money to support a social or environmental issue it is linked to, for example, building schools in disadvantaged areas,

   whereas a private limited company will often just share the profit between its shareholders.

   Students need to show they understand the difference between the two.

2 **Identify** the ways in which a business might change its objectives over time.

   A business may change its objectives over time as the business succeeds or fails. If the business performs well, it may change objectives to focus on keeping up this success. For example, it may set higher sales targets.

3 **Explain** why it is important to a business to set SMART objectives.

Having SMART objectives allows a business to make sure it can clearly judge whether it has achieved the objective or not. The objective has to be **specific** so that there is no misunderstanding about whether or not it has been achieved. For example, an objective of a 10 per cent increase in production of red pens will allow stakeholders to see whether this has been achieved. Using a specific product such as red pens means the objective can be **measured** easily. Stakeholders should **agree** upon all objectives so they all know what the business is trying to achieve. Agreeing on the objectives should motivate the workforce to achieve the objectives. It is important that the objectives are **realistic** so that the business can actually achieve them. Allocating a **time** for when the objective should be achieved is also important because it will give everyone a time frame to work towards. It will also give a finish to the objective so it can be measured.

Students need to define SMART objectives and provide explanation/examples of how the SMART objectives help the business. Students must mention all five aspects of a SMART objective in order.

1.5.1 Business objectives and their importance: Activity A

Activity type

Mini case studies

Content

The aims and objectives of businesses

Time

25–30 minutes

Key terms

aims; objectives

Skills practised

AO1: Knowledge and understanding	✓
AO2: Application	✓
AO3: Analysis	✓
AO4: Evaluation	

Preparation

Make one copy of Activity sheet 1.5.1A for each student in the class.

Aims

To understand the need for business objectives; to outline different business objectives (1.5.1)

Procedure

1. Divide the class into pairs. Ask students to discuss with their partner why businesses need to have aims and objectives. Students should try to think of real businesses as examples of when aims and objectives are needed.
2. Hand out Activity sheet 1.5.1A to each student in the class.
3. Ask students to read each of the scenarios and to discuss and decide on an appropriate objective for that business. They should agree on the reason for choosing this objective and then write their objective and a brief justification in the table.
4. Ask pairs to feed back their answers to the whole class, clearing up any misunderstandings as you listen to their suggestions.
5. In preparation for the next question, you could ask students to identify any issues that might be involved in the objectives they have set.
6. Ask students to complete Question 2; they choose one of the businesses and identify any issues that might be involved in the objective they have chosen.

Teacher tip: Encourage students to think about the size and type of each business and how long it has been running when deciding on an appropriate objective. Allow students to refer to the list of objectives on page 57 of the Student's Book if they need to.

Activity 1.5.1A: Suggested answers

1. **Start-up business: Objective:** Market share. **Justification:** because it is new to the market, it will want to measure how many sales it is achieving within the market.
2. **Pepsi: Objective:** Revenue increases. **Justification:** as an established company, Pepsi will want to see if its promotion and product range is increasing sales.
3. **Wise Revise: Objective:** Increase in customer satisfaction levels. **Justification:** it is in a competitive market, with customer word of mouth a key source of promotion.
4. **IKEA: Objective:** Develop product range. **Justification:** keeping its products modern and up to date will be key in improving the business.
5. **Local shop: Objective:** Growth. **Justification:** the business is doing very well.

1.5.1 Business objectives and their importance: Activity B

Activity type

Case study and questions

Content

The aims and objectives of a social enterprise

Time

25–30 minutes

Key terms

aims; objectives; social enterprise

Aims

To understand the aims and objectives of a social enterprise (1.5.1)

Skills practised

AO1: Knowledge and understanding	✓
AO2: Application	✓
AO3: Analysis	✓
AO4: Evaluation	✓

Preparation

Make one copy of Activity sheet 1.5.1B for each student in the class.

Procedure

1. Explain to students that they will be reading a case study and answering a series of exam-style questions.
2. Hand out Activity sheet 1.5.1B and ask students to read the case study first and highlight the key information.
3. They should then work through the questions, either in pairs or on their own.

Teacher tips: You might want to ask more able students to support less able students to understand and complete the questions.

You could use this activity to formally assess students' understanding of social enterprise objectives.

Extension: Ask students to identify and research another social enterprise and to write a case study about their chosen social enterprise.

Activity 1.5.1B: Suggested answers

1. Students provide a suitable definition and an appropriate example.
2. Students provide two relevant objectives, such as survival or increasing market share, and an appropriate explanation of why each would be relevant.
3. As Divine grows it will change objectives. Initially, it will focus on surviving, as the market is very competitive and has many big companies that already dominate the market, for example, Nestlé and Kraft. As the company gets a larger customer base, it will look to expand the business and make itself better known. This is because it can now compete on a larger scale and will need to increase its market share.
4. Social enterprises still need to make a profit because they use this to fund their social activities. For example, Divine uses its profits to build schools. Without profit a business would struggle to continue. Divine also wants to make a profit so that it can use this money to expand and increase its market share. Divine will want to recruit the best employees and facilities and it will use the profit to do this.

1.5.2 The role of stakeholder groups involved in business activity

Aims (1.5.2)

Knowledge

By the end of this section, students will:

- be able to describe the main internal and external stakeholder groups
- understand the objectives of different stakeholder groups
- be able to explain how these objectives might conflict with each other, using examples.

Resources

- Student's Book pages 59–63
- Activity sheet 1.5.2
- Scissors
- Access to ICT for research tasks (newspaper websites)
- Articles from local or national newspapers about stakeholder conflicts

Key business terms

external stakeholder; internal stakeholder; objectives; stakeholder

Lesson ideas

You should aim to cover the materials in 1.5.2 in a single one-hour lesson, plus, as appropriate, a homework assignment. The homework could be the completion of the Knowledge check questions or end of section assessments. To achieve the Aims for this topic, we recommend doing some of the following activities over the course of the lesson.

Starter suggestion

Discussion: Ask students: 'Which businesses do you shop at?' Ask them to vote on the most popular shop they use. Now ask: 'Which other groups have an interest in this business? Why do they have an interest? Do any of the groups you have identified have the same interests? Do any of them have opposing interests?'

Main lesson activities

Discussion and note-taking (whole class): Use pages 59–63 of the Student's Book to cover what a stakeholder is, the different internal and external stakeholders, and why the objectives of different stakeholders may conflict. Ask students to make notes as necessary.

Discussion: Using the same business as in the starter activity, ask students to use the knowledge they now have of stakeholders to list all the stakeholders of this business. They can discuss this in pairs or small groups before you take feedback from the class. Make a definitive list of all the stakeholders of this business on the board. Praise each pair/group that names a stakeholder than no other group has thought of.

Tip: Alternatively, you could set this as a homework task, perhaps giving students a different business this time.

Student activity: Ask students to complete Activity sheet 1.5.2, which provides practice in identifying internal and external stakeholders and in recognising the different viewpoints of stakeholders.

Class debate: Give students a scenario from the local or national press that involves a conflict between the stakeholders of a business. For example, a local petrol station is going to expand and offer a range of goods that is similar to the goods on sale in a local convenience store. Ask students to first identify the different stakeholders and then to state which stakeholders would support/object to the situation. Allocate different stakeholder roles to pairs or groups of students and ask them to argue their case to the whole class. The class can then vote on the outcome that would best resolve this conflict.

Tip: This activity could be done as a research task. If the class has access to ICT, students could access local or national newspaper websites to find an article about a stakeholder conflict involving a business.

Student activity: Give students a local business to examine and ask them to identify the different stakeholder groups.

Skills activity: Ask students to complete the Skills activity on page 63 of the Student's Book, in which they identify the views of different stakeholders of a planned new airport.

Knowledge check: Ask students to answer the Knowledge check questions on page 63 of the Student's Book.

Tip: This activity could be set as a homework task.

Plenary suggestions

Hot seat: Invite a volunteer to come and sit in the hot seat at the front of the class. The student has to name as many internal and external stakeholders as they can, giving a brief explanation or example of each. When they pause for more than three seconds, invite another student to take their place.

Role play: Give students a scenario, for example, BP is to build a new oil rig in Antarctica. Give students a variety of stakeholders, some of whom would support and some of whom would object to this venture. In small groups, students act as their chosen stakeholder, outlining what that stakeholder might say about the scenario. Alternatively, allocate stakeholder roles to individual students and ask them to present their viewpoint to the class. Encourage students to think about what each stakeholder might say, even if they do not agree with that viewpoint.

Contrast: Ask students to pick two groups or individuals who have an interest in a large company such as Nike, Adidas, Zara, Starbucks or Walmart. They should then contrast what each of their chosen stakeholders wants from the company, first looking at the similarities and then at the differences.

Answers to Student's Book activities

Skills activity (page 63): possible outcomes

Suggested arguments for and against:

For the new airport:	Against the new airport:
• extra jobs for the local community	• increased pollution
• extra revenue for the local area and increased tourism to boost the economy	• reduction in spending elsewhere in the country
• opportunities for new businesses to set up because of better transport links.	• more congestion on roads.
Stakeholders for the new airport:	**Stakeholders against the new airport:**
government, local community, business owners, trade unions and suppliers.	local community, local businesses and pressure groups.

There may be conflict between different members of the local community, with some benefiting from the new jobs created, while others object to the extra pollution and congestion. A key stakeholder conflict might be between the local residents and the government: the government might want to increase employment and wealth in the area, whereas the local community might dislike the noise and other pollution.

Students should identify the key stakeholders in this scenario (local residents, airline and local businesses) and show a clear understanding of their views.

Students should identify the increase in business and positive impact on the local economy, as well as the negative impacts.

Students could make a judgement for either side, as long as their judgement has a clear argument to support it.

Knowledge check (page 63)

1 Define the term internal stakeholder.

   An individual or group that has an interest in the business and that is within the business and normally participates in the day-to-day running of the business; for example, an employee or owner.

2 Define the term external stakeholder.

   An individual or group that has an interest in the business and that is outside of the business and does not work directly for the business; for example, a customer, supplier, member of the local community.

3 **Identify** a possible objective for two stakeholders of a local convenience store.

   Any two stakeholders, such as: employee; owner; supplier; local community; government.

   Students provide an appropriate objective for each stakeholder mentioned.

4 **Identify** two stakeholders of the Exxon oil company.

   Any two stakeholders such as: employee; owner; supplier; local community; government; pressure group; trade union; shareholders.

5 Using an example, explain why stakeholders will often conflict in their objectives.

   Example answer: Different stakeholders will have varying views of what the business should do on a day-to-day basis. For example, customers will often want cheaper prices as this is their priority, whereas, a shareholder will want to see the business make as much profit as possible so they can be paid a high dividend. This means that their objectives will clash.

   Some stakeholders may have short-term objectives for the company (for example, profit) as opposed to longer-term stability.

   Students must use examples of two stakeholders whose objectives conflict and clearly identify why they conflict, with examples.

1.5.2 The role of stakeholder groups involved in business activity: Activity

Activity type
Sorting activity

Content
The difference between internal and external stakeholders

Time
25–30 minutes

Key terms
external stakeholder; internal stakeholder; objectives; stakeholder

Aims
To understand the difference between internal and external stakeholders; to explain why the objectives of some stakeholders conflict (1.5.2)

Skills practised

AO1: Knowledge and understanding	✓
AO2: Application	✓
AO3: Analysis	✓
AO4: Evaluation	✓

Preparation
Make one copy of Activity sheet 1.5.2 for each pair of students in the class. Give pairs of scissors to cut out the cards. (Alternatively, cut them out yourself first.)

Procedure
1. Tell students that Activity 1.5.2 is in two parts: first they will sort stakeholders into internal and external stakeholders; they then identify stakeholders who both support and oppose a variety of situations.
2. Give a copy of Activity sheet 1.5.2 to each pair of students and ask them to cut out the cards in Part 1.
3. For Part 1, students work with their partner to sort their cards into two groups. You could offer a small prize to the pair that does this the fastest.
4. For Part 2, students need to choose two stakeholders who would support each situation, and two who would oppose it.
5. Hold a class discussion based on the feedback from different pairs. Encourage students to discuss, debate and justify their choices.

Teacher tip: For Part 2 of the activity, emphasise that this is not a race, and that students should take time to discuss with their partner the situation and the different stakeholder views.

Variation: You could organise this as a whole-class activity with the two headings on a whiteboard. Enlarge the activity cards to A3 size. Invite individual students to come up and stick each stakeholder card under the correct heading.

Extension: Ask students to identify stakeholders whose views may conflict.

Suggested answers to Activity 1.5.2

Part 1:

Internal stakeholders: employees; business owners.

External stakeholders: trade unions; pressure groups, local residents; government; banks; local businesses; local community.

Part 2: (Other answers are also acceptable, as long as students are able to justify their choices.)

1. Support: new business owners and customers. Object: pressure groups and local residents.
2. Support: business owners and employees. Object: local residents and local businesses.
3. Support: banks and employees. Object: pressure groups and local residents.
4. Support: local businesses and pressure groups. Object: government and trade unions.
5. Support: local community and business owners. Object: pressure groups and local businesses.

1.5.3 Objectives of private and public sector enterprises

Aims (1.5.3)

Knowledge

By the end of this section, students will understand:

- the differences in the aims and objectives of private sector and public sector enterprises.

Resources

- Student's Book pages 64–66
- Activity sheet 1.5.3
- Access to ICT for research tasks (websites that state the objectives of private and public sector organisations)
- Materials to produce a poster

Key business terms

objectives; private sector; public sector

Lesson ideas

You should aim to cover the materials in 1.5.3 in a single one-hour lesson, plus, as appropriate, a homework assignment. The homework could be the completion of the Knowledge check questions or end of section assessments. To achieve the Aims for this topic, we recommend doing some of the following activities over the course of the lesson.

Starter suggestion

Discussion: Ask students to list as many private and public sector businesses/organisations as they can. Students could do this first in pairs and then share their answers with the class. Ask them to identify which sector each of their suggestions belongs to and then write them under the two headings on the board.

Main lesson activities

Discussion and note-taking (whole class): Go through the differences between the private and public sectors and their different objectives, using pages 64–66 of the Student's Book. Ask students to make notes as appropriate.

Make a list: Ask students to choose one of the private sector businesses and one of the public sector organisations that they suggested in the starter activity. Ask them to list the different objectives of these businesses. During feedback, ask students to identify and agree on the key differences between a private and public organisation.

Skills activity: Ask students to do the Skills activity on page 64 of the Student's Book. They produce a poster showing the aims and objectives of a local private sector business.

Research activity: If they have access to ICT, students could research public and private sector businesses/organisations. They should focus on the different aims and objectives of the businesses/organisations they research.

Tip: For homework, you could ask students to write a report based on their research. The report should focus on one organisation from each sector, contrasting the objectives of each organisation.

Student activity: Ask students to complete Activity sheet 1.5.3, which focuses on the differences between public and private enterprises.

Knowledge check: Ask students to answer the Knowledge check questions on page 66 of the Student's Book.

Tip: This activity could be set as a homework task.

Skills activity: Ask students to debate the question in the Skills activity on page 66 of the Student's Book. After the pair-work discussion, develop the discussion into a class debate, with some students arguing for and some against the proposal. Use the Case study feature to help students identify points for the debate.

Plenary suggestions

Exit pass: Tell students that to earn an 'exit pass' from the lesson, they must each write on a small piece of paper their name, one aim/objective of a private sector business and one aim/objective of a public sector business. Once they have done this, collect in the papers. If students' suggestions are correct, allow them to leave.

Answers to Student's Book activities

Skills activities: possible outcomes

Skills activity (page 64)

The poster should focus on a local private business of any size. It should clearly show the aims and objectives of this business. If students choose a larger business, the aims and objectives may be available from the business's website. For smaller businesses, students may only be able to identify broader aims and objectives. The poster should be very clear and include images as well as text.

Skills activity (page 66)

Arguments for: lower prices for consumers; more control over the products; very important in some markets such as fire arms and pharmaceuticals; businesses can be easily regulated and improved.

Arguments against: reduces innovation and entrepreneurism; reduces competition between firms; reduction in quality; lack of choice for consumers.

Reward students who offer alternative valid arguments. Students should identify the key argument for each side and be able to justify this.

Knowledge check (page 66)

1 **Define** the term public sector.

   The public sector is made up of government-owned and funded organisations that deliver services to the public/provide services such as the police and hospitals.

2 **Outline** why businesses in the same industry set different aims and objectives.

   The businesses may have different owners who want to do different things. Every entrepreneur is different and will have a different opinion on how to run a business. Some businesses may be social enterprises and so have an additional aim other than profit. The businesses within an industry may be at different stages, for example, the aim of a start-up business may be survival, whereas more established businesses may focus on reputation, R&D, market share, increasing profit, and so on.

3 **Explain** why the government may set up and run businesses.

   The government may need to run certain services that do not attract private businesses, for example, medical services. Some services may not lend themselves to being operated by a private firm, for example, the police in many countries are public sector. By using government funding, services can be offered on a large scale without the pressure of making a profit. For example, in many countries, the government runs the energy industry, providing electricity and gas to its population. This is because it can run the service at break-even or even a loss to make sure everyone can afford these services.

1.5.3 Objectives of private and public sector enterprises: Activity

Activity type

Case study

Content

The difference between public and private enterprises

Time

30 minutes

Key terms

private sector; public sector

Aims

To understand the difference between public and private enterprises (1.5.3)

Skills practised

AO1: Knowledge and understanding	✓
AO2: Application	✓
AO3: Analysis	✓
AO4: Evaluation	✓

Preparation

Make one copy of Activity sheet 1.5.3 for each student.

Procedure

1. Tell students that they will be reading two scenarios involving the public and private sectors. Explain that they will be working in small groups in Part 1 to help them prepare for answering the exam-style questions in Part 2.
2. Divide the class into small groups, and give each student a copy of Activity sheet 1.5.3.
3. Ask students to read the two scenarios in their groups and to complete Part 1 of the activity sheet.
4. Help students to identify the stakeholders in the oil company scenario if necessary. Make sure that the students in each group select a variety of stakeholders with differing viewpoints.
5. Move around the groups, asking questions to help students develop their ideas about the stakeholders and their views.
6. You may like to take feedback after Part 1 of the activity, and write a list of key stakeholders and their viewpoints on the board. Refer to the suggested answers provided.
7. Ask students to answer the questions in Part 2 individually. Allow about 15 minutes for them to do this.
8. You could either mark students' answers as a formal assessment or take feedback verbally. Alternatively, hand out the suggested answers for students to peer assess.

Teacher tips: *Students often struggle to remember the difference between private and public sector businesses. Encourage them to focus on what private means: owned by a private person.*

Encourage students to link the different stakeholders with the aims and objectives of private and public sector businesses.

Variation: Ask students to design their own case studies that illustrate the differences in aims and objectives of private and public sectors.

Extension: Ask students to write their own question and to swap questions with another student to complete.

Suggested answers to Activity 1.5.3

Part 1

1. In your group, create an argument for or against the government taking over the oil company.

   For: maintains jobs; the government can monitor health and safety, working conditions and pensions.

   Against: the government may not be as efficient as a private owner; the government may be supporting or buying a business that it is not able to run in the long term.

2. Each person in the group should take the role of a different stakeholder who may be affected by this takeover. How do you think your stakeholder feels about the takeover? Prepare your viewpoint and then present it to the group.

   Stakeholders: employee; employer; manager; owner; local community; government; suppliers; trade unions.

Part 2

1. Identify and explain two reasons why the government should take over the failing oil company.

   The takeover will save jobs, which will keep people working and spending in the economy. This is better in the long term as it reduces poverty, unemployment and a possible recession.

2. Choose one stakeholder in the oil company. Why would they support or object to this takeover?

   Students should provide: a suitable stakeholder from those identified in Part 1; why they would object/support with a brief explanation to support this.

3. Explain why a private business such as Wise Revise often aims to expand.

   A private business aims to make a profit and is owned by private individuals. These private individuals may wish to keep increasing the amount of profit a business makes. By expanding the business, the owner hopes to increase market share and profit. In contrast, public sector organisations often aim to stay as they are, and will prioritise other aims above expansion.

4. Evaluate the impact of too many public sector services in one country.

   The public sector is owned and funded by the government, for example, health care. If businesses are owned by the private sector, they often need to be competitive on quality and customer service. This improves the experience for the customer. Too many public sector businesses could reduce competition and entrepreneurship in the country. This could negatively impact on long-term expansion of industries and jobs as businesses do not have to innovate to stay competitive.

1 Understanding business activity: Key terms revision

Define each term and provide an example or explanation. There are 2 marks per definition.

Term	Description/Definition
added value	
entrepreneur	
factors of production	
franchisee	
opportunity cost	
partnership	
private sector organisation	
public sector organisation	
specialisation	
takeover	
tertiary sector	

2 People in business

Introduction

People management is a topic students seem to enjoy. While students often think that managing people is easier than it actually is, the motivation, recruitment and trade union topics are accessible enough to be easily understood while also offering enough challenge for students to feel stretched. Students also love discussing cases related to legal controls, and this is a great way for them to engage with the material and to help them develop skills of analysis and evaluation.

The activities in this section are designed to help scaffold this type of learning. They offer accessible, practical and relevant tasks that students can enjoy, but at the same time they challenge students to think about the subject in depth with greater precision and, importantly, more analytically. They include:

- a categorisation exercise on **motivation** theory
- an examination of **methods of motivation** using a jigsaw reading activity
- a categorisation exercise on **organisation and management**
- a group-work task and matching activity on the **role of management**
- an investigation of **leadership styles** using a categorisation exercise
- a **trade union** role-play exercise
- a **recruitment methods** role-play activity
- a group discussion of different **training methods**
- a pair-work crossword on **reducing the size of the workforce**
- a group-work exercise to explore legal **controls over employment**
- a memory game on types of **internal and external communication**
- a **communication** listening activity.

To introduce students to the concepts they will study and to help gauge prior student knowledge, a useful starter activity might be:

> Put the students in small groups and issue each group with a sheet of A3 paper. Instruct the students to draw an image of a teacher in the centre of the page (if you are brave enough give them a picture of yourself or department colleague to use). Ask the students to think about teachers as 'employees of the school' and then to consider the following questions:
>
> – Are teachers paid too much?
> – What happens if a teacher does something wrong?
> – Who manages teachers/who leads them?
> – Does the school have too many teachers?
> – Do teachers work hard enough?
> – How are schools/teachers organised?
> – How does the school recruit teachers?
>
> These questions should generate some lively conversations that will allow you to prompt each group to think, in technical terms, about some of the key topics within Section 2 – '… so would teachers work harder if we paid them more?', '… so does money really motivate?', '… what else motivates then?', and so on.

The People topic is ideal for introducing and reinforcing the skill of evaluation. Managing people is never easy and answers never simple. Use the **Skills Builder** at the end of Section 2 of the Student's Book to help develop students' ability to weigh up the significance of a firm's actions, to decide which course of action might be most appropriate in a given situation and, importantly, to justify, with detailed explanations, why the recommend action is relevant. Build student confidence by showing that – especially where people are concerned – there is rarely one right answer; sound and reasoned logic to support a recommendation is what matters most.

2.1 Motivating employees

2.1.1 THE IMPORTANCE OF A WELL-MOTIVATED WORKFORCE

Aims (2.1.1)

Knowledge

By the end of this section, students will understand:

- why people work and what motivation means
- the concept of human needs, for example, Maslow's hierarchy
- key motivational theories: Taylor and Herzberg.

Resources

- Student's Book pages 78–85
- Activity sheets 2.1.1A and 2.1.1B
- Small pieces of paper

Key business terms

absenteeism; competitive advantage; higher order needs; hygiene factors; industrial action; labour turnover; lower order needs; Maslow's Hierarchy; motivation; motivators; physiological needs; productivity; safety needs; scientific management; self-actualisation; self-esteem; social needs; two-factor theory

Lesson ideas

You should aim to cover the materials in 2.1.1 in two one-hour lessons, plus, as appropriate, a homework assignment. To achieve the Aims for this topic, we recommend doing some of the following activities over the course of the lessons.

Starter suggestions

Variation before the lesson: As homework before the lesson, ask students to complete the Skills activity on page 79 of the Student's Book, which requires students to consider what motivates them and their friends and to present their findings in visual form.

Lesson 1 Pair-work: Pair students up and ask them to discuss what the word 'motivation' means. Then ask them to interview each other, trying to find out what motivates their partner. They should note down key words (for example, money, friends, popularity) as they go.

Ask each pair to write their key words on the board. Discuss the findings with the group to lead into the topic.

Lesson 2 Question–Answer–Correct: Ask students to write down on a small piece of paper two questions related to the material covered in the previous lesson (an outline of what motivates people and whichever motivation theorists were covered). Collect in the pieces of paper and redistribute them among the class. If students get their own question back, they should swap with another student. Ask students to write an answer to the question on the same piece of paper. Mix the questions/answers up again and redistribute them a third time. This time ask students to check (using the Student's Book) that the answer is correct. Choose a few students to read out their questions and (correct) answers.

Main lesson activities

Discussion and note-taking (whole class): What is motivation? What motivates people? Talk students through each motivational theorist (pages 79–85 of the Student's Book), instructing them to take notes as appropriate.

Group work: Split the class into groups and assign a motivational theorist to each group. Ask each group to research the theorist using both the Student's Book and whatever other resources are available. The group should produce a one-page summary/poster of the theory and then present their research to the whole class. If appropriate, photocopy each summary/poster for the whole group.

Skills activity: As a way of reinforcing Maslow's Hierarchy, ask students to complete the Skills activity on page 82 of the Student's Book.

Investigation: As a stand-alone activity or as an extension of the Skills activity on page 82, ask students to work in groups and investigate a number of different employee roles within the school. If appropriate, allow them a short time to walk around and interview people. Make sure that students consider employees other than just teachers (for example, caterers, cleaners, lab technicians).

They should consider the answers they receive and decide which motivational theorist the answers might be most closely aligned to. Their questions could focus on what motivates the individual, which elements of Maslow's Hierarchy are met or what factors lead to them feeling unmotivated (Herzberg's hygiene factors).

Ask students to present their findings in the form of a short role-play situation to the whole class. For example, they might role-play two cleaners talking to each other about their jobs, explaining in their narrative what motivates them.

Student activity: Ask students to complete Activity 2.1.1. You will need Activity sheets 2.1.1A and 2.1.1B. Students work in small groups and categorise motivational theorists against appropriate elements of each motivational theory.

Plenary suggestions

Discussion: Ask students to define 'motivation' and to list the factors that motivate people. Compare their answers with the responses from the first lesson. Praise students who use key terms and appropriate theory.

Ask students to think about how a business might use knowledge of motivation and motivational theories. To help them prepare for topic 2.1.2, ask them to list all the ways they can think of that a business attempts to motivate its employees.

Skills activity: Ask students to complete the Skills activity on page 85 of the Student's Book. This requires students to examine and summarise the motivational strategies of a company they know about, presenting their findings in report format.

Tip: This exercise could be given as homework.

Answers to Student's Book activities

Skills activities: possible outcomes

Skills activity (page 79)

Students may need prompting to move responses beyond fame and fortune. Encourage them to think about things they do that do not link directly to money or popularity. Allow scope for students to use their imagination to present suitable images. You may wish to prepare some exemplar images in advance, for example, an image of a school-based community service activity to represent self-actualisation.

Skills activity (page 82)

Try to move students' responses beyond direct monetary reward. Encourage them to consider the intrinsic rewards of each job. You could ask students to consider the training (the hours and the personal sacrifice) each job requires. Ask them to consider what this suggests about the link between motivation and money.

Possible levels of Maslow's Hierarchy of Needs might include:

Olympic athlete:	self-actualisation
Rice farmer:	physiological needs; safety needs
Airline steward:	physiological needs; safety needs; belonging needs
Airline pilot:	physiological needs; safety needs; belonging needs; esteem needs
University student:	self-actualisation (through the value of academic study)
University professor:	physiological needs; safety needs; belonging needs; esteem needs
Teacher:	physiological needs; safety needs; belonging needs; esteem needs; self-actualisation
Bank manager:	physiological needs; safety needs; belonging needs; esteem needs

Skills activity (page 85)

Suggest to students that they use the headings and language from the topic to guide their report. You could ask them to include a certain number of relevant key terms in their report. A report of two sides of A4, with some images, should be sufficient.

Knowledge check (page 85)

1 **Identify** the different levels of Maslow's Hierarchy of Needs.

   Physiological needs/basic needs; safety needs; belonging needs; esteem needs; self-actualisation.

2 **Explain** why 'safety needs' are important to employee motivation.

   Any three from: Safety needs help people to work without fear (of physical or emotional harm) or lack of job security. If safety needs are not in place, an individual will not focus on performance (or higher-order needs), productivity may therefore be lower and/or labour turnover higher.

   Accept any appropriate combination of the above or other reasonable suggestions.

3 **Identify** two problems that arise when applying Maslow's theory in practice.

   Accept answers related to the following (any two):

   Generalisation: Not all employees will respond in the same way.

   Applicability: It may be impossible to meet some needs (self-actualisation) in the workplace.

   Work/life: Some employees may simply address the lower-order needs through work and higher-order needs outside of work. This makes it difficult for a firm to motivate beyond a basic level.

4 **Explain** Taylor's view of employee motivation.

   Taylor believed money could motivate; a fair day's pay for a fair day's work; time and motion studies – one best way to perform a task.

5 **Outline** the main points of Herzberg's 'Two-factor theory'.

   Hygiene factors: pay; working conditions; environment.

   Motivators: empowerment; enrichment; teamwork.

6 **Identify** two reasons why having motivated employees is so important to business.

   Any two from: lower labour turnover; improved productivity; customer service benefits; innovation benefits; quality benefits.

2.1.1 The importance of a well-motivated workforce: Activity

Activity type

Categorising activity

Content

Theories of motivation

Time

30 minutes

Key terms

higher order needs; hygiene factors; lower order needs; Maslow's Hierarchy; motivation; motivators; physiological needs; safety needs; scientific management; self-actualisation; self-esteem; social needs; two-factor theory

Aims

To understand the key motivational theories (2.1.1)

Skills practised

AO1: Knowledge and understanding	✓
AO2: Application	
AO3: Analysis	
AO4: Evaluation	

Preparation

Photocopy and cut up one set of the activity cards from Activity sheet 2.1.1A for each group of three students in the class. Make one copy of Activity sheet 2.1.1B enlarged to A3 size for each group of three students.

Procedure

1. Tell students that they are going to complete a categorising activity about the different motivational theories.
2. Divide the class into groups of three students and hand out a set of activity cards (from Activity sheet 2.1.1A) and an enlarged copy of Activity sheet 2.1.1B to each group.
3. Ask students to place the cards in a pile face down on the table in front of them.
4. Explain that they must take turns to take one card from the pile and read it aloud to their group. They must then collectively agree on where to place the card on Activity sheet 2.1.1B.
5. If students cannot agree, or are unsure where to place the card, they may put it to one side and move on to the next card.
6. Move around the class, ensuring that students are doing the activity correctly.
7. Elicit the correct answers from students during the class feedback stage of the activity so students can check their answers.

Teacher tip: Emphasise to students that this is not a competitive activity and the objective is not to be the first to finish. Instead, they should take their time to discuss each card in detail, making sure they back their opinions up with justification.

Extension: Ask students to categorise Herzberg's motivators/hygiene and Taylor's scientific management theory against Maslow's Hierarchy. Following this, ask students to identify the similarities and differences between the different motivational theories. You could ask each group to prepare a poster on one of the motivational theories, which could be used for a classroom wall display on motivation.

Suggested answers to Activity sheet 2.1.1

	Maslow's Hierarchy	Taylor's Scientific Management	Herzberg's Two-Factor Theory
Key terms with explanations or examples	Physiological needs, for example, food, water, clothing and shelter Safety needs, for example, a safe working environment and job security Social needs, for example, good working relationships and being part of a team Esteem needs, for example, promotion, recognition and positive feedback from managers Self-actualisation, for example, achievement through promotion and personal development Lower order needs: physiological, safety and social needs Higher order needs: esteem and self-actualisation needs	Scientific management: employees will be motivated to work hard if they are given specific instructions and they are rewarded with money.	Hygiene factors, for example, basic needs, positive working relationships, safe working conditions, fair pay, job security Motivators, for example, a sense of achievement, recognition, interesting work, responsibility, promotion
Money as a motivator	People are initially motivated by money so that they can satisfy their lower order needs. Once these needs have been met, they will be motivated by other factors.	People are motivated only by money. They will be more productive if they are paid more.	People need money in order to satisfy their basic needs. If their basic needs are not met, they will not be motivated to work hard.
Usefulness for businesses	Helps managers to identify the specific need that motivates each employee. Managers can then focus on satisfying these needs in order to get the best out of their employees.	Works well in manufacturing businesses where the production line is divided into a series of simple tasks which can be completed by unskilled employees.	Businesses must first make sure that employees' basic needs are satisfied if they are to be motivated by factors such as additional responsibility, promotion and achievement.
Limitations of the theory	May not apply to all employees in all situations. Some individuals may be motivated by esteem needs over money. In practice, it is difficult to find a workplace reward for each need of each individual employee.	There are factors other than money which motivate employees. Performing repetitive tasks can lead to boredom and low motivation. This theory is of little use in the service industry in which output is difficult to measure and jobs are highly skilled.	Factors cannot be neatly grouped into categories for every individual or for every situation. Some employees may not respond to motivators such as the opportunity for promotion. Factors change over a person's lifetime. Low pay might not be a demotivator for some people later in life.

2.1.2 Methods of motivation

Aims (2.1.2)

Knowledge

By the end of this section, students will understand:

- financial rewards as a method of motivation
- non-financial methods of motivation
- how to recommend and justify appropriate methods of motivation in given circumstances.

Resources

- Student's Book pages 86–94
- Activity sheets 2.1.2A and 2.1.2B
- Flashcards with key terms related to financial and non-financial methods of motivation (made by the teacher)

Key business terms

motivation; job satisfaction; job rotation; job enlargement; job enrichment; multiskilling; teamwork; training opportunities; financial rewards; non-financial rewards; incentive schemes; fringe benefits; job design; piece rate; time rate; wages; overtime; salary; commission; bonus; performance-related pay; profit sharing; share ownership; teamwork; labour retention; productivity; empowerment

Lesson ideas

You should aim to cover the materials in 2.1.2 in two one-hour lessons, plus, as appropriate, a homework assignment. To achieve the Aims for this topic, we recommend doing some of the following activities over the course of the lessons.

Starter suggestions

Lesson 1 Pair-work: If your students did the Skills activity from 2.1.1 on page 85 of the Student's Book in class or as homework, ask them to share their findings in small groups and discuss what methods of motivational strategies they found in their chosen company.

Half and half: Split the class in half. Ask one half to discuss and justify the statement 'Money motivates'. Ask the other half to discuss and justify the statement 'Money does not motivate'. In a mini-debate, each half should try to convince the other of their position. Write language relevant to the topic on the board for later discussion.

Lesson 2 Flashcards: Produce a set of flashcards with key terms related to financial and non-financial methods of motivation (see the Key business terms list above). Split the students into groups. Give each group a set of flashcards and ask them to sort the cards under the relevant headings.

Main lesson activities

Discussion and note-taking (whole class): Discuss with students the difference between financial and non-financial methods of motivation. Include examples of when each method might be used.

Group work: Split the class into groups and assign a motivational method (financial or non-financial) to each group. Ask the groups to research the method and produce a one-page summary or poster. They should include suggestions of when the method might be used in practice. The group then presents their research to the whole class. If appropriate, photocopy each summary/poster for the whole class.

Tip: If class size allows, you could further sub-divide groups, asking them to focus on, for example, particular elements of financial or non-financial rewards.

Reading exercise: Assign each student in the class a job role (perhaps using those listed in the Skills activity on page 89 of the Student's Book): teacher, manual factory employee, engineer, car salesperson, waitress/waiter, soldier. Ask students to make up a brief biography for their character (children/no children, age, gender, interests, and so on). Ask them to read the topic with that person in mind and to identify which of the motivational methods listed might be appropriate for that person and that role.

Student activity: Ask students to complete Activity sheet 2.1.2B in small groups, using the case studies in Activity sheet 2.1.2A. In this activity, students suggest suitable motivational methods for a variety of situations.

Skills activity: Ask students to complete the Skills activity on page 94 of the Student's Book. Students examine the methods of non-financial motivation used by a business familiar to them.

Tip: This exercise makes a good extended homework task.

Plenary suggestion

Skills activity: Ask students to complete the Skills activity on page 89 of the Student's Book. It requires them to suggest appropriate methods of financial reward for different jobs.

Answers to Student's Book activities

Skills activities: possible outcomes

Skills activity (page 89)

Suggested answers:

- teacher: salary, holidays, discounted school fees for own children, childcare, housing
- manual factory employee: wage, free lunch, free safety clothing, short working week/hours
- engineer: salary, company car, perks such as corporate gym membership
- car salesperson: commission, discounts, company car
- waitress/waiter: wage, free food, flexi-hours
- soldier: salary, housing, travel allowance, extended holidays, pension.

Skills activity (page 94)

Encourage students not just to list methods, but to analyse why these methods are (or are not) appropriate to the context. You could suggest the following headings to guide students' responses: 'Methods used', 'Why these methods?', 'Do the methods work?'

Knowledge check (page 94)

1. **Identify** two methods of financial reward.

   Any two from: salary; wage; time rate; piece rate; bonus; PRP; profit share; share ownership, commission.

2. **Identify** two methods of non-financial reward.

   Any two from: job enlargement; job rotation; job enrichment; empowerment; teamwork.

3. **Explain**, using an example, what is meant by the term commission.

   Accept either: percentage (or fixed fee) related to sale of product(s)

   or: fixed fee for production of a specific piece of work (for example, an artist commission).

   Knowledge: Student demonstrates understanding of commission.

   Analysis: Student uses and explains appropriate example.

4. **Identify** one major advantage of profit share as a method of financial incentive.

   It links employee performance (motivation) to overall company performance.

   Knowledge: Student demonstrates understanding of profit share and its advantages.

5. **Justify** appropriate methods of pay for the following:
   a) nurse: salary or time-rate wage
   b) freelance graphic designer: salary or commission
   c) lawyer: salary
   d) manual production line employee: piece rate
   e) production line manager: salary
   f) hotel cleaner: time rate (hourly wage).

6 **Explain**, using an example, what is meant by the term fringe benefit.

Forms of non-financial reward, such as a company car or discounts on company products, offered as part of an employee's basic package.

Knowledge: Student demonstrates understanding of fringe benefit.

Analysis: Student uses and explains an appropriate example.

7 **Define** the term job rotation.

The process of switching an employee between tasks or jobs over a period of time as a way of introducing job variety.

Knowledge: Student demonstrates some/good understanding of job rotation.

8 **Define** the term job enrichment.

An attempt to make a job more challenging or rewarding through greater variety, scope, training and/or decision-making power; may involve additional pay or access to benefits.

Knowledge: Student demonstrates some/good understanding of job enrichment.

2.1.2 Methods of motivation: Activity

Activity type
- Jigsaw reading

Content
- Methods to motivate employees

Time

25 minutes

Key terms

bonus; commission; empowerment; financial rewards; fringe benefits; incentive schemes; job design; job enlargement; job enrichment; job rotation; job satisfaction; labour retention; motivation; multiskilling; non-financial rewards; overtime; performance-related pay; piece rate; productivity; profit sharing; salary; share ownership; teamwork; time rate; wages

Skills practised

AO1: Knowledge and understanding	✓
AO2: Application	✓
AO3: Analysis	✓
AO4: Evaluation	✓

Preparation

Photocopy and cut up the activity cards from Activity sheet 2.1.2A and make one copy of Activity sheet 2.1.2B for each student in the class.

Aims

To recommend and justify appropriate methods of motivation in given circumstances (2.1.2)

Procedure

1. Tell students that they are going to complete a jigsaw reading task in which they will have to discuss the best way to motivate an employee.
2. Divide the class into three equal groups: A, B and C. From Activity sheet 2.1.2A, hand out Case study 1 to each member of group A, Case study 2 to each member of group B and Case study 3 to each member of group C. Also hand out a copy of Activity sheet 2.1.2B to each student in the class.
3. Explain that each group is going to read a different case study about an employee who is unhappy in their job. Together they should decide on the three best ways to improve the employee's motivation and job satisfaction. They should also make notes in the relevant section of Activity sheet 2.1.2B.
4. Tell students that they will have about 10 minutes to do this, after which time they will be regrouped with students who have read different case studies.
5. Allow students enough time to discuss their allocated case studies in sufficient depth and to make notes.
6. Following this, regroup students so that there is one student from group A, one from group B and one from group C in each group. Give students about 10 minutes to each share the details of their case study with the others in the group and explain the methods they would use to improve motivation and job satisfaction. Students should listen to each other and make brief notes in the relevant sections of Activity sheet 2.1.2B. They should also contribute additional points or ask questions to clarify their understanding.
7. Round off the activity by nominating a few students to share their recommended methods of motivation with the class.

Extension: Students choose one case study and write a response to the following exam question:

Identify and *explain* three methods that could be used to improve the employee's motivation.

2.2 Organisation and management

2.2.1 ORGANISATIONAL CHARTS

Aims (2.2.1)

Knowledge	Resources
By the end of this section, students will understand: • simple hierarchical structures: span of control, levels of hierarchy, chain of command • the roles and responsibilities of directors, managers, supervisors, other employees in an organisation and the inter-relationships between them.	• Student's Book pages 95–99 • Activity sheet 2.2.1 • Organisational chart of the school/institution • Presentation software or materials to make a poster

Key business terms

organisational chart, departments, hierarchy, chain of command, span of control, subordinates, flat structure, tall structure, de-layering

Lesson ideas

You should aim to cover the materials in 2.2.1 in a single one-hour lesson, plus, as appropriate, a homework assignment. To achieve the Aims for this topic, we recommend doing some of the following activities over the course of the lesson.

Starter suggestion

Skills activity: Start the lesson with the Skills activity on page 98 of the Student's Book. Display an organisational chart of your school/institution and discuss the various positions/departments. Start at the top and make the link between the head teacher's role and the CEO or managing director of a business organisation. Ask students if the head teacher is at the top of the hierarchy – explain the role of a governing body (if applicable) that employs the head teacher to run the school/institution on their behalf. Link this to the shareholders of a business who employ the managing director to run the business.

Main lesson activities

Discussion and note-taking (whole class): Ask students to copy the organisational chart of the school/institution. Explain the key features of the organisational chart: departments, hierarchy, chain of command, span of control, the roles of individuals and the inter-relationship between the various departments. Students should annotate the organisational chart, making notes where necessary.

Student activity: Ask students to complete Activity sheet 2.2.1, in which they produce two versions of a business's organisational chart both before and after structural changes within the company. Students could produce either a presentation of their charts and annotations or two posters (one for each chart).

Flat and tall structures: Explain flat and tall structures and de-layering, including the benefits and problems of each type of structure, using pages 96–98 of the Student's Book. Students should make notes.

Review: Ask students to review the school's/institution's organisational chart covered at the beginning of the lesson, adding any further annotations in the light of what they have learned about span of control.

Knowledge check: Ask students to answer the Knowledge check questions on page 99 of the Student's Book.

Tip: This exercise could be given as homework.

Plenary suggestions

Feedback: Students present their findings from Activity sheet 2.2.1 to the rest of the class. Question the groups about the type of structure (tall or flat) and the key features.

Knowledge check review: Go through the suggested answers for the Knowledge check questions, asking students to self-assess their work.

Answers to Student's Book activities

Skills activity (page 98): possible outcomes

The organisational chart may look like the following:

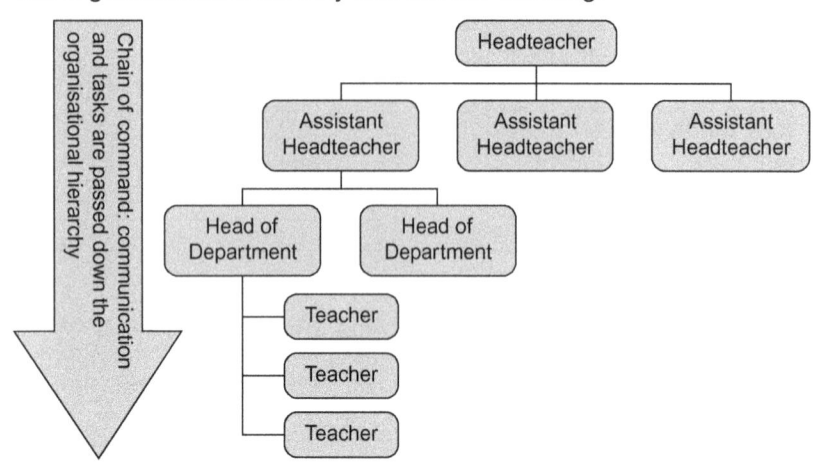

```
                    Headteacher
         ┌──────────────┼──────────────┐
    Assistant      Assistant      Assistant
   Headteacher   Headteacher    Headteacher
    ┌─────┴─────┐
 Head of    Head of
Department  Department
              ├── Teacher
              ├── Teacher
              └── Teacher
```

Chain of command: communication and tasks are passed down the organisational hierarchy

Knowledge check (page 99)

1 Outline the term chain of command.

The chain of command is the path that is used to pass tasks/communication down the organisation, from top to bottom.

The chain of command shows the chain of authority within the organisation: who is responsible for which employees.

Bolanle is a project manager for a Nigerian building firm, BuildTech. He has a deadline in two weeks' time, so he wants to pass the authority of completing some of his tasks to one of his subordinates. BuildTech has a tall structure, Bolanle is one of many project managers.

a) Explain what is meant by the term subordinate.

An employee who is under the control of another.

b) Identify Bolanle's span of control.

Three people.

c) Explain one advantage and one disadvantage to Bolanle of his company having a tall organisational structure.

Any one of the following advantages and explanations:

More managerial positions; this can make it is easier to monitor subordinates' performance.

More layers in the hierarchy; this can mean more promotion opportunities for employees.

More chance of promotion for employees; this can mean higher motivation.

Any one of the following disadvantages and explanations:

Chains of command are longer, so communication can take longer.

There are more management roles, so the business has to pay more for management salaries.

Spans of control tend to be narrow, so managers have fewer subordinates to delegate to.

d) Explain the differences between a tall and a flat structure in an organisational chart.

Tall structures have long chains of command, whereas flat structures have shorter chains of command. Tall structures have narrow spans of control, whereas flat structures have wide spans of control. Flat structures have fewer management roles, whereas tall structures have more management roles. Managers find it easier to delegate tasks in flat structures. There are fewer subordinates for managers to delegate to in tall structures.

2.2.1 Organisational charts: Activity

Activity type

Categorising activity

Content

Features of an organisational chart

Time

45 minutes

Key terms

chain of command; departments; flat structure; hierarchy; organisational chart; span of control; subordinates; tall structure

Aims

To understand the main features of an organisational chart (2.2.1)

Skills practised

AO1: Knowledge and understanding	✓
AO2: Application	✓
AO3: Analysis	
AO4: Evaluation	

Preparation

Make one copy of Activity sheet 2.2.1 for every student in the class or one copy for every two students, if students are working in pairs.

Procedure

1. Ask students to read about organisational charts on pages 95–99 of the Student's Book.
2. Read the case study, Suits for You Ltd, together as a class (Activity sheet 2.2.1).
3. Explain that students need to use the information about the organisation to construct two organisational charts for Suits for You Ltd: one chart for before their change of structure, and one chart for after their change of structure. They can work individually or in pairs to do this.
4. Help students by asking them questions about the roles given in the case study and pointing out any relevant information to them as necessary.
5. Students annotate their charts to explain the key terms: 'chain of command', 'hierarchy' and 'span of control' as they apply to Suits for You Ltd.
6. Tell students that they should be prepared to feed back to the class and display their organisational charts as part of the lesson plenary.

Teacher tip: Make links to related areas of the syllabus so students can see how the organisational structure of an organisation impacts on how the human resources department is managed. Make links to motivation, communication, training, management and leadership.

Extension: Ask students to evaluate why the new organisation chart represents a more effective way of organising the employees of Suits For You Ltd.

2.2.2 Role of management

Aims (2.2.2)

Knowledge

By the end of this section, students will understand:

- the functions of management, for example, planning, organising, coordinating, commanding and controlling
- the importance of delegation and trust versus control.

Resources

- Student's Book pages 100–102
- Activity sheets 2.2.2A, 2.2.2B, 2.2.2C, 2.2.2D and 2.2.2E
- Photo of a well-known manager (for example, from sport, industry or the head teacher)
- Newspapers, scissors, sticky tape, a tennis ball

Key business terms

commanding; controlling; coordinating; organising; planning

Lesson ideas

You should aim to cover the materials in 2.2.2 in a single one-hour lesson, plus, as appropriate, a homework assignment. To achieve the Aims for this topic, we recommend doing some of the following activities over the course of the lesson.

Starter suggestion

Management skills: Put on the board a photo of a well-known manager that students will recognise and relate to. This could be a manager from the sporting world, from industry or from within the school (for example, the head teacher). Ask students to suggest skills that make this manager good at their job. Use students' suggestions and make a definitive list of key skills a manager might need around the photo. Ask students to make notes.

Main lesson activities

Discussion and note-taking (whole class): Building on the starter activity, explain the key features of a good manager (introduced on page 100 of the Student's Book), emphasising the importance of delegation (pages 101–102) in order to manage the manager's resources (employees) effectively. Ask students to make notes as necessary.

Case study: Use the case study on page 100 of the Student's Book to give students a real example of a good manager. Ask students to give examples of other good managers that they know of and/or provide them with further examples.

Spider diagram: Using the Student's Book to help them, ask students to create their own spider diagram of what makes a good manager.

Skills activity: Ask students to do the Skills activity on page 101 of the Student's Book. Allow students sufficient time to complete this, as they will need to interview a manager within the school/institution to find out what makes this person a good manager.

Student activity: Ask students to carry out the group work task on Activity sheet 2.2.2A (see the Activity 1 notes). This requires students to work in groups to plan and construct a bridge. The activity is designed to develop their understanding of the need to plan, delegate, control and coordinate to complete a particular project. Students review the task using Activity sheets 2.2.2B and 2.2.2C.

Knowledge check: Ask students to answer the Knowledge check questions on page 102 of the Student's Book.

Tip: This exercise could be given as homework.

Plenary suggestion

Student activity: In order to consolidate students' learning from this topic, ask them to carry out the matching exercise on Activity sheet 2.2.2D or the gap-fill exercise on Activity sheet 2.2.2E, according to ability (see the Activity 2 notes). Students can then peer assess each other's work.

Answers to Student's Book activities

Skills activity (page 101) possible outcomes

Students' questions should cover the key points, and might include:

- Do you delegate work to employees within your span of control?
- If yes, how do you manage each subordinate effectively to ensure they know what to do?
- How do you organise your time to make sure you manage your workload?
- Have you ever had to make any decisions that were unpopular? If so, how did you manage this?

Students' reports should cover the results all of the questions they asked. Award higher marks for linking the manager's responses to the main skills of a good manager: coordination (managing subordinates); controlling (reviewing the progress of tasks/subordinates); organising (in order to manage their workload effectively); commanding (ensuring that all subordinates understand their tasks).

Encourage students to include a judgement at the end of their report, outlining whether they think the person they interviewed is a good manager.

Knowledge check (page 102)

1 **Explain** two characteristics that would make Fawaz a good manager.

   Any two characteristics and explanations from:

   Planning: Managers have to plan how they aim to achieve a specific objective that they have set.

   Organising: Managers have to organise their resources effectively, for example, time, employees, finance and the day-to-day running of a project or a business.

   Commanding: A good manager must set clear expectations of how his or her employees should perform.

   Controlling: Managers need to control the day-to-day activities and continually evaluate their effectiveness.

   Coordinating: Managers have to effectively coordinate their employees to ensure that enough resources are allocated to particular tasks.

2 **Explain** how coordinating is an important characteristic for a manager like Fawaz.

   Coordinating is important for Fawaz to ensure that he makes the best use of his employees. This is important as 60 per cent of his employees work part time, so he needs to ensure that there are enough employees on a shift to help the business run effectively. This might include ensuring that there are enough employees on the shift at times of high demand such as weekends.

3 Define the term delegation.

   When a manager gives authority to a subordinate to complete a task, but the manager is still responsible for making sure that the task is completed.

4 **Explain** two benefits to benefits to Fawaz of delegating tasks to his supervisors.

   Any two benefits and explanations from: Delegation can allow Fawaz more time to spend on other tasks. This will enable him to complete these other tasks more quickly or to a higher standard

   Delegating will allow Fawaz to assess his subordinates' abilities, which will allow him to manage his resources more effectively in the future as he will be aware of his subordinates' capabilities.

5 **Explain** one disadvantage to Fawaz of delegating tasks to his supervisors.

   Any one disadvantage and explanation from: A subordinate may not complete the task on time, which will delay the project or mean Fawaz has to take the task off the subordinate in order to complete it on time.

   A subordinate may not complete the task to the required standard. However, Fawaz is still responsible for the task so he would be held accountable for its success or failure.

2.2.2 Role of management: Activity 1

Activity type

Group work

Content

Building a bridge

Time

45 minutes

Key terms

control and trust; commanding; controlling; coordinating; delegation; organising; planning

Aims

To understand the role of management – planning, organising, coordinating, commanding and controlling and to recognise the importance of delegation: trust versus control (2.2.2)

Skills practised

AO1: Knowledge and understanding	✓
AO2: Application	✓
AO3: Analysis	✓
AO4: Evaluation	✓

Preparation

Make one copy of Activity sheet 2.2.2A for each group of four or five students and enough copies of Activity sheets 2.2.2B and 2.2.2C for all the students in the class (one copy of the manager's review form for each group manager, and one copy of the team's review form for each of the other group members). Provide enough resources for students to complete the activity: four newspapers, one pair of scissors and a roll of sticky tape for each group of four or five students.

Procedure

1. Tell students that they are going to take part in a bridge-building activity that will allow them to experience what a manager's role involves. Their task is to work in groups to build as large a bridge as they can from newspaper, with one of the group members acting as project manager.

2. Organise students into groups of four or five.

3. Ask students to choose one student in their group to act as project manager. Explain that the manager's task is to organise the group into clear tasks, coordinate the timings, control the outcome and direct the group. The role of the manager is to supervise the task; he or she must not take part in the planning or building.

4. Tell students that they will need to do the following:
   - plan their bridge, given the resources available
   - build the bridge
   - review the effectiveness of the manager.

5. Tell the managers that they will need to do the following:
   - allocate students for the planning task
   - allocate students for the building task
   - make changes as necessary during the task
   - review the success of both tasks.

6. Ask students to evaluate the effectiveness of the manager in their group. Each group member should complete the appropriate form.

Teacher tip: You may wish to use a tennis ball to check how strong each bridge is; you could include it as one of the judging criteria on the review forms.

Extension: Ask students to write up their review of the task as a report.

2.2.2 Role of management: Activity 2

Activity type
Matching activity

Content
The main features of a manager's role

Time
10 minutes

Key terms
commanding; controlling; coordinating; delegation; organising; planning

Aims
To understand the role of management (2.2.2)

Skills practised

AO1: Knowledge and understanding	✓
AO2: Application	
AO3: Analysis	
AO4: Evaluation	

Preparation
Make one copy of Activity sheet 2.2.2D or Activity sheet 2.2.2E (as appropriate) for every student in the class.

Procedure
1. Tell students that they are going to carry out a matching activity to check their learning from this topic.
2. Give a copy of Activity sheet 2.2.2D to each student in the class.
3. Ask students to identify the correct definition for each aspect of the role of manager.
4. Go through the answers with the class. Students can peer assess each other's work.

Variation: Cut out the key terms and definitions from Activity sheet 2.2.2D and mix them up. Divide the class into pairs or small groups and give a set of cards to each pair/group. Ask students to work together to match up the key terms and definitions.

Extension: Use Activity sheet 2.2.2E instead, which requires students to identify the missing definitions/terms and fill in the gaps.

Answers to Activity sheet 2.2.2D

Delegating: Giving authority to a subordinate to complete a particular task, while still being responsible for the successful completion of the task

Controlling: Supervising tasks to make sure that employees meet a particular aim or objective; making decisions during the task if it is not going as planned

Organising: Using his or her own time and the team's time in the most efficient way

Coordinating: Ensuring that all the employees understand how their role impacts on other employees or departments in the business, in order to achieve a particular aim or objective

Planning: Preparing a number of different strategies to complete a particular task, including any necessary backup plans if a particular strategy fails

Directing: Communicating tasks and instructions to employees in the most appropriate way

2.2.3 Leadership styles

Aims 2.2.3

Knowledge

By the end of this section, students will understand:

- the features of the main leadership styles, for example, autocratic, democratic and laissez-faire
- how to recommend and justify an appropriate leadership style in given circumstances.

Resources

- Student's Book pages 103–107
- Activity sheet 2.2.3
- Flashcards with characteristics of the three main leadership styles (made by the teacher with suitable adjectives to describe each leadership style, for example, firm, relaxed, inclusive, and so on.)
- Flashcards in three colours, with the three different leadership styles on them (made by the teacher with one leadership style on each, using a different colour card for each style).
- Newspaper cuttings/print-outs from the internet of stories about the people in the Skills activity (Richard Branson, Sheikh Khalifa bin Zayed Al Nahyan, Aung San Suu Kyi, Angela Merkel, Sheryl Sandberg, Alex Ferguson)

Key business terms

autocratic leadership; democratic leadership; laissez-faire leadership

Lesson ideas

You should aim to cover the materials in 2.2.3 in a single one-hour lesson, plus, as appropriate, a homework assignment. To achieve the Aims for this topic, we recommend doing some of the following activities over the course of the lesson.

Starter suggestion

Modelling: Start the lesson by modelling the three leadership styles. For example, demonstrate, as appropriate, autocratic or laissez-faire leadership as students enter the room. Then model each of the other leadership styles. Follow this up by asking students to vote on whether they should do any work this lesson or not.

Ask students to describe the different styles you modelled. Write key terms and appropriate adjectives on the board.

Tip: Depending on the ability of your class, you may want to ask students to identify each style immediately after you have modelled it.

Main lesson activities

Discussion and note-taking (whole class): Talk students through each leadership style, instructing them to take notes as appropriate. Make sure that you cover the appropriateness of different styles in different contexts. Refer to the case studies on pages 105 and 106 of the Student's Book for examples of different styles in context.

Group work: Split the class into three (or, if you have a large class, six) groups and assign a leadership theory to each group. Ask each group to research the theory they have been assigned and to produce a one-page summary/poster of the theory. Each group should present their research to the whole class. If appropriate, photocopy each summary/poster for the whole class.

Role play: Put students in small groups and ask them, to devise short role plays for each of the leadership styles, referring to the Student's Book if necessary. Ask one group for each style to act out their role play to the whole class.

Set the scene: Split the class into pairs. Ask students to take each leadership style and to create two situations (a short story/scene) – one where the leadership style might be appropriate and one where it might be inappropriate. Ask pairs for each leadership style to present their situations to the whole class.

Student activity: Ask students to complete Activity 2.2.3, in which they categorise statements about each of the leadership styles under the correct headings.

Knowledge check: Ask students to answer the Knowledge check questions on page 107 of the Student's Book.

Tip: This exercise could be given as homework.

Skills activity: As a useful summary exercise to this topic, ask students to complete the Skills activity on page 107 of the Student's Book. The activity requires students to investigate and evaluate the leadership styles of several famous leaders. Show students the newspaper cuttings/print-outs you have brought in to help with this.

Tip: This exercise could be given as homework.

Plenary suggestions

Word wall: Give each student one of the flashcards you have made and a small piece of sticky tape. Write the three leadership styles on the board and ask students to stick their flashcard under the appropriate heading. Use this 'word wall' as the basis for a discussion.

Which type of leadership? Give each student the three leadership flashcards you have made. Using PowerPoint, show different management situations or managers and ask students to respond by holding up the flashcard which they think is the most appropriate leadership style. The colours will help you to easily identify any general misunderstandings and areas for clarification.

Answers to Student's Book activities

Skills activity (page 107): possible outcomes

Students may interpret the leaders' styles differently. Accept any reasoned answer, but encourage students to consider alternative styles. To support this activity, you could collect newspaper cuttings on the various leaders both as source material and as a guide to presentation style.

Knowledge check (page 107)

1. Using appropriate examples, **outline** the differences between management and leadership.

    Leaders set the vision, direction and mission of an organisation; they inspire others to follow their vision.

    Managers put a leader's vision into action; they plan the business activities and implement the business strategy.

2. **Identify** one situation when an autocratic management style might be the most appropriate

    Any one from: crisis situation; military organisation; low-skill/low-pay manual labour situations.

3. **Outline** the differences between democratic and laissez-faire management styles.

    Democratic: managers value employee opinion and see they input on decisions; Laissez-faire: managers control/interfere with employees in only a limited way, employees are left to achieve tasks in the best way they think suitable.

4. **Outline** a suitable leadership style for each of the following situations:

    a) creative design agency: laissez-faire

    b) law firm: democratic

    c) car production factory; autocratic/democratic

    d) hospital surgery: autocratic.

2.2.3 Leadership styles: Activity

Activity type

Categorising activity

Content

Features of the main leadership styles

Time

20 minutes

Key terms

autocratic leadership; democratic leadership; laissez-faire leadership

Aims

To identify the features of the main leadership styles and the conditions in which each style might or might not be appropriate (2.2.3)

Skills practised

AO1: Knowledge and understanding	✓
AO2: Application	
AO3: Analysis	
AO4: Evaluation	

Preparation

Photocopy and cut up one set of the cards on Activity sheet 2.2.3 for every three students in the class.

Procedure

1. Ask students to read about the different styles of leadership on pages 103–105 of the Student's Book.
2. Tell students that they are going to work together in groups of three to categorise statements under each of the three styles of leadership: autocratic, democratic and laissez-faire.
3. Divide the class into groups of three and give a set of cards to each group (see the *Teacher tip* below).
4. Explain that students should take turns to pick up a card and read it aloud to their group before agreeing where to place it. Emphasise that this is not a competitive activity and they should take their time to consider each card carefully.
5. Move around the room, making sure that students are doing the activity correctly.
6. Allow students sufficient time to complete the task. Round off the activity by eliciting the correct answers from the class.

Teacher tip: It is a good idea to store sets of cards in resealable zip lock plastic bags. Students can then draw one card at a time from the bag to discuss with their group. This also allows you to store sets of cards for later use in another lesson.

Extension: Using what they have learned from this activity, students think of situations in which each type of leadership would be appropriate or inappropriate. Some possible contexts: a doctor in a hospital; a manager of a McDonald's restaurant; scientists developing new medicines for a pharmaceutical company; a marketing team designing an advertising campaign for a new sports shoe.

2.2.4 Trade unions

Aims (2.2.4)

Knowledge

By the end of this section, students will understand:

- what a trade union is and the effects of employees being union members.

Resources

- Student's Book pages 108–109
- Activity sheets 2.2.4A and 2.2.4B
- Video clips of industrial action (optional)
- Websites or other information about trade unions in the students' country

Key business terms

collective bargaining; trade union

Lesson ideas

You should aim to cover the materials in 2.2.4 in a single one-hour lesson, plus, as appropriate, a homework assignment. To achieve the Aims for this topic, we recommend doing some of the following activities over the course of the lesson.

Starter suggestions

Discussion: If you are a member of a trade union, discuss the role of trade unions from your own point of view. Make sure you cover why you joined, the cost of joining and the benefit of being a member of your union.

Video clips: Use video clips from YouTube (www.youtube.com) to show students examples of industrial action. Try searching for 'public sector march [name of country]' or 'strike action [name of country]'. Ask students to suggest why they think the strike action took place.

Main lesson activities

Discussion and note-taking (whole class): Explain the role of trade unions and collective bargaining using pages 108–109 of the Student's Book, asking students to make notes as necessary.

Skills activity: Ask students to do the skills activity on page 108 of the Student's Book. Ideally, they need access to the internet to research two trade unions. Alternatively, provide students with materials giving information about a number of different trade unions, including the benefits to employees of joining, and the cost of membership.

Student activity: Ask students to do the role play in Activity 2.2.4. They take the role of one of the stakeholders in an industrial dispute and present their arguments. They then complete a judgement grid evaluating the arguments presented for each stakeholder group.

Knowledge check: Ask students to answer the Knowledge check questions on page 109 of the Student's Book.

Tip: This exercise could be given as homework.

Plenary suggestion

Ask students to feed back on Activity 2.2.4 using their judgement grids. Lead a discussion on the impacts of strikes on employees, employers and customers. After the discussion, ask students to write down three impacts on each of these stakeholder groups.

Answers to Student's Book activities

Skills activity (page 108): possible outcomes

Students could produce a brief table of the benefits and costs for two of these trade unions and then recommend which union they would join.

Example trade union: Unite (public sector trade union in the UK)

Benefits of joining:

- representation in the workplace
- free legal advice
- reduced rates on mortgages
- cheaper insurance rates.

Cost to the member:

- £12.05 per month.

Example trade union: Transport Workers' Union of Australia

Benefits of joining:

- the union aims to secure employees the best pay, conditions and safety standards
- it is a national trade union so has a large collective power
- it campaigns for employees through national and local media.

Cost to the member:

- 10 Australian dollars per month.

Knowledge check (page 109)

1 **Explain** two benefits to an employee who joins a trade union.

   Any two benefits and explanations from:

   Trade unions work to protect employees' pay and conditions, so businesses have to offer employees a fair employment contract.

   Trade unions often provide legal advice and support for their members, which makes it cheaper for members to have access to legal support if necessary.

   Collective bargaining allows employees to have more of a voice; the more members who join the union, the more power the union has in industrial disputes.

2 **Outline** what is meant by collective bargaining.

   Collective bargaining is the negotiations between employers and a trade union. A trade union will negotiate on behalf of its members. The more members a trade union has, the stronger the bargaining position.

3 **Explain** two reasons why you think it might be beneficial to employees, such as Mutya, if everyone joined the same union.

   The union would have more members, so it would have more power with collective bargaining.

   Communication between the union and the employer would be easier because the employer would only have to negotiate with one union.

2.2.4 Trade unions: Activity

Activity type
Role play

Content
Considering the roles of stakeholders in an industrial dispute

Time
45 minutes

Key terms
collective bargaining; trade union

Aims
To understand the role of trade unions in industrial disputes (2.2.4)

Skills practised

AO1: Knowledge and understanding	✓
AO2: Application	✓
AO3: Analysis	✓
AO4: Evaluation	✓

Preparation
Make one copy of Activity sheet 2.2.4A for each group of three or four students in the class and one copy of Activity sheet 2.2.4B for every student in the class.

Procedure

1. Split the class into groups of three or four students.
2. Explain that students will read a case study about an industrial dispute and take the role of different stakeholder groups.
3. Give one copy of Activity sheet 2.2.4A to each group and one copy of Activity sheet 2.2.4B to each individual student.
4. Ask students to read through the scenario. Alternatively, you could read the scenario to the class to make sure that all students understand the context.
5. Within each group, students need to decide who will take the role of each stakeholder group (employers, customers and employees).
6. Depending on the size of the groups, students work either individually or in pairs to prepare arguments for their stakeholder group. Tell them that they have 20 minutes to prepare their argument based on the scenario.
7. When all of the students are ready, they should present their arguments to the rest of their group, who should complete the judgement grid on Activity sheet 2.2.4B.
8. Finish by holding a feedback session. Each group should give their judgement on the situation to the whole class. Listen to all of the groups' feedback and then give an overall judgement on which stakeholder group has presented the best arguments.

Teacher tip: Stress that the refuse collectors offer a public service. Because they work in the public sector, there is little alternative for customers if they want their refuse taken away.

Extension: Give students the following scenario, explaining that the stakeholder groups are the same. Ask students to repeat the activity using this new scenario.

Teachers in [insert a country of your choice] *have decided to go on strike to protest against a five-year pay freeze (salaries have not increased for five years) and changes to their working conditions that mean they will have to work longer hours. Teachers are complaining that the employers are asking them to work longer hours for less pay. The government (the employer) believes that the changes are necessary as teachers are costing taxpayers too much money.*

2.3 Recruitment, selection and training of employees

2.3.1 RECRUITING AND SELECTING EMPLOYEES

Aims (2.3.1)

Knowledge	Resources
By the end of this section, students will understand: • methods of recruitment and selection • the difference between internal and external recruitment • the main stages in recruitment and selection of employees • how to recommend and justify who to employ in given circumstances • the benefits and limitations of part-time and full-time employees.	• Student's Book pages 110–117 • Activity sheets 2.3.1A, 2.3.1B and 2.3.1C • Flashcards of the different stages of the recruitment process (made by the teacher – see below) • Small cards with short statements relating to internal or external recruitment (made by the teacher – see below) • A4 paper • Examples of job descriptions, person specifications and job advertisements from newspapers or job websites

Key business terms

aptitude test; assessment centre; employment contract; external recruitment; full time; induction; internal recruitment; interview; job advertisement; job application; job description; part time; person specification; psychometric test; recruitment; shortlist

Lesson ideas

You should aim to cover the materials in 2.3.1 in two one-hour lessons, plus, as appropriate, a homework assignment. To achieve the Aims for this topic, we recommend doing some of the following activities over the course of the lessons.

Starter suggestions

Lesson 1 Their shoes: Depending on your context, ask students to indicate if they have (or have had) a part-time job. Ask if they needed to apply for that job and, if so, how they applied. Write any key terms on the board.

Your shoes: In contexts where few students have part-time jobs, ask them to describe what they think the process of recruitment is for a teacher in the school. Write any key terms on the board.

Lesson 2 Recap: Prepare a series of flashcards showing the different stages of the recruitment process. Ask students to put the flashcards in order. For a higher-ability group, you may wish to remove cards and ask students to identify which stages are missing. Alternatively, you could add in new stages not yet introduced.

Main lesson activities

Discussion and note-taking (whole class): Talk students through the methods of recruiting and selecting employees, asking them to take notes as appropriate. Ensure that you cover the advantages and disadvantages of the different approaches.

Find a friend: Prepare a series of short statements on small cards, each of which **either** describes internal or external recruitment **or** gives an advantage or disadvantage of either type of recruitment. Give students one statement each. Ask them to walk around the room, comparing statements with each other, and to organise themselves into two groups according to their statements: one group for internal recruitment and one for external. Once completed, ask each student to read the text on their card aloud in order to introduce the differences between internal and external recruitment to the whole group.

Skills activities: To reinforce understanding of job descriptions and person specifications, ask students to complete the Skills activity on page 112 of the Student's Book.

Following on from this, ask students to complete the Skills activity on page 114 of the Student's Book. They draw up a job advertisement based on their person specification/job description.

Tip: This exercise makes a useful homework task.

Tweet it: Put students into pairs. Ask them to draw a copy of the recruitment and selection flowchart on page 110 of the Student's Book on the left side of a page of paper (or photocopy a version of the flowchart on A4 paper and give one copy to each pair). Using no more than 140 characters, students should describe each stage of the process. You may wish to follow this up by asking students to Snapchat or Tweet their definitions to each other. The receiver should identify the stage of recruitment described in the Snapchat or Tweet.

Student activity: Ask students to do the recruitment role play in Activity 2.3.1. They need to know the stages of recruitment for this activity.

Debate: Split students into appropriate groups and ask them to debate part-time versus full-time employment. Ask some groups to take the point of view of employees and others the point of view of a business. Discuss responses with the whole group once complete.

Knowledge check: Ask students to complete the Knowledge check questions on page 117 of the Student's Book.

Tip: This exercise could be given as homework.

Plenary suggestion

Recruitment strategy: Using suitable examples of jobs (such as manual factory employee, car salesperson, waitress/waiter, soldier, engineer), ask students to outline a suitable recruitment strategy (including appropriate stages of recruitment and selection). Encourage them to apply their knowledge to the particular context of the job. They should consider internal and external recruitment, and whether a part-time or full-time employee might be appropriate.

Answers to Student's Book activities

Skills activities: possible outcomes

Skills activity (page 112)

Students should refer to the Student's Book, and you may also want to give them examples of job descriptions and person specifications from newspapers or job websites. In order to draw out application skills, focus on comparisons between the different descriptions and person specifications. Ask students to consider why the jobs may require different types of skills/different types of people.

Skills activity (page 114)

Students should refer to the Student's Book, and you may also want to give them examples of job advertisements from newspapers or job websites. Ensure that students make the advertisement applicable to the particular job and don't write a generic advertisement.

Knowledge check (page 117)

1 **Explain** two differences between a job description and a person specification.

Job description: A description of the tasks, role and responsibilities of a particular position.

Person specification: A description of the type of person, their skills qualifications and experience, required to fill a particular vacancy.

Knowledge: Student demonstrates some understanding of job descriptions and person specifications. Student demonstrates good understanding of job descriptions and person specifications, using appropriate examples and terminology.

2. **Explain** two items that might appear in a job description and two that would appear in a person specification for a teaching position.

   Person specification: required skills, qualifications or attributes; previous experience.

   Job description: job title, role description, location of job, responsibilities.

3. **Explain** why a business might prefer internal recruitment.

   Any three from: cheaper; faster; less risk; motivating for employees.

4. **Outline two** advantages of external recruitment.

   External recruitment is employing people from outside of the business. This can bring fresh ideas into the business and possibly encourage current employees to work harder meaning that the workforce is more productive and aware of ideas from outside the business.

5. **Explain** what psychometric tests are used for.

   Testing the suitability of personality and/or aptitude for a firm/position.

6. **Explain** the factors a firm will need to consider when selecting an appropriate method of recruitment.

   Cost; length of time; type of position; skills/suitability of current employees.

   Knowledge: Student demonstrates some/good understanding of McGregor Theory X–Y.

   Analysis: Student uses and explains an appropriate example/gives a suitable explanation.

2.3.1 Recruiting and selecting employees: Activity

Activity type
Role play

Time
40 minutes

Content
Recruitment process

Key terms
aptitude test; assessment centre; employment contract; external recruitment; full time; induction; internal recruitment; interview; job advertisement; job application; job description; part time; person specification; psychometric test; recruitment; shortlist

Aims
To understand the main stages of the recruitment and selection process (2.3.1)

Skills practised

AO1: Knowledge and understanding	✓
AO2: Application	✓
AO3: Analysis	✓
AO4: Evaluation	

Preparation
Make one copy of Activity sheet 2.3.1A for each student in the class. Photocopy and cut out enough role-play cards from Activity sheets 2.3.1B and 2.3.1C, see below.

Procedure

1. Tell students that they are going to do a role play in which some students will interview others for a job as a manager in a small hotel.
2. Ask students to work in small groups and write down the different stages of the external recruitment process. Elicit these and write them on the board.
3. Give a copy of Activity sheet 2.3.1A (job advertisement, job description and person specification) to each student and explain the context of the role play by reading the introduction aloud. Allow a few minutes for students to read through the other information.
4. Divide the class into two equal groups: A and B. Allocate the role of interviewer to group A and the role of applicant to group B. Following this, divide group B into two again and allocate the role of applicant 1 to one half and the role of applicant 2 to the other half.
5. Give each student in group A Activity sheet 2.3.1B, the interviewer card, and each student in group B one of the applicant cards on Activity sheet 2.3.1C (either applicant 1 or 2).
6. Explain that each interviewer will interview two candidates and then decide on the best person for the job. Students will have 10 minutes to prepare for the role play in their group. Interviewers should use the information on Activity sheet 2.3.1A to prepare 10 interview questions, while applicants 1 and 2 use the same information to prepare possible responses to interview questions based on their backgrounds and experience.
7. After 10 minutes, pair each interviewer with either applicant 1 or 2 and allow them sufficient time to complete the interview. Encourage applicants to extend their responses to the questions.
8. After students have completed the first interview, pair up each interviewer with an applicant from the other group. For example, if an interviewer interviewed an applicant 1 previously, they should then interview an applicant 2.
9. Following the second interview, ask interviewers to explain who they think would be the best person for the job. Ensure that they provide justification for their decision.

Teacher tip: Try to ensure that the interviewers do not 'offer' the job to their friends. Try to mix up friendship groups and encourage students to evaluate their reasons for selecting a particular candidate.

2.3.2 The importance of training and methods of training

Aims (2.3.2)

Knowledge

By the end of this section, students will understand:

- the importance of training to a business and employees
- the benefits and limitations of induction training, on-the-job and off-the-job training.

Resources

- Student's Book pages 118–122
- Activity sheets 2.3.2A and 2.3.2B

Key business terms

coaching; college/university course; conference; induction training; labour turnover; Maslow's self-esteem needs; mentoring; off-the-job training; on-the-job training; job rotation; in-house course

Lesson ideas

You should aim to cover the materials in 2.3.2 in a single one-hour lesson, plus, as appropriate, a homework assignment. To achieve the Aims for this topic, we recommend doing some of the following activities over the course of the lesson.

Starter suggestions

Discussion: Write 'Why is training important?' on the board and discuss it as a whole class, or ask students to consider the question in pairs.

Training for school: Introduce the concept of induction by asking students to consider what 'training' they had when they joined the school, for example, a tour of the school, a talk from a teacher on where to find certain facilities, a list of things to bring to school, and so on.

Main lesson activities

Discussion and note-taking (whole class): Talk students through the methods of training, asking them to take notes as appropriate. Ensure that you cover the benefits and limitations of the different approaches.

Half and half: Split the class into two groups of equal size. Ask one group to review the value of training from the point of view of employees and the other half to review training from a business's point of view. Ask them to consider the advantages and disadvantages of training from the relevant perspective. Once they have done this, the two groups should share their findings.

Skills activity: Ask students to complete the Skills activity on page 122 of the Student's Book. This requires students to analyse the advantages and disadvantages of on-the-job and off-the-job training.

Student activity: Ask students to complete the small group discussion in Activity 2.3.2. They will need to know the different methods of training and the possible limitations of these methods.

Plenary suggestion

Knowledge check: Ask students to complete the Knowledge check questions on page 122 of the Student's Book.

Tip: This could be given as homework.

Answers to Student's Book activities

Skills activity (page 122): possible outcomes

Students should present a report based on the advantages/disadvantages given in the table on page 121 of the Student's Book.

Knowledge check (page 122)

1. **Explain** why training is important to employers.

   Productivity; motivation; improved labour retention; improved quality; improved service.

2. **Explain** why training is important to employees.

   Improved performance leading to self-esteem (Maslow); chance of promotion; increased employability.

3. **Identify** two things that might be included in induction training.

   Any two from: basic elements of the job; safety training; an introduction to company systems.

4. **Outline** the differences, using examples, between on-the-job and off-the-job training.

   On-the-job training: Training is undertaken at the place of work; usually involves the trainee being observed and guided by an experienced employee.

   Off-the-job training: Training is undertaken away from the place of work; involves conferences, courses, online learning, and so on.

5. **Discuss** two benefits of on-the-job training.

   Any two from: employee(s) remain productive (no lost production); no travel time; the skills learned are directly applicable to the job/task; it is motivating for experienced employees to train new employees; low cost.

6. **Consider** two limitations of on-the-job training.

   Any two from: trainee may pick up bad habits from experienced employee; limited source of new ideas/new approaches; productivity may suffer; trainee may make costly mistakes.

7. **Define** the term induction.

   Induction is training undertaken when a new employee first joins a firm; it is designed to familiarise the employee with routines, rules and the basics of the job.

2.3.2 The importance of training and methods of training: Activity

Activity type

Group discussion

Time

30 minutes

Content

Methods of training

Key terms

induction training; off-the-job training; on-the-job training

Aims

To identify appropriate methods of training for given situations and the benefits and limitations of each method (2.3.2)

Skills practised

AO1: Knowledge and understanding	✓
AO2: Application	✓
AO3: Analysis	✓
AO4: Evaluation	✓

Preparation

Make one copy of Activity sheet 2.3.2A for each student in the class. You may also want to make a copy of Activity sheet 2.3.2B for each student, see below.

Procedure

1 Discuss the different forms of training described in the Student's Book.
2 Tell students that they are going to evaluate methods of training for different employees and discuss their ideas in groups.
3 Give a copy of Activity sheet 2.3.2A to each student.
4 Use the example in the first row of the table to demonstrate the activity to the class.
5 Tell students that they have five minutes to individually complete as much of the table as they can.
6 Allow students exactly five minutes and then ask them to stop writing, even if some have not fully completed the table.
7 Arrange students into groups of three. Tell them that they have 10 minutes to compare their answers with the others in their group and add relevant points to their own table. Together, they should agree on the most appropriate method of training for each situation.
8 To round off the activity, either ask students to share their group's ideas with the class or hand out Activity sheet 2.3.2B and ask them to discuss the suggested answers.

Teacher tip: Ask students to start at different points in the table so that all questions are covered by the time it comes to the group discussion phase of the activity. For example, some students start at situation 1, while others start at situation 3.

Variation: Do this activity as a jigsaw reading task. First, cut up the table on the suggested answer sheet (Activity 2.3.2B) into different sections. Then give students different parts of the table. For example, give one student the advantages and another the disadvantages. Students must read their text to each other (without looking at each other's text) and match up the appropriate texts.

Extension: Students choose one of the job situations on the activity sheet and write a response to the following exam-style question:

Identify the appropriate method of training for this employee and discuss the advantages and disadvantages of this method for the business.

2.3.3 Reducing the workforce

Aims (2.3.3)

Knowledge

By the end of this section, students will understand:

- the difference between dismissal and redundancy, with examples
- situations in which downsizing the workforce might be necessary, for example, automation or reduced demand for products
- how to recommend and justify which employees to make redundant in given circumstances.

Resources

- Student's Book pages 123–126
- Activity sheets 2.3.3A and 2.3.3B
- Small pieces of paper
- Presentation software for the Skills activity, if available

Key business terms

automation; capital intensive; cash flow; dismissal; downsize; employee/labour turnover; gross misconduct; headcount; labour intensive; outsourcing; production; productivity; reduced demand; redundancy; redundancy pay; salary; severance pay; underperformance; unfair dismissal; wage; workforce

Lesson ideas

You should aim to cover the materials in 2.3.3 in a single one-hour lesson, plus, as appropriate, a homework assignment. To achieve the Aims for this topic, we recommend doing some of the following activities over the course of the lesson.

Starter suggestions

What's the difference? Write 'redundancy' and 'dismissal' on the board. Ask students if there is a difference between the two. Use their responses to guide the depth of your introduction to the topic.

Reasons for redundancy/dismissal: If appropriate, tell students that the school needs to 'get rid of 10 per cent of the teachers'. Ask them to list the possible reasons why this might be the case. Write 'redundancy' and 'dismissal' on the board and ask students to group their ideas under the headings.

Main lesson activities

Discussion and note-taking (whole class): Talk students through downsizing, dismissal and redundancy, asking them to take notes as appropriate. Ensure that you cover the consequences of such workforce decisions.

Create a character: Split the class into small groups. Ask each group to create profiles of characters who work for a fictional company. Each character's 'story' should relate to redundancy or dismissal. (Some, but not all, characters should be in danger of dismissal or redundancy.) Encourage students to use appropriate business language and to base their situations within the context of the subject. Collect students' 'character profiles' and read some out to the class, asking them to recommend an appropriate action (dismissal, redundancy or no action) for each character. The group that created the character should not respond initially, but should be asked to justify their character's reactions.

Student activity: Ask students to complete Activity sheets 2.3.3A and 2.3.3B, a crossword activity that reinforces understanding of the key business terms related to reducing the workforce.

Skills activity: Ask students to complete the Skills activity on page 126 of the Student's Book. This activity asks students to analyse the implications of a headcount reduction in a company they are familiar with. Encourage them to use presentation software, if available.

Knowledge check: Ask students to complete the Knowledge check questions on page 126 of the Student's Book.

Tip: This exercise could be given as homework.

Plenary suggestion

Exit/Entry pass: Tell students that to earn an 'exit pass' they must write an exam-style knowledge question on the content of the lesson on a small piece of paper. If necessary, allow them to refer to the Knowledge check questions in the Student's Book. Collect students' questions as they leave the room, checking that they are appropriate.

Use these questions as an 'entry pass' (recap) for the next lesson, issued at random as students enter the classroom.

Answers to Student's Book activities

Skills activity (page 126): possible outcomes

A wide range of responses is possible, although the questions suggest a negative impact. Student responses might include reference to: low morale; increased labour turnover; reduced productivity; negative PR; a decline in sales; difficulty re-adjusting if demand increases.

Importantly, encourage students to apply their answers to the context. Ask if all companies will be affected similarly. How will the company they have chosen be affected?

Knowledge check (page 126)

1 **Define** the term downsize.

   To reduce the total number of employees within a firm.

2 **Identify** two reasons why a firm may need to downsize.

   Any two from: poor sales; merger; relocation; business closure; automation; outsourcing.

3 **Explain** what workforce planning involves.

   Assessing the current workforce (age profile, skills, labour turnover, longevity, and so on) and comparing this against predicted future labour needs.

4 **Define** the term redundancy.

   Where a firm has too many employees for its current needs and wants to downsize, or where the skills of an employee are no longer needed.

5 **Explain** how redundancy differs from dismissal.

   Dismissal is where an employee is told to leave the job because of poor behaviour or unsatisfactory performance. Redundancy is not related to an individual's performance.

6 'An employee can be dismissed if their job is surplus to requirements.' **Outline** why this statement is false.

   The statement should refer to redundancy, NOT dismissal.

2.3.3 Reducing the workforce: Activity

Activity type

Pair-work crossword

Time

30 minutes

Content

Key business terms related to workforce

Key terms

automation; capital intensive; cash flow; dismissal; downsize; employee/labour turnover; gross misconduct; headcount; labour intensive; outsourcing; production; productivity; reduced demand; redundancy; redundancy pay; salary; severance pay; underperformance; unfair dismissal; wage; workforce

Skills practised

AO1: Knowledge and understanding	✓
AO2: Application	
AO3: Analysis	
AO4: Evaluation	

Preparation

Make one copy of Activity sheet 2.3.3A and Activity sheet 2.3.3B for each pair of students in the class.

Aims

To understand the key business terms related to workforce size reduction (2.3.3)

Procedure

1. Write the definitions below on the board and elicit the correct terms (in brackets) from students. Allow students to ask clarifying questions, if necessary.
   - *Money that is paid to employees for the hours they have worked* (wages)
   - *A fixed amount of money that is usually paid to employees monthly* (salary)
2. Tell students that they are going to write similar clues and definitions for a range of business terms to do with the workforce of a business.
3. Divide the class into two equal groups (A and B), with each group sitting together.
4. Explain that you are going to give each group a different part of the same crossword, with some of the words already filled in. Give a copy of Activity sheet 2.3.3A to each student in group A and a copy of Activity sheet 2.3.3B to each student in group B.
5. Students work with one or two other students in their group to write a clue/definition for each word in their part of the crossword. They have 10 minutes to do this. Encourage them to write clues in their own words and only to use the Student's Book to check that their definitions are correct.
6. When they have finished writing their clues, pair up each student from group A with a student from group B. Students must not look at each other's crossword (see *Teacher tip*).
7. Students take turns to read out one of the clues from their crossword. They listen to each other's clues and identify the correct business terms, then write them on their sheet. Encourage them to ask questions if they can't guess the word from the initial clue. They continue the activity until both crosswords are complete.

Teacher tip: During the information-sharing phase, it helps if students have a barrier, for example, a folder or book between them, so they aren't tempted to look at each other's crosswords.

Extension: Once they have completed the activity, students could create a mind-map linking each of the business terms in the activity to the concept of 'workforce size reduction'. In their mind-map, students should link the business concepts using arrows and make a note saying what the relationship is between each pair of terms or concepts.

Answers to Activity 2.3.3

			¹R	E	D	U	C	E	D	D	E	M	²A	N	D				
		³W											U						
		A					⁴O		⁵P				T						
		G					U		R				O						
	⁶H	E	A	D	C	O	U	N	T		O		M						
							S		D		A								
							O		U		T						⁷L		
							U		C		I		⁸W				A		
⁹G							R		T		O		O				B		
R			¹⁰P	¹¹R	O	¹²D	U	C	T	I	O	N		R				O	
O				E		I		E	V				K					U	
S		¹³R		D		S			I				F					R	
S		E		U		M			T				O					T	
M		¹⁴D		N		I			Y				R					U	
I		U		D		S							C					R	
S		N		A		¹⁵S	E	V	E	R	A	N	C	E	P	A	Y	N	
C		D		N		A												O	
O		A		C		¹⁶L	A	B	O	U	R	I	N	T	E	N	¹⁷S	I	V	E
N		N		Y													A		E
D		C															L		R
U		Y															A		
⁹C	A	P	I	T	A	L	I	N	T	E	N	S	I	V	E		R		
T		A															Y		
		Y																	

2.3.4 Legal controls over employment and their impact

Aims (2.3.4)

Knowledge

By the end of this section, students will understand:

- legal controls over employment contracts, unfair dismissal, discrimination, health and safety, legal minimum wage.

Resources

- Student's Book pages 127–131
- Activity sheets 2.3.4A and 2.3.4B
- Sticky notes
- Websites (or other reference materials) giving information on the local minimum wage

Key business terms

discrimination; employment contract; equal pay; gross misconduct; health and safety; labour turnover; legal minimum wage; motivation; unfair dismissal

Lesson ideas

You should aim to cover the materials in 2.3.4 in a single one-hour lesson, plus, as appropriate, a homework assignment. To achieve the Aims for this topic, we recommend doing some of the following activities over the course of the lesson.

Starter suggestion

Board work: Introduce the term 'discrimination' and ask students to list as many types of discrimination as they can think of. Write these forms of discrimination (age, gender, and so on) down the left-hand side of the board. Split the class into small groups and assign one form of discrimination to each group. Ask students to write a workplace-based example of that type of discrimination on the board, next to the discrimination type. Use this list to begin a discussion of legal controls.

Main lesson activities

Discussion and note-taking (whole class): Talk students through the legal controls over employment issues, asking them to take notes as appropriate. Ensure that you cover the consequences and costs of such legal issues.

Stick-up: Put up coloured cards around the classroom with the titles of various legal controls on them: Health and Safety Law, Employment Contract, Unfair Dismissal Law, Minimum Pay Law, Equal Pay Law, Gender Discrimination Law, Race Relations Laws, Pregnancy Discrimination Law, Disability Discrimination Law.

Give each student a small number of sticky notes. Ask them individually (without using the Student's Book) to write a brief definition of what each legal control might involve; they should stick their definitions on the appropriate cards. Arrange students in small groups and assign one legal control per group. Ask them to read all the definitions for their legal control and to move those definitions they feel are stronger to the top of the card and those that are weaker lower down. Ask the groups to read out the 'best' definition to the whole class. Correct any misinterpretations.

Skills activity: To encourage a more detailed analysis of the minimum wage (and its impacts), ask students to complete the Skills activity on page 131 of the Student's Book.

Student activity: Ask students to complete Activity sheets 2.3.4A and 2.3.4B. Students read case studies and discuss a variety of legal controls over employment and decide what legal controls might apply in different situations, and the possible outcomes.

Tip: Homework could be preparation for the debate.

Half and half: Split the class into two equal groups. Ask one group to consider the implications of legal controls from the employees' point of view and the other half to look at the implications for employers. Once complete, discuss students' responses as a whole class.

Plenary suggestion

Knowledge check: Ask students to complete the Knowledge check questions on page 131 of the Student's Book.

Tip: This exercise could be given as homework.

Answers to Student's Book activities

Skills activity (page 131): possible outcomes

If students have access to the internet, guide them to websites where they will find details of the local minimum wage (or the minimum wage in their own country). Alternatively, provide them with appropriate reference information. Give them enough time to prepare for the debate; move around the group helping students to develop more detailed arguments. Encourage them to present reasoned arguments in their debate as well as a well-justified summary.

Knowledge check (page 131)

1 **Identify** two examples of legal controls on employment.

   Accept any two appropriate acts of law or general terms such as discrimination or health and safety.

2 **Explain** one factor that may affect the extent to which legal controls impact on a particular firm.

   Any one from: size; nature of business; number of employees; countries of operation.

3 **Consider** two positive implications of health and safety law for a business.

   Any two from: reduction in workplace accidents and therefore fewer legal claims for injury; less lost time caused by accident/injury (maintaining productivity); avoidance of negative publicity associated with accidents at work; more motivated employees if they feel the working environment is safe.

4 **Identify** three 'rights' provided under employment contract law.

   Any three from:
   - the right to a written employment contract
   - the right to be paid the national minimum wage
   - the right to reasonable notice before dismissal
   - the right to take statutory (legal minimum) holiday leave
   - the right to redundancy payments.

5 **Outline**, using examples, what is meant by discrimination.

   Discrimination is the unfair treatment of a person or a group of people as compared to others. Examples include discrimination because of: age, gender, disability, race, sexual orientation, marital status, pregnancy, religion.

2.3.4 Legal controls over employment and their impact: Activity

Activity type
Group discussion

Time
30 minutes

Content
Legal controls over employment issues

Key terms
discrimination; employment contract; equal pay; gross misconduct; health and safety; labour turnover; legal minimum wage; motivation; unfair dismissal

Skills practised

AO1: Knowledge and understanding	✓
AO2: Application	✓
AO3: Analysis	✓
AO4: Evaluation	✓

Preparation
Make one copy of Activity sheet 2.3.4A and Activity sheet 2.3.4B for each pair of students in the class.

Aims
To understand legal controls over employment issues and their impact on employers and employees (2.3.4)

Procedure

1 Tell students that they are going to read short cases studies about employment issues between employees and employers.

2 Divide the class into two groups (A and B). Give a copy of Activity sheet 2.3.4A to each student in group A and a copy of Activity sheet 2.3.4B to each student in group B.

3 Explain that each group has different case studies and that they are going to discuss their case studies using the questions on their activity sheet. After this, they will have to explain and discuss their case studies with a student from the other group.

4 If necessary, divide each larger group into smaller groups of three or four students. Allow students 15 minutes to read and discuss each of the case studies with their group members. They should make brief notes on the activity sheet.

5 Pair up each student from group A with a student from group B. Allow them 15 minutes to discuss each of their case studies with their partner and summarise their group's responses to the questions. The other student should listen and say if they agree or disagree with the group's analysis and why.

6 Round off the activity by sharing the outcomes of each case (see below) with the class. During the class discussion, elicit the main points from the Student's Book (pages 127–131) using the contexts of the case studies.

Variation: Step 5 could be done with two students from each group rather than as a one-to-one discussion. This could help to provide more scaffolding and support for ESL learners and lower ability students.

Extension: Students search online for a story about an employment dispute in their own country. Ask them to read the story and make notes on the legal controls in place and what impact they might have on employees and employers. They should be ready to share their story with the class in the next lesson.

Outcomes of the cases

A	The case went to court and the fast food restaurant was ordered to pay the waitress more than €4200 ($5430) in lost wages. The court ruled that the decision to dismiss the employee was too severe and a written warning would have been more appropriate.
B	The Employment Relations Authority ruled that the woman was unfairly dismissed and discriminated against because she was a member of a trade union. She was also unfairly treated by having her hours cut and not being given an employment contract. They ordered the supermarket to pay $10 000NZ ($8215) for lost wages and hurt and humiliation.
C	In 2012, the employment tribunal ruled in favour of the footballer, saying that he was unfairly dismissed by his former football club, after suffering from racial discrimination.
D	The fish restaurant claimed that none of its employees were paid below the legal minimum wage after tips had been included in the calculation of their earnings. While this is acceptable under UK law, it has been criticised for being unethical. Unite is pressing the government to stop restaurants from calculating wages in this way.
E	Following the investigation by the FLA, the sportswear store increased the wages of its employees by 25 per cent and agreed to comply with the legal limit of a 49-hour working week for employees.
F	The employment tribunal awarded the woman £8000 ($12 182) in compensation. However, it found that, while she had been unlawfully harassed, there was not enough evidence to suggest that it was a case of direct disability discrimination. The court also found that the way in which the clothing retailer handled the case failed to comply with employment law.

2.4 Internal and external communication

2.4.1 ACHIEVING EFFECTIVE COMMUNICATION

Aims (2.4.1)

Knowledge

By the end of this section, students will understand:

- effective communication and its importance to business
- the benefits and limitations of different communication methods, including those based on information technology (IT)
- how to recommend and justify which communication method to use in given circumstances.

Resources

- Student's Book pages 132–144
- Activity sheet 2.4.1
- Small pieces of paper

Key business terms

communication; electronic; external; formal; informal; internal; stakeholders; verbal; written

Lesson ideas

You should aim to cover the materials in 2.4.1 in a single one-hour lesson, plus, as appropriate, a homework assignment. To achieve the Aims for this topic, we recommend doing some of the following activities over the course of the lesson.

Starter suggestion

Board work: Ask students to think of all of the different ways that they receive communication at school. Ask each student to come to the board and write one idea under the heading 'Methods of communication'. As scaffolding, you could add the subheadings 'Written', 'Verbal' and 'Electronic'. Once all students have contributed an idea, ask them if businesses use any other methods to communicate and add these ideas to the lists.

Main lesson activities

Discussion and note-taking (whole class): Talk students through the various methods of communication and the benefits and drawbacks of each method. If you have done the starter activity, add to the list of methods on the board as appropriate. Ask students to take notes. Focus on the importance of communication in business and on recommending which communication methods to use in different circumstances.

Group activity: Divide the class into small groups. Give each group one or two methods of communication from the list created in the starter activity. Ask students to consider the benefits and drawbacks of their methods. Each group should then share their ideas with the rest of the class.

Skills activity: Building on the starter activity, ask students to complete the Skills activity on page 142 of the Student's Book.

Note: The starter activity is the first part of this Skills activity.

Student activity: In groups of two or three, ask students to do Activity 2.4.1. They look at different communication methods and make suggestions for different contexts.

Skills activity: Ask students to complete the Skills activity on page 144 of the Student's Book, which reinforces their understanding of communication methods and barriers, and how a business might improve communication.

Plenary suggestion

Exit pass: Tell students that to earn an exit pass from the lesson, they must each write on a small piece of paper their name, one method of communication, one benefit of that method and one drawback. Once they have done this, collect in the papers. If the student's suggestions are correct, allow them to leave.

Answers to Student's Book activities

Skills activities: possible outcomes

Skills activity (page 134)

- Members of the local community write an email to a shoe factory complaining about the increase in noise.

    Answer: The message may not be received by the correct person/people. The message may not be clear or may not be written in a way that encourages the firm to change. Email is easily ignored. The local community may fail to get the action it wants (less noise pollution) if the message is not received.

- The local sports shop receives some emails from their suppliers about some poorly made equipment. The suppliers have sent a fax with the product codes on.

    Answer: The two different messages (emails and fax) may not be put together, so the purpose of the message may be unclear or action not possible. Emails are easily ignored. A fax may be missed or may be disposed of in error. The sports shop may remove the wrong product from display, losing sales on those items and, potentially, selling faulty items to customers.

- A customer demands to see the manager of the local coffee shop about the service they have received.

    Answer: The manager may not be present at the time. The manager may listen to the complaint but forget to complete the required action (as the complaint is verbal, there will be no record of the message).

Skills activity (page 142)

A wide range of responses is possible depending on the context. Ensure that students identify appropriate benefits and drawbacks of the external method they use as an example. (Refer to the Student's Book pages 139–141 for a summary of communication methods and their benefits and drawbacks.) Encourage students to evaluate whether the methods they listed were appropriate.

Skills activity (page 144)

A wide range of responses is possible depending on the context. Ensure that students identify appropriate benefits and drawbacks of the methods they have mentioned in their case studies. (Refer to the Student's Book pages 139–141 for a summary of external communication methods and their benefits and drawbacks.) Encourage students to evaluate whether the methods they listed were appropriate and, in particular, what went well, what went poorly and what could have been done to improve communication.

Knowledge check (page 144)

1. **Identify** two reasons why it is very important for a business to communicate effectively.

    Any two from: employees may enjoy their job and feel valued; employees may work more efficiently; customers may be more loyal; sales may result from good communication; tasks are completed correctly and quickly.

2. **Explain** why feedback from the receiver is an important part of communication.

    It is important to check that a message has been received and understood. Instant feedback can improve communication and avoid mistakes.

3. **Outline** the reasons behind the success of social media and apps in helping businesses communicate with customers.

    Reasons: social media allows businesses to communicate directly with customers; apps and social media enable a business to tailor their marketing and promotions for their different customer types.

4. **Explain** one benefit and one drawback of using emails to respond to customer questions.

    Benefits: *Any one from:* speed of response; written record of communication; two-way; easy to include others in communication (using the cc function).

    Drawbacks: *Any one from:* may be ignored; may be treated as junk mail; may not be considered formal enough.

5. Outline why you think many businesses now use social media to communicate with stakeholders.

    Social media are popular with younger consumers; easy method to reach large numbers of people; can be focused on target markets; a creative and fun way to communicate; quick; can accurately target customers (specific).

2.4.1 Achieving effective communication: Activity

Activity type

Matching/Memory game

Time

20 minutes

Content

Communication methods and recommendation of communication methods

Key terms

communication; electronic; external; formal; informal; internal; stakeholders; verbal; written

Aims

To understand methods of communication and be able to recommend appropriate methods (2.4.1)

Skills practised

AO1: Knowledge and understanding	✓
AO2: Application	
AO3: Analysis	
AO4: Evaluation	

Preparation

Make one copy of Activity sheet 2.4.1 for each pair of students in the class. If possible, photocopy the Activity sheet onto card. Cut out the cards in advance of the lesson. You may also wish to photocopy intact versions of Activity sheet 2.4.1 (not cut up into cards) to give to students as an answer sheet.

Procedure

1. Split the class into pairs. Tell students they are going to play a memory game that relies on their knowledge of which communication methods are appropriate in different situations.
2. Give each pair a set of playing cards from Activity sheet 2.4.1. Ask students to remove the grey communication method cards and lay them out face up on the table in front of them. They should place the remaining white situation cards in a pile face down on the table.
3. Students take turns to draw one situation card from the pile and read it aloud to their partner. They then discuss the card and match it with the correct communication method, continuing until they have matched all the situation cards with the appropriate communication method.
4. Display a copy of the complete Activity sheet on the classroom projector for groups to check their answers. Discuss any inconsistencies with the class.
5. Following this, ask students to shuffle all the cards together (both the communication method and situation cards) and lay them out face down in a square pattern in front of them.
6. Students then take turns to each draw two cards. The intention is to match the situation (white card) with the appropriate communication method (grey card).
7. If the cards match, the student keeps these cards. If they don't match, they should replace both cards in the square pattern on the table.
8. Students should attempt to memorise where the different situations and communication methods are so that they can select appropriately when it is their turn.
9. A student can challenge a match by declaring 'Challenge' and asking you to confirm.
10. When students have matched up all the cards, the winning student is the one with the most cards.

Teacher tip: To scaffold this activity, instruct students to place the cards in two separate squares (one for communication method and one for situation).

Extension: Give students several blank cards and ask them to create their own situations and matching communication methods. They can then play the game with the larger number of cards.

2.4.2 Communication barriers

Aims (2.4.2)

Knowledge

By the end of this section, students will understand:

- how communication barriers arise and problems of ineffective communication; how communication barriers can be reduced or removed.

Resources

- Student's Book pages 145–148
- Activity sheet 2.4.2
- Square sheets of coloured paper for Activity 2.4.2

Key business terms

method of communication; language; culture; distractions; enthusiasm and emotion; amount; chain of command; barrier to communication

Lesson ideas

You should aim to cover the materials in 2.4.2 in a single one-hour lesson, plus, as appropriate, a homework assignment. To achieve the Aims for this section, we recommend doing some of the following activities over the course of the lesson.

Starter suggestion

Recap: Recap methods of communication by asking each student (or small groups of students) to recall one method of communication and one benefit and one drawback of that method.

Main lesson activities

Discussion and note-taking (whole class): Talk students through the various barriers to communication, the issues such barriers cause for business and how training can be used to improve communication. Instruct students to take notes as appropriate. Focus on how communication barriers can be removed or reduced.

Student activity: Ask students to do Activity 2.4.2 as a whole class, in which they follow instructions to make an origami bird. It supports students' understanding of barriers to communication and afterwards they suggest how the barriers might be removed.

Plenary suggestion

Sign language: Ask each student to think of a barrier to communication and to come up with a matching hand action that represents that barrier. Ask students to perform their actions to each other and guess the barrier to communication being shown.

Answers to Student's Book activities

Skills activity (page 148): possible outcomes

A wide range of responses is possible depending on the situation the students choose. Ensure that students role-play appropriate benefits and drawbacks of their chosen communication methods. (Refer to the Student's Book pages 136–141 for a summary of communication methods and their benefits and drawbacks.) Encourage students to evaluate why the communication method would fail, and ensure that they recommend ways to correct it.

Knowledge check (page 148)

1 Define the term barrier.

   An obstacle or complication that prevents or inhibits effective communication.

2. **Identify** one way in which a business can overcome a language communication barrier.

   Any one from: language training for employees; insistence that all communication is undertaken in a language common to all employees/customers; provide translations of as many documents as possible.

3. Consider the likely impacts of bad communication for a relatively new small business.

   Employee motivation may suffer; tasks may be completed slowly or incorrectly; sales opportunities may be missed; slow response to customer enquires; damage to business reputation. However, the impact on a small firm may be minimal.

4. **Explain** two barriers to communication that may stop a message being delivered.

   Any two from: method of communication; language; culture; distractions; enthusiasm and emotion; amount; length of chain; losing message.

2.4.2 Communication barriers: Activity

Activity type

Listening/Recording activity

Time

20 minutes

Content

Barriers to effective communication

Key terms

amount; barrier to communication; chain of command; culture; distractions; enthusiasm and emotion; language; method of communication

Aims

To understand barriers to effective communication (2.4.2)

Skills practised

AO1: Knowledge and understanding	✓
AO2: Application	✓
AO3: Analysis	
AO4: Evaluation	

Preparation

You will need one square sheet of coloured paper for each pair of students in the class. Make two copies of Activity sheet 2.4.2. Music and something to play it on. For the extension activity, you may wish to make a class set of the Activity sheet.

Procedure

1. Tell students that they are going to take part in a communication exercise and that it involves making an origami bird.
2. Put the students into pairs. One student will act as the Manufacturer and the other will be the Recorder. You can allow students to change roles halfway through the exercise if appropriate. Give each pair a square sheet of coloured paper.
3. Choose one, ideally confident, student to act as the Instructor for the whole class. Ideally, the chosen student should be able to speak in a language not understood by the majority of the class.
4. Give the Instructor the script (Activity sheet 2.4.2). Ask the Instructor to stand at the front of the class with his/her back to the group (i.e. facing away from his/her classmates).
5. Ensure that the Instructor only reads from the script. He/She must not turn around and face the group. He/She should not demonstrate with his/her hands.
6. Ensure that the Instructor follows the instructions on the script correctly. Assist by prompting as necessary. It will be useful to have a copy of the script to follow yourself.
7. The Manufacturer in each pair should follow the instructions given by the Instructor.
8. During each stage of the process, the Recorder should make a note of the communication issues that are presenting barriers to effective completion of the task.
9. Regardless of whether the previous instruction was followed correctly, the Manufacturers should attempt the next instruction. Part of the fun of this is enjoying the variety of interpretations.
10. Once the Instructor has read out all the instructions, he/she can turn around and look at the Manufacturers' results.
11. Use the Recorders' notes to discuss barriers to communication.

Teacher tip: Depending on the ability profile of your class, you may need to be the Instructor.

Extension: If time allows, ask students what would make communication more effective in this task. Students could then repeat the exercise with their suggestions in place.

2. People in business: Key terms revision

Define each term and provide an example or explanation. There are 2 marks per definition.

Term	Description/Definition
autocratic leadership	
delegation	
democratic leadership	
empowerment	
fringe benefit	
induction	
job enrichment	
labour turnover	
laissez-faire leadership	
off-the-job training	
overtime	
piece rate	
redundancy pay	
span of control	
trade union	

3 Marketing

Introduction

The beauty of the marketing topic is that students tend to have plenty of prior knowledge – they usually know about branding, promotion and customer sensitivity to price, for example. This makes marketing a great topic for student-led activities, practical exercises and lots of real-life case studies.

The key, though, when teaching marketing is to ensure that students don't take their prior knowledge for granted – marketing deserves the same respect as other topics, and having a 'feel' for it is not enough.

The activities in this section aim to help students build on their prior knowledge and to develop a technical understanding of marketing. Each section includes a substantive activity that can be used, in a fun and engaging way, to develop knowledge, understanding and skills. These activities include:

- a pair work exercise on the **role of marketing**
- an investigation into the impact of **market changes**
- an investigation task to analyse **niche** and **mass marketing**
- an examination of **market segmentation** using a jigsaw reading activity
- a focus group role play to examine **market research**
- a data gathering and analysis exercise enabling **presentation of results**
- a categorisation exercise examining **product**
- a categorisation task to analyse **pricing** methods
- an examination of **place** using a jigsaw reading activity
- an investigation into types of **promotion**
- an evaluation of the **impact of technology** on the marketing mix
- marketing strategy examined through an investigation task
- an evaluation activity on **legal controls related to marketing**
- a snakes and ladders game requiring knowledge on **entering markets abroad**.

To introduce students to the various marketing concepts and to help gauge prior knowledge, a useful starter activity might be the Journey journal.

> **Journey journal**
>
> Before the first lesson on marketing, ask students to record all examples of marketing they see on their journey to/from school. If possible, ask them to take photographs or to bring into class examples of any particularly good marketing they notice. Don't explain what marketing is at this stage, but do instruct students to think about more than just promotion.
>
> At the start of the next lesson ask students to share their examples. Use their responses to introduce the various topics and, importantly, to reinforce that marketing is not just about promotion.

As marketing is often delivered early in the course, students may not yet be familiar with the required examination skills. At this stage, it might be appropriate to focus on knowledge (encouraging students to write concise and technically correct answers rather than rely on general knowledge) and application (encouraging students to think about what types of marketing might be most relevant in different contexts).

3.1 Marketing, competition and the customer

3.1.1 THE ROLE OF MARKETING

Aims (3.1.1)

Knowledge

By the end of this section, students will understand:

- the role of marketing in identifying customer needs
- the role of marketing in satisfying customer needs
- the role of marketing in maintaining customer loyalty
- the role of marketing in building customer relationships.

Resources

- Student's Book pages 160–163
- Activity sheet 3.1.1
- Video clips of TV advertising; examples of other forms of promotion
- Presentation software for Activity 3.1.1 (optional)

Key business terms

added value; brand; brand image; brand loyalty; building relationships; competitive advantage; customer loyalty; differentiation; first mover advantage; market orientation; place; price; product; promotion; relationship marketing; unique selling point (USP)

Lesson ideas

You should aim to cover the materials in 3.1.1 in a single one-hour lesson, plus, as appropriate, a homework assignment. To achieve the Aims for this topic, we recommend doing some of the following activities over the course of the lesson.

Starter suggestions

Discussion: Start the lesson by showing students clips of TV advertising and other forms of promotion. Discuss other forms of promotion and broaden the conversation into other aspects of marketing. Ask questions such as: 'Why is popcorn so expensive at cinemas?' Use the answers to introduce price and place as aspects of marketing.

Definition: Write the word 'Marketing' on the board and ask students (without referring to the Student's Book) to define marketing. Use their responses to make a list of key terms on the board. Refer them to the definitions in the Student's Book (pages 160–163).

Main lesson activities

Discussion and note-taking (whole class): Talk students through the role of marketing, asking them to take notes as appropriate. Make sure that you cover customers' needs, customer loyalty and building customer relationships.

Customer loyalty and building customer relationships – create a character: Split the class into small groups. Assign each group a character (teenager, middle-aged parent, young single person, elderly couple, wealthy individual, and so on). Ask each group to create a story of what that character might buy and what they might do (hobbies, and so on). The purpose is to focus on these fictional consumers' 'needs'. Once students have created the characters, ask them to consider how a soft drinks manufacturer might attempt to meet these needs and how they might establish customer loyalty. Allow the conversation to be general and broad ranging at this point.

You as customer: Ask students to list three products they buy regularly, together with the reasons why they buy them. Then ask students to highlight how many of those reasons have been created by the company. Use this to discuss marketing as a creator of need and a satisfier of need. Develop the discussion by referring to brand loyalty and building customer relationships.

Skills activity: Ask students to do the investigation in the Skills activity on page 163 of the Student's Book. They choose a famous company from the list provided and analyse the marketing activities of their chosen company.

Student activity: Ask students to complete Activity 3.1.1, in which, they examine the role of marketing in creating customer loyalty and building customer relationships for a brand of their choice.

Knowledge check: Ask students to complete the Knowledge check questions on page 163 of the Student's Book.

Tip: This exercise could be given as a homework task.

Plenary suggestion

Write key terms from the lesson on the board and ask students to consider these questions:

- How do firms find out what makes customers loyal?
- What tactics will build relationships with customers?
- How can firms identify what customer needs actually are? (i.e. market research)

Conclude by indicating that it is marketing that satisfies those needs.

Answers to Student's Book activities

Skills activity (page 163): possible outcomes

Encourage students to refer to Section 3 in the Student's Book as part of this activity. At this stage, however, expect general answers focused on promotion. Use students' responses to lead into discussions of other elements of marketing and the role of marketing in satisfying customer needs.

Knowledge check (page 163)

1 **Define** marketing and **explain** how it is used to develop/maintain customer loyalty.

   Marketing is the management process that identifies, anticipates and satisfies customer requirements profitably. Modern marketing, however, is not just about getting new customers; it is also about maintaining customer loyalty and building relationships with those customers. Many firms now use social media (such as Facebook and Twitter) to communicate with customers in an attempt to develop trust and loyalty. The two-way nature of internet marketing allows firms to listen to customers and respond to their needs much faster than they could previously. By engaging customers with websites, blogs, tweets and even online games, firms can build brand image, develop relationships with customers and improve brand loyalty. Relationship marketing involves communicating with customers regularly and encouraging repeat purchase (brand loyalty). Developing and maintaining customer loyalty means not just selling a product to customers and forgetting about them. Firms need to engage their customers with the brand regularly.

   Accept other suitable definitions.

2 **Define**, using a suitable example, market orientation.

   A business that is customer-driven: finding out what customers want before making decisions about product, price or promotion. Examples are McDonalds and Virgin Limited.

3 **Identify** one example of how marketing adds value.

   Accept any reasonable example: branding; packaging; distribution; design; convenience.

4 **Define** the term unique selling point.

   A USP is a feature of a product that makes it unique/different from competitors' products.

5 **Explain** the term first mover advantage. Why is being 'first mover' considered an advantage?

   First mover advantage is being the first to enter a market with a new product. It is an advantage to securing an early market share, brand identity and (potentially) long-term brand loyalty.

6 **Explain** how marketing helps a firm to identify customer needs.

   Marketing focuses the attention of managers on customer needs and, through market research, attempts to find out what those needs are (and identify when they have changed).

3.1.1 The role of marketing: Activity

Activity type

Pair-work information gap

Time

20 minutes

Content

The role of marketing in creating customer loyalty

Key terms

added value; brand; brand image; brand loyalty; building relationships; competitive advantage; customer loyalty; differentiation; first mover advantage; market orientation; place; price; product; promotion; relationship marketing; unique selling point (USP)

Skills practised

AO1: Knowledge and understanding	✓
AO2: Application	✓
AO3: Analysis	✓
AO4: Evaluation	✓

Preparation

Make one copy of Activity sheet 3.1.1 for each student in the class.

Aims

To introduce students to the role of marketing within a context they are familiar with (3.1.1)

1. Check that students understand the key terms in bold on Activity sheet 3.1.1. If necessary, elicit the meanings of these words.
2. Ask students to think of a particular product or brand that they like and are loyal to, for example, Apple, KitKat, Billabong, and so on.
3. Explain to students that they will use their experience as a loyal customer of this brand to individually answer the questions on the activity sheet. They will then share their answers with another student. Demonstrate the activity using one of the brands mentioned in step 2 above.
4. Allow students 10 minutes to answer the questions. Move around the room, ensuring that students are answering the questions correctly and in sufficient detail.
5. Following this, pair students up and give them 10 minutes to interview each other using the questions on the activity sheet. Students should listen to each other's responses and make brief notes in the second column.
6. Round off the activity by nominating students to share information about their partner's brand/product with the class. Use this to lead in to a discussion of the broader role of marketing and the main points presented in topic 3.1.1 of the Student's Book (pages 160–163).

Extension: Students could prepare a PowerPoint presentation on their brand/product using the questions on Activity sheet 3.1.1.

Teacher tip: As a way of reinforcing the key terms required for this topic, you could split the terms between the groups. Ask each group to define a few of the terms and then share their responses with other groups.

3.1.2 Market changes

Aims (3.1.2)

Knowledge

By the end of this section, students will understand:

- why customer/consumer spending patterns may change
- the importance of changing customer needs
- why some markets have become more competitive
- how business can respond to changing spending patterns and increased competition.

Resources

- Student's Book pages 164–167
- Activity sheet 3.1.2
- Newspaper articles or internet print-outs about a business's changing consumer spending and increased competition (optional)
- Websites of book and ebook retailers
- Presentation software (optional)

Key business terms

competition; competitive advantage; customer needs; customer spending patterns; disposable income

Lesson ideas

You should aim to cover the materials in 3.1.2 in two one-hour lessons, plus, as appropriate, a homework assignment. To achieve the Aims for this topic, we recommend doing some of the following activities over the course of the lessons.

Starter suggestions

Lesson 1 – Timeline: To introduce the concept of changing customer spending patterns, split the class into small groups.

Ask one third of the groups to draw a timeline for a person's life (from age 10 to age 90), indicating how an individual's purchasing habits might change.

Ask another third of the groups to draw a timeline of the last 20 years and to map the technological changes that have affected consumer behaviour and consumer spending.

Ask the remaining groups to draw a timeline of the mobile phone or computer market over the last 20 years, considering the extent of competition within the market. At this stage, discussion should be general and broad ranging; encourage students to use appropriate business language as required.

Ask students to keep copies of their timelines for the next lesson.

Lesson 2 – Timeline: Ask students to map onto their timelines some general thoughts about how a business might respond (or how businesses they know of have responded) to changing consumer spending patterns or changes in competition.

It may be useful to mix up the groups from the previous lesson and encourage students to question any aspects of the original timelines they are unsure of.

Main lesson activities

Discussion and note-taking (whole class): Talk students through market changes, instructing them to take notes as appropriate. Make sure you cover changing customer needs and market competitiveness.

Story time: Ask students to write a short story (maximum 300 words) of either changing consumer needs, changing spending patterns or increased competition. They should use their timelines from the starter activity as a guide and refer to the Student's Book (pages 164–167). Give students a series of topic-related key terms that they must include in the story, for example, customer spending patterns; customer needs;

disposable income; competition; competitive advantage. Ask some students to read their 'stories' to the whole class.

How, what, why?: Write the three headings 'How?' 'What?' and 'Why?' on the board. Ask students: 'How have businesses responded to changing consumer spending and increased competition?' Students use the headings to help them consider how a company they know has responded to consumer/market change, what the implications of the response have been and why the company chose that particular response.

Tip: Depending on the ability profile of your group, you may wish to choose a case study company and provide students with source material such as newspaper articles.

Student activity: Ask students to complete Activity 3.1.2, in which students analyse the changes that have taken place in their own country for a product/market of their choice. They present their findings in the form of a report.

Skills activity: Ask students to complete the Skills activity on page 167 of the Student's Book. They consider the market changes that have made publishing an increasingly competitive industry and present their findings in the form of a newspaper article.

Plenary suggestion

Knowledge check: Ask students to answer the Knowledge check questions on page 167 of the Student's Book. This could be done individually or you could allocate different questions to different groups of students, who then share their answers with the whole class.

Tip: This exercise could be given as homework.

Answers to Student's Book activities

Skills activity (page 167): possible outcomes

You may need to lead into this activity by demonstrating Amazon (or a similar website) to students, or confirming their general understanding through questions. Discuss the challenges facing these retailers in general terms. Ask students to use the questions from the activity (or close variations) as section titles for their newspaper/magazine article.

Tip: This activity makes a good extended homework task. You could also link it to the concepts of niche and mass marketing, which are covered in the next topic.

Knowledge check (page 167)

1 **Identify** two reasons why consumer spending patterns change.

   Any two from: the economy; technology; fashion; age of consumer; life stage; income.

2 **Explain**, using an example, how life stages change consumer spending patterns.

   Accept life stages such as single people, empty-nesters and DINKIES (Double Income, No Kids), with suitable example(s) of spending habits.

3 **Explain** why a competitive market may benefit consumers.

   Answers should include: lower prices; greater choice; higher bargaining power; better service; frequent promotions; faster pace of invention/innovation.

4 **Outline**, using examples, two ways in which a firm might respond to a competitive market.

   Accept any two from: branding; price reduction; USP; distribution strategy; promotional campaign; market exit; investing in employee training to improve quality of service; improving operations management to speed up delivery times; conducting research to develop new product; launching a promotional campaign to increase sales; using relationship marketing to develop brand loyalty; using pricing strategy to increase competitiveness.

5 **Explain** why knowledge of changing consumer spending patterns is vital to business success.

   Knowledge of spending patterns is essential to: remaining relevant to the market; knowing how to adapt products to changing markets; knowing when and how to launch new products (and what those products should be); identifying possible new market opportunities; knowing when to close down unprofitable products/locations.

3.1.2 Market changes: Activity

Activity type

Investigation

Time

60 minutes

Content

Changing customer needs and spending patterns

Key terms

competition; competitive advantage; customer needs; customer spending patterns; disposable income

Aims

To investigate how customer needs and spending patterns have changed in the market for a product and the impact this has had on businesses in the industry (3.1.2)

Skills practised

AO1: Knowledge and understanding	
AO2: Application	✓
AO3: Analysis	✓
AO4: Evaluation	

Preparation

Make one copy of Activity Sheet 3.1.2 for each student in the class

Procedure

1. Tell students they are going to use what they have learned about market changes to investigate an industry of their choice. They will prepare a written report on the changes that have taken place in their chosen industry. Provide the following suggestions for students to investigate: fast food, organic food, health care, air travel or cars.

2. Give Activity sheet 3.1.2 to students and discuss the example about the market for TVs. Start by finding out what students already know about the TV industry by asking them questions, such as: 'How have TVs changed over recent years?' 'Which are the most popular brands of TV in your country?' 'Have these always been the leading brands?' 'Do people spend more on their TVs now than in the past?'

3. Allow students a few minutes to decide on a focus for their investigation.

4. Explain that students should use the information from Topic 3.1.2 (pages 164–167 in the Student's Book), as well as information from the internet (or other sources) to make notes on the changing market for their product. They should use the questions on the activity sheet to guide them.

5. Students then write the final version of their report.

Variation: Instead of a written report, you could ask students to present their findings in the form of a poster or PowerPoint presentation.

Teacher tip: Ask students to highlight the language devices used to link ideas and sentences together in the example report on the TV market. Examples include: 'this is due to'; 'have resulted from', 'such as', and so on. Encourage students to use similar linking words when preparing their final written reports.

3.1.3 Niche marketing and mass marketing

Aims (3.1.3)

Knowledge

By the end of this section, students will understand:

- the benefits and limitations of niche and mass marketing.

Resources

- Student's Book pages 168–170
- Activity sheets 3.1.3A and 3.1.3B
- Flashcards with the characteristics of niche and mass markets (made by the teacher – see below)
- A range of products used by students

Key business terms

economies of scale; focused marketing; mass market; niche market; product recall; target market; undifferentiated marketing

Lesson ideas

You should aim to cover the materials in 3.1.3 in a single one-hour lesson, plus, as appropriate, a homework assignment. To achieve the Aims for this topic, we recommend doing some of the following activities over the course of the lesson.

Starter suggestion

Product characteristics: Write suitable examples of niche and mass market products on the board. Write the niche products on one side and the mass market products on the other – don't indicate to students how you have organised the products. Without using the terms niche or mass market, ask students to identify the characteristics of the different products and to explain why you have grouped them in this way. Write the relevant adjectives used by the students next to each list of products and use these lists to introduce the terms 'niche marketing' and 'mass marketing'.

Main lesson activities

Discussion and note-taking (whole class): Talk students through niche and mass marketing approaches, asking them to take notes as appropriate. Make sure you cover the benefits and limitations of each marketing approach.

Props: Make a series of flashcards with the characteristics of niche and mass markets from pages 168 and 169 of the Student's Book (one characteristic per card). Make enough sets for students to work in groups on the following task:

Either ask students to bring to class or bring in yourself a range of different items they use (school bags and items of stationery can be used as well); one or two items per student is sufficient. Give out the flashcards and ask students to analyse each product using the characteristics. Ask them to write down their findings under the name of each item. They should finish by identifying each item as either a niche or mass market product.

Extension: Ask students to consider how each of the characteristics might change if the product they are analysing changed from a mass to a niche market product or from a niche to a mass market product.

Student activity: Ask students to complete Activity sheets 3.1.3A and 3.1.3B. It is an investigation of niche **or** mass markets with reference to a company of the students' choice.

Plenary suggestion

Skills activity: Ask students to complete the niche and mass market compare/contrast Skills activity on page 170 of the Student's Book.

Tip: This could be given as a homework task and linked to marketing strategy and/or the marketing mix.

Answers to Student's Book activities

Skills activity (page 170): possible outcomes

The main features of niche markets include: premium prices; small sales volumes; highly differentiated products; a high skills base. Mass markets, on the other hand, feature: low prices, high sales volumes, generic/undifferentiated products and a low skills base requirement.

Knowledge check (page 170)

1 **Identify** two characteristics of a mass market.

   Any two from: low prices; high sales volume; undifferentiated/generic products; similar customer needs across the market; a wide range of sales outlets/wide availability; extensive promotion.

2 **Identify** one advantage of mass marketing.

   Any one from: economies of scale; lower costs per unit (production, marketing and distribution); high sales volume with potential for large profits.

3 **Explain** one disadvantage of Coca-Cola's mass marketing approach.

   Any one from: product not adapted to local markets; production mistakes affect large numbers of products; strategic overexposure to one product category.

4 **Explain**, using an example, what is meant by niche marketing.

   Niche marketing means marketing to a small, clearly identifiable segment of a larger market.

   Students should provide a suitable example.

5 'The toothpaste market is a good example of a niche market.' **Explain** this statement. To what extent do you believe it to be true?

   The toothpaste market is highly segmented; niche products might include those for babies, sensitive teeth or dentures. The whole market can be considered mass, but there are niches within it.

3.1.3 Niche marketing and mass marketing: Activity

Activity type

Investigation

Time

40 minutes

Content

Niche and mass markets

Key terms

economies of scale; focused marketing; mass market; niche market; target market; undifferentiated marketing

Aims

To understand the concepts of niche marketing and mass marketing and the benefits and limitations of each approach (3.1.3)

Skills practised

AO1: Knowledge and understanding	✓
AO2: Application	✓
AO3: Analysis	✓
AO4: Evaluation	

Preparation

Make enough copies of Activity sheet 3.1.3A for half the students in the class and enough copies of Activity sheet 3.1.3B for the other half.

Procedure

1. Tell students that they are going to investigate a business of their choice that operates in either a mass or a niche market. They will then share this information with another student.

2. Divide the class into two halves, A and B. Give a copy of Activity sheet 3.1.3A to all the students in group A and a copy of Activity sheet 3.1.3B to all the students in group B. Explain that the students in group A will be investigating a mass market product, while the students in group B will be investigating a niche market product.

3. Working with two other students in their group, ask students to decide on a product and answer the questions on their activity sheet. They should use their own knowledge of the product as well as information they can find on the internet (or from other sources).

4. Once students have completed their investigation, pair up each student from group A with a student from group B. Explain that each student will have a few minutes to explain the market for their product to their partner.

5. When students have completed their discussions, round off the activity by asking students to identify the main differences between mass markets and niche markets. Encourage them to use the contexts of their discussions when doing this.

Teacher tip: Encourage students to give detailed answers. If possible, avoid too much repetition of product types between students. The more varied the product types, the more valuable the sharing of ideas towards the end of the activity.

Extension: Once students have finished discussing their product with their partner (step 4), pair them up with another partner (from either group, but who analysed a different product) and ask them to discuss their products again. After their first discussion, students should be talking about the markets for their products with a higher level of confidence and fluency, which will enable them to complete their discussion in a shorter time. Ask students to repeat the process again with a new partner, if they are still enjoying the activity and benefiting from their discussions.

3.1.4 Market segmentation

Aims (3.1.4)

Knowledge

By the end of this section, students will understand:

- how markets can be segmented, for example, according to age, socio-economic groupings, location, gender
- the potential benefits of segmentation to businesses
- how to recommend and justify an appropriate method of segmentation in given circumstances.

Resources

- Student's Book pages 171–173
- Activity sheet 3.1.4

Key business terms

demographic segmentation; differentiated; geographical segmentation; market segmentation; market segments; mass market; socio-demographic segmentation; target market

Lesson ideas

You should aim to cover the materials in 3.1.4 in a single one-hour lesson, plus, as appropriate, a homework assignment. To achieve the Aims for this topic, we recommend doing some of the following activities over the course of the lesson.

Starter suggestion

Reader profile (1): Display/write the segmentation statement from the Skills activity (page 173 of the Student's Book) on the board. Without introducing the concept of segmentation, ask students to identify the different ways in which the magazine reader is characterised. Write words such as age, gender, income, and so on, on the board. Tell students that such categorisation is known as 'segmentation'.

Tip: You can repeat this activity once students have studied this topic, using specific rather than general business language (see plenary suggestion).

Main lesson activities

Discussion and note-taking (whole class): Talk students through the different methods of market segmentation, asking them to take notes as appropriate. Make sure you cover the benefits of segmentation.

Student activity: Ask students to complete Activity 3.1.4, in which they analyse the target market of some well-known products and brands.

Segmenting the market: Write a list of products that will be familiar to students on the board. Ask them to work individually to recommend an appropriate method of segmentation for each product. Once they have finished, ask them to discuss their responses with a partner, adding to their list of recommendations as appropriate.

Extension: If time allows, ask students to justify why they made the recommendations.

Skills activity: To reinforce their understanding of the different methods of segmentation, ask students to complete the second part of the Skills activity on page 173 of the Student's Book, in which they prepare segmentation statements for different products.

Tip: This activity could be given as homework following on from the lesson plenary (see below).

Evaluation activity: Ask students to evaluate whether social class is a good way to segment the market. Ask them to consider issues such as whether occupation really determines social class and whether all people in similar occupations buy similar products. Ask students to debate these questions with a partner: one partner should argue that social class is a good way of segmenting markets, the other that it is not.

The simple answer is clearly no. The social class groupings are too simplistic and too narrow to be of significant practical use. That said, encourage students to balance their arguments by considering how segmentation like this might be useful. The groupings may not be relevant in every case, but they are arguably generally applicable and therefore of some use, especially for firms with mass market products.

Plenary suggestion

Reader profile (2): Display/write the segmentation statement from the Skills activity (page 173 of the Student's Book) on the board. Ask students to identify the different ways in which the magazine reader is segmented. Write topic-specific words such as demographic, geographic, and so on, on the board. If students also did this activity as the lesson starter, refer to their understanding at the beginning of the lesson and their (hopefully) more technical and precise knowledge at the end.

Answers to Student's Book activities

Skills activity (page 173): possible outcomes

Encourage students to be inventive and to use appropriate language. Allow their first attempt to mirror the example closely, but encourage them to develop a more sophisticated response using as many types of segmentation as possible.

Extension: Ask students to show their work to a partner, who should identify the different types of segmentation that have been used. If relevant, encourage the partner to recommend additions.

Knowledge check (page 173)

1 **Explain**, using an example, what is meant by a market segment.

   The division (by age, gender, location, purchasing habits, and so on) of a larger market into smaller clearly identifiable segments.

2 **Explain** the key advantages of market segmentation.

   Allows a company to: use marketing budgets effectively; target marketing campaigns accurately; spot gaps in the market and identify new opportunities; differentiate products from those of competitors (allowing higher prices to be charged).

3 **Identify** two examples of markets that might be segmented by age.

   Examples include: transport; toothpaste; movies; magazines; clothing.

4 **Identify** two examples of markets that might be segmented by gender.

   Examples include: hair care products; clothing; cars; exercise programmes; magazines.

5 *'Segmentation is especially important for large firms.'* **Explain** why this might be the case.

   Reasons include: potentially selling to larger markets; may be selling multiple yet similar products across many segments; market may be more competitive and thus greater segmentation required for accurate/ effective marketing.

3.1.4 Market segmentation: Activity

Activity type

Jigsaw discussion activity

Time

30 minutes

Content

Market segmentation

Key terms

demographic segmentation; differentiated; geographical segmentation; market segmentation; market segments; mass market; socio-demographic segmentation; target market

Skills practised

AO1: Knowledge and understanding	✓
AO2: Application	✓
AO3: Analysis	✓
AO4: Evaluation	

Preparation

Make one copy of Activity Sheet 3.1.4 for each student in the class.

Aims

To understand and recommend how markets can be segmented, for example, according to age, income, location and gender (3.1.4)

Procedure

1. Tell students that they are going to analyse how some businesses segment the market for their products.
2. Divide the class into two groups, A and B, and give a copy of Activity sheet 3.1.4 to each student.
3. Demonstrate what students need to do using Sony PlayStation 4 Pro as an example.
4. Explain that the students in group A will complete the table for products/brands 1 and 2, while the students in group B will complete it for products/brands 3 and 4. Following this, each student from group A will be paired with a student from group B. Students will then take turns to explain the target market segmentation of the products/brands they analysed to their partner.
5. Students should listen to their partner and make brief notes. They should also offer their own opinions and ask clarifying questions if they don't understand.
6. Round off the activity by nominating students to share their analysis with the class.

Teacher tips: Remind students that this is a speaking activity and they should not simply give their completed activity sheet to their partner to copy. The objective here is for students to discuss marketing concepts in a meaningful context, not to complete the activity in the minimum time possible!

If any of the products/brands on the activity sheet are likely to be unfamiliar to your students, you may wish to change them to other examples.

Extension: Students discuss the potential benefits to each of these businesses of segmenting their markets. Ask them to write a response to the following question for one of the businesses on Activity sheet 3.1.4.

Discuss the potential benefits for [name of business] of segmenting the markets for its products.

3.2 Market research

3.2.1 THE ROLE AND METHODS OF MARKET RESEARCH

Aims (3.2.1)

Knowledge

By the end of this section, students will understand:

- market-oriented businesses – uses of market research information to a business
- the benefits and limitations of primary research and secondary research
- different methods of primary research, for example, postal questionnaires, online surveys, interviews, focus groups
- the need for sampling
- the methods of secondary research, for example, online, accessing government sources, paying for commercial market research reports
- the factors influencing the accuracy of market research data.

Resources

- Student's Book pages 174–181
- Activity sheet 3.2.1
- Packaging of popular snack foods
- Students' mobile phones (optional)

Key business terms

cluster sampling; customer satisfaction survey; desk research; field research; focus group; market orientation; market research; market segment; marketing mix; primary research; prototype; qualitative data; quantitative data; questionnaire; quota sampling; random sampling; reliability; sampling; secondary data; secondary research; specificity; stratified sampling; systematic random sample; test marketing

Lesson ideas

You should aim to cover the materials in 3.2.1 in two or three one-hour lessons, plus, as appropriate, homework assignments. To achieve the Aims for this topic, we recommend doing some of the following activities over the course of the lessons.

Starter suggestion

Tweet it: As a recap, ask students to define market-orientation in fewer than 140 characters. If possible, encourage them to use a mobile phone to do this. You may wish to ask students to Tweet or Snapchat the definitions to one another, encouraging discussion as students pass the messages around the class. Alternatively, students could write their definitions on a card. Use the concept of market-orientation (understanding consumer needs) to introduce market research.

Main lesson activities

Discussion and note-taking (whole class): Talk students through market research, the different research methods and methods of sampling, asking students to take notes as appropriate. Make sure that you cover the limitations of the different methods and the factors influencing accuracy.

Half and half: Set students a small (imaginary) challenge. Tell them that they are going to conduct some market research. One half of the group will conduct primary research and the other half secondary research. Tell students that they are going to (pretend to) research the ages of all the teachers in the school.

Ask the two halves to consider how they will do the research. Once they have discussed their methods (with you guiding them), ask them to consider the benefits and limitations of the approaches. Use this as the basis for discussing the benefits and limitations of primary and secondary research.

Match it: Photocopy or print out a section of notes on the different types of market research, including both primary and secondary methods (see pages 176–180 of the Student's Book). Photocopy enough sets of these notes to give to small groups within your class. Cut up the titles, descriptions and limitations of each method, mix them up and place each set in an envelope.

Divide the class into small groups and give each group one envelope. Ask students to match up the titles, descriptions and limitations.

Student activity: Ask students to do Activity 3.2.1, in which they role-play a focus group and consider how certain products could be improved.

Class activity: Divide the class into small groups and assign a different method of primary research to each group. Ask students to consider how they would use that method to research the cinema-going habits of students in the school. Once they have decided on how they would use that method, ask them to consider how accurate their method would be.

Ask each group to present their method and justify its accuracy to the whole class. Using the terms 'reliability' and 'accuracy' as a guide, ask the whole class to vote on which method they think would be the best.

Use the issues that arise from this exercise (time, sample size, and so on) to introduce the concept of sampling (and the methods of sampling). Have students consider the benefits and limitations of sampling.

Skills activity: Ask students to complete the Skills activity on page 178 the Student's Book. Students consider the most appropriate primary research method for a variety of products and present their findings as a short report.

Plenary suggestion

Snowball: Ask students to write down one factor that influences the accuracy of market research data. Tell them to walk around the room adding influences from different classmates. Tell them that they can't use the same classmate twice and that they must write down four or five different factors.

Knowledge check: Ask students to answer the Knowledge check questions on page 181 of the Student's Book.

Answers to Student's Book activities

Skills activity (page 178): possible outcomes

Possible answers include:

- a new brand of female cosmetics: in-store questionnaire; observation; survey in female magazine
- a magazine for students: focus groups of 14–16-year-old students, small but focused sample
- a new tablet computer: online survey to computer buyers (linked to computer related websites); narrow sample
- a new Pixar movie: focus groups with children and parents OR observation of children watching Pixar movie clips.

Encourage students to justify their choices.

Knowledge check (page 181)

1   **Identify** the differences between primary and secondary research, supporting your answer with examples.

   Secondary research (also accept desk research) is the process of gathering data that has already been collected or published. Secondary data may already exist within the business or may be gathered from elsewhere. Primary research (also accept field research) is the gathering of new and original, first-hand information.

2   **Explain** the difference between quantitative and qualitative data.

   Quantitative data is data from a large group of respondents showing numbers, proportions or trends within a market (for example, sales data). Qualitative data is in-depth research into the reasons behind consumer decisions.

3   **Identify** two key advantages of secondary research.

   Any two from: cheaper; easy to access; faster; potentially accurate (depending on source).

4 Define the term sampling.

Sampling is selecting a smaller research group from a larger population. The sample needs to be large enough to provide data that is reliable and representative of the attitudes and characteristics of the total population, but small enough to make research cost-effective.

5 **Outline** one limitation of primary research and one limitation of secondary research.

Primary research: *Any one from:* expensive; time-consuming; may contain interviewer bias; difficult to conduct accurately.

Secondary research: *Any one from:* may not be specific to a firm's needs; may be out of date; may not be reliable; large amount of data that needs sorting carefully.

6 **Outline** two reasons why market research may *not* be useful for a firm selling technology products.

Any two from: technology markets change rapidly so research may become quickly out of date; research may not be accurate; purchasing behaviour may not reflect survey response (a person who claims to 'dislike Apple' may still own an Apple phone); rapidly falling technology prices can affect purchasing decisions.

3.2.1 The role and methods of market research: Activity

Activity type
Focus group activity

Content
Market research: focus group

Time
30 minutes

Key terms
brand; brand image; field research; focus group; market orientation; market research; market segment; marketing mix; primary research; qualitative data; unique selling point

Skills practised

AO1: Knowledge and understanding	✓
AO2: Application	✓
AO3: Analysis	✓
AO4: Evaluation	

Preparation
Before the lesson, ask each student to bring a packet of their favourite snack food to class. Make one copy of Activity sheet 3.2.1 for each student in the class.

Aims
To understand the role and purpose of focus groups as one form of market research (3.2.1)

Procedure

1. Tell students they are going to be part of a focus group in which they will discuss a type of snack food. Elicit the meaning of 'focus group' and ask students what the purpose of a focus group is. Refer them to the section on primary research on pages 176–179 of the Student's Book.
2. Divide the class into groups of four and give a copy of Activity sheet 3.2.1 to each student.
3. In their groups, students choose one of the snack foods they have brought to class and discuss it, using the questions on the activity sheet. They should note down the main points of their discussion on the sheet.
4. Allow students 20 minutes to complete this task. If they finish discussing the first type of snack food, they should move on and discuss another type of snack, making notes on a second copy of the activity sheet.
5. To round off the activity, elicit suggestions from students as to how the snack foods each group discussed could be improved. Finally, discuss the possible value of this information to the business.

Variation: After discussing and making notes on a type of snack food in their group, ask students to briefly share their analysis with other groups.

Extension: Students summarise their findings in the form of a poster, listing what was good about the product and what the groups thought could be improved. You could use the posters to create a wall display.

Teacher tip: Ensure that students stay focused. The focus group discussion could easily move off-task. Redirect and encourage on-task analysis as necessary.

3.2.2 Presentation and use of market research results

Aims (3.2.2)

Skills

By the end of this section, students will understand:

- how to analyse market research data shown in the form of graphs, charts and diagrams, and draw simple conclusions from such data.

Resources

- Student's Book pages 182–183
- Activity sheet 3.2.2
- Examples of graphs and charts from newspapers/magazines or the internet – see below
- Photographs and pictures of toothbrushes from the past; a selection of new toothbrushes of different types
- Spreadsheet/presentation software (optional)

Key business terms

bar chart; closed questions; line graph; open questions; pictogram; pie chart; primary research; qualitative data; quantitative data; secondary research; table; tally chart

Lesson ideas

You should aim to cover the materials in 3.2.2 in two one-hour lessons, plus, as appropriate, homework assignments. You could assign some elements of Activity 3.2.2 as homework and/or as an activity during break/lunchtimes.

To achieve the Aims for this topic, we recommend doing some of the following activities over the course of the lessons.

Starter suggestion

How is it presented? Take into the class examples of graphs and charts from newspapers/magazines or the internet showing the different ways in which data can be presented visually. Hand out the examples to groups of students and ask them to identify and label each form of presentation (pie chart, pictogram, and so on).

Main lesson activities

Discussion and note-taking (whole class): Talk students through the various methods of presentation, asking them to take notes as appropriate. Make sure that you cover how to analyse data and draw simple conclusions.

Group activity: Using the materials from the starter activity, ask small groups of students to analyse the advantages and disadvantages of each form of presentation.

Extension: Ask students to consider the possible accuracy of the data, including both presenter and reader bias.

Skills activity: Ask students to complete the Skills activity (an analysis of a set of data) on page 183 of the Student's Book. Make sure that students focus on drawing conclusions from the data as well as on creating the graphs/charts.

Student activity: Ask students to complete the school-based survey in Activity 3.2.2, and ensure they present their findings in an appropriate format. You will need to carry out this activity over two lessons, with students conducting the survey as homework in between the lessons.

Plenary suggestion

Knowledge check: Ask students to answer the Knowledge check questions on page 183 of the Student's Book.

Tip: This could be given as a homework task.

Answers to Student's Book activities

Skills activity (page 183): possible outcomes

The most obvious forms that students might choose are bar charts or line graphs. Ensure that students draw their charts accurately and label them appropriately. The key to this exercise is to ensure that students focus on analysis of the data. Key issues they may draw attention should include:

Product A: very static sales.

Product B: decline in sales seems directly correlated (linked) to growth of product D sales.

Product C: seems correlated (linked) to sales of product E.

Product D: possibly a new product in direct competition with product B.

Product E: possibly an established product in competition with product C.

The implications for Product B might be the need to change, adapt or market the product to challenge the growing presence of Product D in the market.

Knowledge check (page 183)

1 **Identify** when a pictogram might be the most appropriate form of data presentation.

   Answers might include: to present simple data; to include in a presentation; for a newspaper/ TV report.

2 **Identify** appropriate methods of presentation for the following:
   a) the sales of a product over time
   b) a comparison of multiple product sales for one month
   c) percentage responses to questions about movies viewed in the last month.

   a) line graph b) bar chart c) pie chart

3 Present the following data in a suitable format (other than a table) and **identify** any conclusions that can be drawn.

Sales projections	Month 1	Month 2	Month 3
Sales @ $1000	400 000	1 200 000	2 400 000
Sales @ $750	300 000	900 000	1 800 000

Bar chart or comparison pie charts, but accept any appropriate method.

3.2.2 Presentation and use of market research results: Activity

Activity type
Data gathering and analysis

Time
90 minutes (over two lessons) plus homework

Content
Market research and presentation of data

Key terms
bar chart; closed questions; line graph; open questions; pictogram; pie chart; primary research; qualitative data; quantitative data; secondary research; table; tally chart

Skills practised

AO1: Knowledge and understanding	
AO2: Application	✓
AO3: Analysis	✓
AO4: Evaluation	

Preparation
Make one copy of Activity sheet 3.2.2 for each student in the class. Prepare a selection of pictures showing different types of toothbrush from the past and present. If possible, bring a few different types of toothbrush to class.

Aims
To gather market research data, present it in the form of graphs, charts and diagrams and draw simple conclusions (3.2.2)

Procedure

1. Tell students that they are going to design a questionnaire that they will use to gather market data. They will then present their findings using graphs, charts and diagrams and draw conclusions from the data.

2. Using the information on pages 176 and 182 of the Student's Book, discuss the difference between qualitative and quantitative data and the different ways in which quantitative data can be presented.

3. Explain that students are going to create a questionnaire designed to gather quantitative data on the teenage market for toothbrushes.

4. Show some pictures of different types of toothbrush and discuss how the design of toothbrushes has changed over time. If available, hand out a selection of (new) toothbrushes to students to prompt discussion.

5. Divide the class into groups of five and give a copy of Activity sheet 3.2.2 to each student. Explain that in their groups they should agree on five questions to gather quantitative data.

6. Explain that Questions 1 to 3 have been done for them as examples and they should design Questions 4 to 8 based on the areas suggested at the top of the activity sheet.

7. Allow groups 10 minutes to agree on their questions. While they are doing this, move around the room, checking that their questions are quantitative in nature and they have a clear purpose.

8. Explain that each group will have to survey at least 20 teenagers in their school using their completed questionnaire before the next lesson. Students may either interview respondents face-to-face or administer their questionnaire in another way, such as by email or Facebook. If necessary, make additional copies of the questionnaire for each group.

9. In the next lesson, ask each group to prepare a tally chart of their responses for each question using an Excel spreadsheet.

10. Groups then present their information graphically in Excel using at least one bar chart, one pie chart and one pictogram.

11. Finally, ask students to share their charts with the class and draw simple conclusions from the data.

Extension: Ask students to do some secondary research for homework. Using the internet (or other sources), they should find out useful information about the toothbrush industry in their home country, such as: the main competitors in the market; how companies differentiate their products; how they promote their products; how they innovate and add value to their products. Students should share their findings with the class at the beginning of the next lesson.

Teacher tip: *Ensure that students' questions are focused enough to be presentable in graphical form. They should, where possible, stick to closed questions and should provide limited response options as much as possible.*

3.3 Marketing mix

3.3.1 PRODUCT

Aims (3.3.1)

Knowledge

By the end of this section, students will understand:

- the costs and benefits of developing new products
- brand image and its impact on sales and customer loyalty
- the role of packaging
- the product life cycle: the main stages and extension strategies; how to draw and interpret a product life cycle diagram
- how stages of the product life cycle can influence marketing decisions, for example, promotion and pricing decisions.

Resources

- Student's Book pages 184–191
- Activity sheet 3.3.1
- Examples of product packaging

Key business terms

brand image/branding; cash flow; competitive advantage; decline; economies of scale; extension strategy; growth; introduction; market segment; marketing expenditure; maturity; packaging; place; price; price flexibility; product; product life cycle; profit; promotion; research and development (R&D); unit cost

Lesson ideas

You should aim to cover the materials in 3.3.1 in two one-hour lessons, plus, as appropriate, homework assignments. To achieve the Aims for this topic, we recommend doing some of the following activities over the course of the lessons.

Starter suggestions

Pre-lesson Skills activity: As an introduction to the Marketing mix topic, ask students to consider the marketing activities of their school/institution (Skills activity on page 184 of the Student's Book). Use students' responses at the start of this series of lessons to draw out key topic-related themes. Encourage them not just to describe the marketing activities of the school/institution, but also to evaluate whether they think they are successful.

Lesson 1 Playing favourites: Ask students to work individually to list their five favourite products. Ask them to identify what it is about each product that they like (design, features, brand, and so on). Use their ideas to generate a list of topic-related key words on the board. Ensure that you discuss the impact on sales and customer loyalty.

Lesson 2 Props: Ask students to bring into the lesson various examples of product packaging from home. Organise them into small groups and ask them to analyse the packaging. Ask them to consider the following questions: 'How does the packaging help to promote the product; differentiate the product; protect the product from damage; make the product convenient to use; communicate information; make the product easy to store/display?'

Main lesson activities

Discussion and note-taking (whole class): Talk students through various aspects of product (knowledge of brand image and its impact on sales and customer loyalty, the role of packaging, the product life cycle), asking them to take notes as appropriate.

Flowchart: Ask students to work individually to draw a flowchart of what they think happens between a business having an idea for a new product and that product going on sale to customers. Use students' responses to introduce the concept of R&D. Link this understanding to the costs and benefits of developing new products.

Skills activity: Ask students to work in small groups on the Skills activity on page 187 of the Student's Book. They consider which elements of the brand and/or packaging make a range of famous products and services successful.

Student activity: Introduce the students to the concept of product life cycle (pages 188–191 of the Student's Book) and ask them to complete Activity 3.3.1. They categorise explanations of the different stages of the product life cycle.

Skills activity: Introduce students to alternative forms of the product life cycle (page 190 of the Student's Book). Ask them to work in pairs on the Skills activity on page 191 (identification of different forms of life cycle for different products). If group size allows, ask pairs to draw a copy of one of the diagrams on the board. Use their responses to reinforce how product life cycle might influence marketing decisions.

Knowledge check: Students answer the Knowledge check questions on page 191 of the Student's Book.

Tip: This exercise could be given as a homework task.

Plenary suggestion

Product profile: Ask students to select one product from their list of five favourites (from the starter activity). Instruct them to write a profile for that product using appropriate key terms from the topic. For example, they could write a short analysis of the product's marketing-related features (brand, design, packaging, and so on), draw a product life cycle for the product and prepare a brief evaluation of the product's strengths and weaknesses (from a competitive, market-focused perspective).

Answers to Student's Book activities

Skills activities: possible outcomes

Skills activity (Introduction to Marketing mix: page 184)

This activity would make a useful starter or plenary for the Marketing mix topic. As a starter, use students' responses to draw out key topic-related themes. As a plenary, ensure that students use appropriate marketing-specific language appropriately. Encourage students not just to describe the marketing activities of the school, but also to evaluate whether they think they are successful.

Skills activity (page 187)

A wide range of answers is possible here. Responses may depend on students' interests and product knowledge. Encourage them to research the brands and to use business-specific language when defining what makes each product successful. The following list of possible responses is not exhaustive:

- Mercedes-Benz: design, quality
- Justin Bieber: brand image
- Hilton Hotels: brand name, brand loyalty
- LUXE travel guides: design, brand, niche product
- Kellogg's breakfast cereal: brand loyalty
- Real Madrid football shirt: brand image, design.

Skills activity (page 191)

Suggested answers:

- PlayStation 4: slow start; multiple extension strategies
- iPad 3: rapid growth; multiple extension strategies
- skinny jeans: rapid growth; some extension strategies (carrot style, turn-ups); likely to be short/fashion life cycle
- DVD players: rapid growth; many extension strategies; long period of maturity/saturation but now (arguably) in decline
- Mars bar: rapid growth; possible fad.

Knowledge check (page 191)

1. **Explain**, using an example, what is meant by the term brand image.

    The personality and values associated with a particular brand.

2. **Identify** one advantage of 'brand loyalty'.

    Any one from: repeat purchase; word-of-mouth promotion; price inelasticity.

3. **Identify** the main stages of the product life cycle.

    Introduction; growth; maturity/saturation; decline.

4. Outline the details and draw product life cycle diagrams for the following: a) a failed product; b) a successful extension strategy.

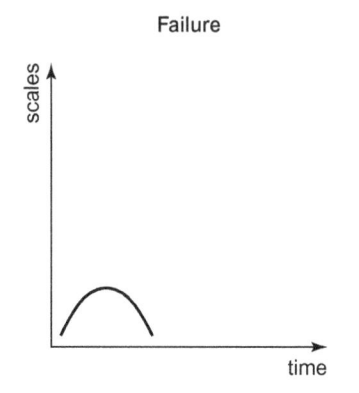

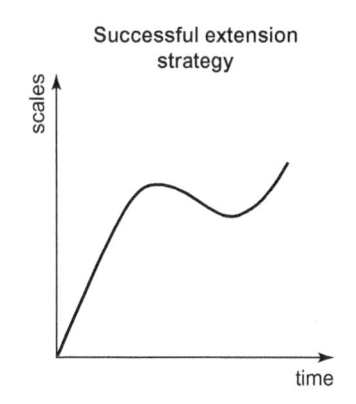

    a) Failure — graph with scales on y-axis and time on x-axis, showing a small hump that quickly declines.

    b) Successful extension strategy — graph with scales on y-axis and time on x-axis, showing a rise, slight dip, then rise again.

5. **Identify** one reason why packaging is an important additional element of the marketing mix.

    Any one from: promote the product; differentiate the product; protect the product from damage; communicate information (ingredients, usage); make the product convenient to use; make the product easy to store/display.

6. **Outline** how the promotion of a product might be different in each stage of its life cycle.

    Introduction: focus on awareness; Growth: generate brand preference; Maturity: retain brand loyalty; Decline: targeted promotions.

7. **Explain**, using an example, what is meant by the term R&D.

    Research and development: the process of generating/developing new product ideas, inventing completely new technologies, making prototypes and testing products with consumers.

3.3.1 Product: Activity

Activity type
Categorisation activity

Time
30 minutes

Content
Characteristics of the product life cycle

Key terms
brand image/branding; cash flow; competitive advantage; decline; economies of scale; extension strategy; growth; introduction; market segment; marketing expenditure; maturity; packaging; place; price; price flexibility; product; product life cycle; profit; promotion; research and development (R&D); unit cost

Skills practised

AO1: Knowledge and understanding	✓
AO2: Application	
AO3: Analysis	
AO4: Evaluation	

Preparation
Photocopy and cut up one set of the cards on Activity sheet 3.3.1 for each group of three students. Make one copy of Activity sheet 3.3.1 for each student for the answers.

Aims
To discuss the various characteristics at each stage of the product life cycle (introduction, growth, maturity and decline) (3.3.1)

Procedure

1. Tell students that they are going to complete a categorisation activity about the different stages of the product life cycle in small groups.
2. Divide the class into groups of three and give each group a set of cards from Activity sheet 3.3.1.
3. Students place the black cards (Introduction, Growth, Maturity, Decline) in the order of the product life cycle. They place the category cards (Product, Price, Promotion, Place (distribution), Marketing expenditure, Cash flow, Profit, Competitors, Unit cost) down the left-hand side to form a grid. You could draw the grid on the board. Students place the remaining cards face down in a pile.
4. Students take turns to draw one card from the pile and read it aloud to their group. They then discuss where to place the card in the grid. Students must collectively agree on the best place for each card. Debate is to be encouraged!
5. If students can't agree, or are unsure where to place a card, they can move on to the next card.
6. Emphasise that this is not a competitive activity; the objective is not to be the first to finish. Students should take time to discuss each card in detail, and support their opinions with sound justification.
7. Move around the class, ensuring that students are doing the activity correctly.
8. At the end of the activity, hand out complete copies of Activity sheet 3.3.1 so students can check their answers.
9. Round off the activity by reading a card aloud and nominating a student to identify the stage of the product life cycle which it belongs to, preferably without looking at their completed grid.

Teacher tip: You can make the activity cards more durable by photocopying them onto card before cutting them up.

Variation: If students have not yet covered topics such as cash flow and unit cost, you could remove these cards from the set. Similarly, you could remove the marketing expenditure and profit cards if EAL or ability needs are likely to make these cards too challenging. Alternatively, you could leave them in as extension for the more able members of the class.

Extension: In groups, students identify examples of specific products at each stage of the product life cycle. They must be prepared to justify their examples.

3.3.2 Price

Aims (3.3.2)

Knowledge

By the end of this section, students will understand:

- pricing methods, for example, cost plus, competitive, penetration, skimming, promotional; and their benefits and limitations
- how to recommend and justify an appropriate pricing method in given circumstances
- the benefits and limitations of different pricing strategies
- the significance of price elasticity: difference between price elastic demand and price inelastic demand; importance of the concept in pricing decisions.

Resources

- Student's Book pages 192–198
- Activity sheet 3.3.2
- A variety of snack products

Key business terms

competitive pricing; cost plus; discriminatory pricing; geographical pricing; mark-up; penetration pricing; premium pricing; price elastic demand; price elasticity of demand; price inelastic demand; price skimming; promotional pricing; selling price; substitutes

Lesson ideas

You should aim to cover the materials in 3.3.2 in two one-hour lessons, plus, as appropriate, homework assignments. Cover pricing strategies in the first lesson and price elasticity of demand in the second. To achieve the Aims for this topic, we recommend doing some of the following activities over the course of the lessons.

Starter suggestions

Lesson 1: List five products on the board, the prices of which will be familiar to students (snack products, cinema tickets, and so on). Ask them to write down the approximate price of each product. Then ask them to talk in pairs about why they think the firm has priced each product at that level. Make sure they focus on marketing issues and not just the cost of production. Use their responses to introduce the concept of pricing strategy and the different methods of pricing.

Lesson 2: Take into the lesson some snacks that students are likely to want and some that they are likely to want less (or not at all). At the start of the lesson, set up a mock situation where you offer to sell the snacks to the students. Start at a low price and record the level of demand in the class. Increase the price until demand is close to zero. Do this for the different types of snack and use the student demand profiles to introduce sensitivity to price changes and (if time allows) the factors that affect that sensitivity.

Main lesson activities

Discussion and note-taking (whole class): Talk students through the various pricing strategies and the concept of price elasticity of demand. Ask them to take notes as appropriate. Ensure that you cover the need to recommend pricing strategies in different contexts and the significance of price elasticity of demand in pricing decisions.

Student activity: Introduce students to the concept of pricing strategy and ask them to complete Activity sheet 3.3.2, a categorisation activity. They group features of the various pricing strategies under the appropriate strategy headings.

Skills activity: Ask students to complete the Skills activity on page 195 on the Student's Book. They suggest an appropriate pricing strategy for different products/services.

Skills activity: Introduce the concept of price elasticity of demand and ask students to work in pairs on the Skills activity on page 198 of the Student's Book. Ask them to consider how their answer might affect the pricing strategy for each product.

Homework: A possible homework activity for this topic is included in the Extension at the end of the notes about Activity sheet 3.3.2; students find real-world examples on the various pricing strategies.

Plenary suggestion

Exit pass: Using the Knowledge check questions on page 198 of the Student's Book, ask pairs or small groups to answer a topic-related question. They should share their answers with the whole class. Allow other groups to 'steal' answers if the first group's response is incorrect or insufficient. This can be a fun activity, if context allows, before lunch, break or at the end of the school day. Students are motivated to answer a question correctly in order to be the first group out of the classroom.

Answers to Student's Book activities

Skills activities: possible outcomes

Skills activity (page 195)

A range of answers is possible. Encourage students to justify their choices. Possible responses include:

- a new magazine aimed at teenagers: penetration pricing
- a new concept mobile phone with a strong USP: price skimming
- a breakfast cereal re-launching in new packaging: competitive pricing, discounting
- a hair care product manufacturer with *excess* (too much) stock: promotional pricing.

Skills activity (page 197)

A range of answers is possible. Encourage students to justify their choices. Possible responses include:

- unbranded rice: price inelastic (low price so any percentage change would have to be significant to affect demand to a great extent)
- BMW cars: price inelastic
- Prada clothing: price inelastic
- iTunes music tracks: price elastic (many competing brands), though switching costs may lower the elasticity
- headache tablets: price elastic (many competing brands)
- IMAX cinema tickets: price elastic.

Knowledge check (page 198)

1 **Identify** three factors that will affect a firm's pricing decision.

   Any three from: cost of production; market segment; amount of competition; business objectives; where the product is in its life cycle.

2 **Explain** when a firm might use price skimming.

   When entering a new market with a new/unique product.

3 **Explain** an advantage and a disadvantage of using competitive pricing.

   Advantage: *Any one from:* ensures product price is in line with competitor products; set at a level customers expect; demand is proven at that price point.

   Disadvantage: *Any one from:* offers no advantage over competition; competitors may lower the price; takes no account of costs or other factors.

4 **Identify** which pricing strategy a firm might use when trying to gain a foothold in a competitive market.

   Penetration pricing

5 **Explain** what the term price elasticity measures.

   The responsiveness of demand to changes in a product's price.

6 **Identify** two types of goods that might be price inelastic.

   Examples include: petrol; essential services (electricity, gas); cigarettes; basic/essential foodstuffs.

3.3.2 Price: Activity

Activity type
Categorising activity

Time
30 minutes

Content
Pricing methods

Key terms
competitive pricing; cost plus; discriminatory pricing; geographical pricing; mark-up; penetration pricing; premium pricing; price skimming; promotional pricing

Aims
To demonstrate an understanding of the different pricing methods as well as their benefits and limitations (3.3.2)

Skills practised

AO1: Knowledge and understanding	✓
AO2: Application	
AO3: Analysis	
AO4: Evaluation	

Preparation
Photocopy and cut up one set of the cards on Activity sheet 3.3.2 for each group of three students. Make one copy of Activity sheet 3.3.2 for each student for the answers (optional).

Procedure

1. Tell students that they are going to work in small groups to complete a categorisation activity about the different pricing methods used by businesses.
2. Divide the class into groups of three and give a set of the activity cards to each group.
3. Students remove the black title cards (Cost plus pricing, Competitive pricing, Penetration pricing, Price skimming, Promotional pricing) and put them on the desk in front of them. They place the remaining cards face down in a pile on the desk.
4. Students take turns to draw one card from the pile and read it aloud to their group. They then match the card with the correct pricing method and place it in the appropriate category. Students should collectively agree on the best place for each card.
5. If students can't agree or are unsure about where to place a card, they can put it to one side and move on to the next card.
6. Emphasise to students that this is not a competitive activity and the objective is not to be the first to finish. Instead, they should take their time to discuss each card in detail, making sure they support their opinions with sound justification.
7. Move around the class to ensure that students are doing the activity correctly.
8. Elicit the correct answers during the feedback stage of the activity. Alternatively, give students a complete photocopy of Activity sheet 3.3.2 so they can check their answers in their group.

Teacher tip: Before the final feedback stage of the activity, ask groups to briefly compare their answers with another group. This should encourage more discussion and debate among students, thereby enhancing their understanding of the different pricing methods.

Note: Although this activity is designed so there is an equal number of cards under each pricing method, some features can be matched to more than one method. For example, both penetration and promotional pricing may signal inferior quality to consumers, thereby harming the image of the brand. Both alternatives should be accepted. The important thing is that students are able justify their decision.

Extension: For homework, ask students to find evidence of each of these pricing strategies being used by businesses. They could find these online or by taking photographs of promotional materials such as brochures, billboards, newspaper advertisements, and so on, on their mobile phones.

3.3.3 Place – distribution channels

Aims (3.3.3)

Knowledge

By the end of this section, students will understand:

- the advantages and disadvantages of different channels, for example, use of wholesalers, retailers or direct to consumers
- how to recommend and justify an appropriate distribution channel in given circumstances.

Resources

- Student's Book pages 199–204
- Activity sheet 3.3.3

Key business terms

agent; direct distribution; disintermediation; distribution channel; intermediaries; retail distribution; wholesale distribution

Lesson ideas

You should aim to cover the materials in 3.3.3 in a single one-hour lesson, plus, as appropriate, homework assignments. To achieve the Aims for this topic, we recommend doing some of the following activities over the course of the lesson.

Starter suggestion

Hot seat: Write 'Product distribution' on the board. Explain that distribution is about how products get from producer to consumer, not about location. Without giving any explanation, write the key terms for this topic on the board. Put yourself in the 'hot seat'. Students need to ask you questions about the meanings of the terms, but they can't ask direct questions (such as 'What is an agent?'). This is to help students develop questioning skills and make them think about the topic in analytical rather than knowledge terms. If they ask closed questions, give short, closed answers. Encourage them to develop their questioning and don't allow direct questions about the meaning of the key terms.

Main lesson activities

Discussion and note taking (whole class): Talk students through the various distribution strategies, asking them to take notes as appropriate. Make sure you focus on the need to recommend and justify appropriate distribution channels for different contexts.

Student activity: Introduce students to the various distribution strategies and ask them to complete Activity sheet 3.3.3. They read pages 199–202 in the Student's Book and make notes on an assigned method of distribution in the table on the sheet.

Tip: Once students have completed the activity in class, you could ask them to correct and expand on their notes as a homework exercise.

Skills activity: Ask students to work individually to complete the Skills activity on page 204 of the Student's Book. In this activity students suggest and justify distribution strategies for different products.

Plenary suggestion

Role play: Split the class into groups of three. Tell students that they are going to 'role-play' each distribution channel. For each channel, ask the students to take a role (producer, retailer, customer, and so on) and to explain their role. For example, 'I am a wholesaler. My role is …' Students should rotate the roles around the group so that each member has the chance to role-play one of the key roles (retailer, wholesaler or agent).

Note: For the purpose of this exercise, exclude direct distribution, as there is no intermediary role for students to play.

Answers to Student's Book activities

Skills activity (page 204): possible outcomes

a) a new breakfast snack: wholesale distribution

b) a new book: direct distribution or wholesale distribution

c) a Vietnamese firm exporting Vietnamese art: agent

d) a Honda motorbike: retail distribution

Knowledge check (page 204)

1 Define the term intermediary.

An intermediary is a step/stage in the distribution chain (for example, a retailer).

2 **Explain** two factors that influence the choice of distribution channel.

Any two from: marketing aims; product characteristics; market coverage; cost considerations; customer expectations/brand image; stage of product life cycle.

3 **Explain** the role of a wholesaler.

Wholesalers buy in large quantities from manufactures and then sell these products in smaller quantities to retailers.

4 **Identify** one disadvantage of using a wholesaler.

Any one from: wholesalers add their own mark-up to the price of the product (making the product uncompetitive); the additional stage in distribution increases the time for a product to reach consumers; increased handling increases the chance of product damage; loss of control over product storage environment (potentially leading to mishandling and damage).

5 **Explain** the role of a distribution agent.

Agents connect buyers and sellers and manage the transfer of the product. This distribution method is most often used by businesses involved in import/export.

6 **Explain** two benefits of using direct distribution methods.

Any two from: by cutting out the intermediaries products can be sold at a lower (and potentially more competitive) price; the producer is able to develop a direct relationship with consumers; the producer is able to react faster to consumers' needs and to changing market conditions.

7 **Identify** and **explain** the impact of the internet on distribution.

Lower prices for consumers; wider choice; lower profit margins for firms; buyers have perfect knowledge; more competitive markets; new distribution options (downloading).

8 **Identify** the relationship between cost of distribution and product price.

The longer the chain of distribution, the higher the price of the product and vice versa.

3.3.3 Place – distribution channels: Activity

Activity type

Jigsaw reading activity

Time

30 minutes

Content

Channels of distribution

Key terms

agent; direct distribution; disintermediation; distribution channel; intermediaries; retail distribution; wholesale distribution

Aims

To understand the advantages/disadvantages of different distribution channels (3.3.3)

Skills practised

AO1: Knowledge and understanding	✓
AO2: Application	✓
AO3: Analysis	
AO4: Evaluation	

Preparation

Make one copy of Activity sheet 3.3.3 for each student.

Procedure

1. Tell students that they are going to read about one of the methods that businesses use to distribute their products and explain it to other students.
2. Divide the class into four equal groups, A, B, C and D, and give a copy of Activity sheet 3.3.3 to each student.
3. Assign a different distribution channel to each group and ask them to read about their assigned channel in the Student's Book and make notes using the table on the activity sheet. For example, the students in group A read about direct distribution on pages 199–200 and complete the relevant section of their table, while the students in group B read about retail distribution on page 200, and so on.
4. Allow students 10 minutes to complete the relevant section of the activity sheet and compare their notes in their group.
5. Following this, reorganise students so there is one student from group A, one from B, one from C and one from D in each new group.
6. Tell students that they have three to four minutes each to describe their allocated channel of distribution to the members of their new group and explain its advantages and disadvantages. Other group members should listen and ask for clarification if they don't understand. Allow them to make brief notes if they want, but they don't need to write down every word as the information is in their Student's Book. Emphasise that the focus of this activity should be on listening and speaking, not reading and writing. They must not simply copy what each group member has written about a particular channel of distribution.
7. Move around the room, ensuring that students are following instructions and doing the activity correctly.
8. To round off the activity, and ask different students to outline the differences between the various distribution channels. Refer to the Suggested answers provided.

Teacher tip: You can organise step 5 of the activity by numbering the students in each group and asking the number 1s to form a new group in one part of the classroom, the number 2s to form a new group in another part of the classroom, and so on.

Extension: For homework, you could ask students to complete the table on Activity sheet 3.3.3, using what they learned from their discussion and the information on pages 199–202 of the Student's Book.

3.3.3 Place – distribution channels: Activity: Suggested answers

	Direct distribution	Retail distribution	Wholesale distribution	Distribution through agents
Explanation	The producer sells goods directly to the end customer.	Goods are sold to a retailer, who then sells them on to the end customer.	Goods are sold to a wholesaler, who then sells them on to retailers in smaller quantities (breaking bulk).	An agent connects a producer with a retailer and manages the transfer of the goods, usually to overseas markets.
Example	A small local baker or a firm that sells products directly to customers over the internet.	The majority of goods are sold in this way.	Large supermarket chains.	Distribution of goods in overseas markets.
Advantages for producers	By cutting out intermediaries, the product can be sold at a lower price. Producers benefit from feedback about the product from customers and are able to respond to their changing needs quickly. A direct relationship may lead to increased customer loyalty.	Producers are able to achieve a wide distribution. Selling through specialist or high-end retail outlets could help to improve the image of the brand. Retailers can help to promote and merchandise a producer's products. Retailers may allow consumers to purchase items on credit.	Increases the number of smaller retailers able to stock the product. Reduces the cost of distributing the products to retailers for the producer. Wholesalers are sometimes able to store large quantities of the product, which reduces storage costs for the producer.	Agents have knowledge of the distribution network in their country and know how to get the product to the consumer as quickly and efficiently as possible. Agents understand the language, culture and tastes of the local market. They also understand the laws and regulations involved in selling goods in their country.
Disadvantages for producers	Many consumers will not be able or willing to travel to the producer to purchase products. It may be impractical or expensive to send items ordered over the internet by post.	Retailers also sell competing brands. Retailers add a mark-up, which makes products more expensive.	As each intermediary adds a mark-up, the price charged to consumers increases. This method increases the time for goods to reach the customer, which may result in more wastage, especially in the case of perishable items.	The producer may have little or no control over where the product is sold, which may affect brand image. Due to transport costs and the mark-ups taken by the agent and other intermediaries, the price charged to the consumer may be high and uncompetitive.

3.3.4 Promotion

Aims (3.3.4)

Knowledge

By the end of this section, students will understand:

- the aims of promotion
- the different forms of promotion and how they influence sales, for example, advertising, sales promotion
- the need for cost effectiveness in spending the marketing budget on promotion.

Resources

- Student's Book pages 205–213
- Activity sheet 3.3.4
- A range of promotional materials: an advertisement from a newspaper or magazine, a brochure or leaflet, a photo of a billboard taken on a mobile phone, a TV commercial on YouTube, a free sample, and so on.

Key business terms

advertising media; customer service; direct mailing; informative advertising; marketing budget; merchandising; personal selling; persuasive advertising; promotional strategies; public relations; relationship marketing; sponsorship; target market; viral marketing

Lesson ideas

You should aim to cover the materials in 3.3.4 in two one-hour lessons, plus, as appropriate, homework assignments. To achieve the Aims for this topic, we recommend doing some of the following activities over the course of the lessons.

Starter suggestion

Snowball: Ask students to individually list all the types of promotion they can think of. Make sure they focus on promotion generally and not just advertising.

Ask them to move around the room, swapping ideas with classmates and trying to develop as large a list as possible.

Use students' responses to introduce promotion and to reinforce the fact that promotion is not just advertising.

Main lesson activities

Discussion and note-taking (whole class): Talk students through the aims of promotion, the various methods and the importance of the marketing budget. Tell them to take notes. Make sure you focus on the need for cost-effectiveness in spending the marketing budget.

Taboo: Students should work in pairs to discuss as many aims of promotion as they can think of. Add challenge (and fun) to the activity by telling them they are not allowed to say 'improve sales' (or similar).

Student activity: Introduce the various methods of promotion and ask students to complete Activity 3.3.4. They should bring examples of various promotional campaigns to the lesson. They will then analyse this promotional material in terms of topic theory (refer to pages 205–213 of the Student's Book).

Skills activity: If Activity 3.3.4 is not practical, ask students to work in small groups to complete the Skills activity on page 211 of the Student's Book. They will need to analyse appropriate promotion methods for a product of their choice.

Tip: This exercise could be given as homework.

Budget allocation: Put the students into small groups and ask them to complete the following budget allocation exercise:

Project: Marketing campaign for local school (to attract new students)					
Budget: $100 000					
Promotion options					
TV campaign	$1 000 000	Internet advertising	$20 000	Billboard campaign	$100 000
Radio campaign	$500 000	Direct mailing	$10 000	PR event	$5000
Magazine advert	$50 000	Sponsorship of local hockey team	$25 000	Cinema campaign	$500 000

Encourage students to consider the effectiveness of each method given the context. A PR event supported by a direct mailing campaign may, for example, be both the cheapest option and the most effective.

Exam-style question: Ask students to think about the following evaluation question and discuss in pairs:

'Marketing can never be truly cost-effective.' To what extent do you agree with this statement?

Student responses are likely to be broad; teacher support and guidance will be vital. Encourage the development of exam-related skills by getting students to focus on the need to evaluate. Ask them to develop arguments in support of the statement and arguments against.

Plenary suggestion

Knowledge check: Split the class into four groups. Ask each group to consider one product from Question 7 of the Knowledge check questions (page 213 of the Student's Book). Each group should present their suggestions and justification to the whole class.

Answers to Student's Book activities

Skills activity (page 211): possible outcomes

The following table summarises some of the key advantages and disadvantages of the different promotion methods. You could photocopy the table and give it to students to support their notes once they have completed this exercise.

Promotional media – advantages and disadvantages		
Media type	**Advantages**	**Disadvantages**
Television	• Reaches a wide audience • Product demonstration possible • Colour, movement, sound and special effects possible • High impact ads possible • Can be targeted regionally • High repetition value • Good consumer recall rates • Cost-effective	• Expensive production and air-time (though low cost per 1000) • Difficult to win new customers – consumers may ignore ads • Message must be brief and simple • Difficult for consumers to retain important information • Long lead times
Radio	• Wide coverage • Regional and specific interest group targeting possible • Short lead times • Use of sound • Relatively cheap	• No movement or colour • Commercial stations often disliked due to advertisements • Ads may be ignored • Difficult for consumers to retain important information

Promotional media – advantages and disadvantages

Media type	Advantages	Disadvantages
National newspapers	<ul><li>National coverage</li><li>Colour possible</li><li>Consumer can retain a copy of the advert</li><li>Ads can be detailed</li><li>Relatively cheap</li></ul>	<ul><li>'Noisy medium' – lots of other advertisements competing for attention</li><li>No movement or sound</li><li>Younger audience not reached</li></ul>
Regional newspapers	<ul><li>Very cheap</li><li>Closely targeted/can be adapted to suit specific region</li></ul>	<ul><li>Limited circulation</li><li>Occasionally poor quality</li><li>Limited readership data</li></ul>
Magazines	<ul><li>Colour possible</li><li>Targeting possible</li><li>Information can be retained</li><li>Often read by more than one person</li><li>Message has a long life (i.e. one month)</li><li>Advertisements can be linked to or designed as features</li></ul>	<ul><li>No movement or sound</li><li>Very 'noisy' medium</li><li>Long lead times (advertisements have to be booked and designed months before publication)</li><li>Specific placement is expensive (i.e. opposite a related article)</li></ul>
Cinema	<ul><li>Young audience</li><li>Colour, movement, sound and special effects possible</li><li>Captive audience – ads often watched</li><li>High impact</li><li>Targeting possible</li><li>Relatively cheap (if combined with TV)</li></ul>	<ul><li>Limited coverage</li><li>Some segments not reached</li><li>Difficult for consumers to retain important information</li><li>Expensive to produce advertisements just for cinema</li><li>No repetition of message</li></ul>
Outdoor	<ul><li>National coverage</li><li>Colour possible</li><li>Can be regionally targeted</li><li>Can be innovative (for example, London taxi designs)</li><li>Relatively cheap</li></ul>	<ul><li>Message must be short</li><li>Difficult for consumers to retain important information</li><li>'Noisy' medium</li><li>Often ignored</li></ul>
Internet	<ul><li>Very close targeting possible – can be linked to direct marketing</li><li>Cheap and easy to produce/maintain</li><li>Colour and movement possible</li></ul>	<ul><li>Very low 'hit' rate</li><li>Advertisements can be filtered out</li><li>'Pop-up' ads considered a nuisance</li></ul>
Trade journals	<ul><li>Very close targeting possible</li><li>Relatively cheap</li><li>Colour possible</li><li>Journal may convey 'authority'</li></ul>	<ul><li>Critical, knowledgeable readership</li><li>Advertising alongside competition</li><li>Trade only</li><li>Sometimes low production values</li></ul>

Knowledge check (page 213)

1. **Identify** the aims of promotion.

   To increase demand for products; to establish a price for products; to create, enhance or maintain a brand image; to raise awareness, emotion or concern for an issue or product; to maintain, protect or increase market share.

2. **Identify** three methods of promotion.

   Any three from: TV, radio, magazines, internet, new media, newspaper, billboards (and other outdoor methods), cinema, viral marketing.

3. **Explain**, using an example, one of the benefits offered by TV advertising.

   Any one from: easy to reach mass market; can show product in action; easy to build brand image; can be targeted to particular viewers (depending on programming slot).

4. **Explain** the role of public relations.

   Press releases and press conferences, and so on, designed to ensure constant communication with a firm's stakeholders.

5. **Explain** why promotion might be important early in a product's life cycle.

   To develop brand awareness; to inform customers about the product/its usage.

6. **Explain** why new media advertising might be important to a firm targeting teenagers.

   Teenagers engage frequently with new media and less frequently with other forms; new media can help viral marketing and thus appeal to teenagers; a product may benefit from modern status if promoted using new media.

7. **Justify** appropriate methods of promotion for the following:

   a) a new brand of shampoo: TV, radio, magazines

   b) a new smartphone aimed at teenagers: internet/new media (Facebook, Twitter, SMS promotion)

   c) holidays for the over 60s: magazine, newspaper, direct mail, radio

   d) the latest James Bond movie: TV, internet, magazines

8. Define the term marketing budget.

   The marketing budget outlines how much money is allocated to the marketing function and on what types of marketing it will be spent.

   Student demonstrates basic/good understanding of marketing budget.

9. **Explain** two factors that determine how much a firm allocates to its marketing budget.

   Any two from: the firm's marketing objectives; how much competitors spend; the nature of the market (how disbursed, and so on); how much money the firm has; the cost of different promotion methods; where a product is in its life cycle.

3.3.4 Promotion: Activity

Activity type
Investigation

Content
Advertisements and advertising media

Time
50 minutes

Key terms
advertising media; customer service; direct mailing; informative advertising; marketing budget; merchandising; personal selling; persuasive advertising; promotional strategies; public relations; relationship marketing; sponsorship; target market; viral marketing

Aims
To understand the aims of promotion and the different forms of promotion and how they influence sales, for example, advertising, sales promotion (3.3.4)

Skills practised

AO1: Knowledge and understanding	✓
AO2: Application	✓
AO3: Analysis	✓
AO4: Evaluation	✓

Preparation
Make one copy of Activity sheet 3.3.4 for each student in the class. Before the lesson, ask students to bring two or three examples of different promotional materials to the lesson. These could include an advertisement from a newspaper or magazine, a brochure or leaflet, a photo of a billboard taken on their mobile phone, a TV commercial on YouTube, a free sample, and so on. It is also a good idea for you to gather a range of promotional materials yourself to give to any students who do not bring any examples.

Procedure

1. Tell students they are going to analyse a range of different promotional methods and discuss the advantages and disadvantages of each.
2. Before starting the activity, ask students to review the advantages and disadvantages outlined on pages 207–211 of the Student's Book.
3. Divide the class into groups of three or four and give each student a copy of Activity sheet 3.3.4.
4. Ask students to select four different forms of promotion from the examples they have brought to class. They should discuss each method of promotion in their groups and complete the activity sheet by answering the questions and making brief notes.
5. Give students 25 minutes to complete this task. Move around the room, making sure students are on task and correctly identifying and elaborating on the main advantages and disadvantages.
6. To round off the activity, ask each group to present to the class one of the promotional methods they discussed in their group. They should speak for one minute, summarising their responses to the questions on the activity sheet.

Teacher tip: Allow students to use their mobile phones or computers to view commercials on YouTube or photos they have taken of promotional methods and advertising media in preparation for this lesson.

Variation: Organise the activity as a jigsaw discussion activity.

- After they have discussed at least two promotional methods in their initial group, pair students up with a student from another group.
- Students discuss the promotional methods they analysed previously with their new partner.
- For variety, ask students to share one promotional method with one student before moving on to discuss another promotional method with another student.
- Give each student exactly one minute of speaking time (two minutes in total), before asking them to change partners.

Extension: Students could prepare a more detailed presentation in their group (using PowerPoint if possible) evaluating one of the promotional methods they examined. They could prepare this for homework and deliver it in the next lesson.

3.3.5 Technology and the marketing mix

Aims (3.3.5)

Knowledge

By the end of this section, students will understand:

- how to define and explain the concept of e-commerce
- the opportunities and threats of e-commerce to business and consumers
- the use of the internet and social networks for promotion.

Resources

- Student's Book pages 214–220
- Activity sheet 3.3.5
- Good-quality card

Key business terms

blog; business to business (B2B); business to consumer (B2C); consumer to consumer (C2C); e-commerce; email; internet; newsletter; social media; social networks

Lesson ideas

You should aim to cover the materials in 3.3.5 in a single one-hour lesson, plus, as appropriate, a homework assignment. To achieve the Aims for this topic, we recommend doing some of the following activities over the course of the one-hour lesson.

Pre-lesson task: As students will be familiar with the content of this topic, consider setting Skills activity 1 on page 217 of the Student's Book as a pre-lesson task. Students will review their favourite e-commerce websites and could then feed back their findings after the lesson starter.

Starter suggestion

Internet shopping: Ask students to make a list of all the times when they (or their parents) use the internet for commercial purposes (for example, buying cinema tickets). Use their lists to define and explain the scope of e-commerce.

Main lesson activities

Discussion and note-taking (whole class): Talk students through the concept of e-commerce, the opportunities and threats it poses to businesses and consumers, and the use of the internet/social networks for promotion. Ask them to take notes as appropriate.

Student activity: Students should complete Activity 3.3.5 to help them evaluate the opportunities and threats to business and consumers of e-commerce.

Log on: If appropriate, ask students to log on to their Facebook, Twitter, Instagram and/or Pinterest account(s). They should review the sites as tools for promotion.

- What types of promotion(s) are found on the different sites?
- How effective do students find promotions on the different sites?
- Why do firms choose to use these social sites?
- What are the advantages of social marketing?

Use students' answers as the basis for a class discussion on social marketing.

Skills activity: As an alternative to the Log on activity (or perhaps as a homework extension), students could complete Skills activity 2 on page 220 of the Student's Book. They should design their own e-commerce promotional campaign.

Plenary suggestion

Knowledge check: Ask students to answer the Knowledge check questions on page 220 of the Student's Book.

Tip: *This task could be given as a homework activity.*

Answers to Student's Book activities

Skills activities: possible outcomes

Skills activity 1 (page 217)

A wide range of responses is possible here. Encourage students to use topic-specific vocabulary.

Skills activity 2 (page 220)

A wide range of responses is possible here. Students should focus their suggestions on aspects that relate to elements of the Business Studies specification. Encourage them to use topic-specific vocabulary.

Knowledge check (page 220)

1. Define the term e-commerce.

   The buying and selling of goods over the internet or via similar electronic means.

2. **Explain** two benefits to a business of e-commerce.

   Any two from: direct access to customers; lower costs; reduction in the number of intermediaries lowering prices at point of sale; customers get better information faster, and are therefore more likely to purchase; use of modern media helps to target younger consumers; can include images, sounds and movies as part of marketing activities; allows cheap access to a global customer base.

3. **Explain** two potential threats to a customer from e-commerce.

   Any two from: closure of local (physical) branches of firm; danger of internet fraud; difficulty of returning faulty or damaged goods; online identify theft.

4. **Identify** two important features of a successful website for a business.

   Any two from: up-to-date; relevant; easy to navigate; easy to place orders; includes company contact details; error free.

3.3.5 Technology and the marketing mix: Activity

Activity type
Evaluation activity

Time
20 minutes (or at teacher's discretion)

Content
Opportunities and threats of e-commerce to business and consumers

Key terms
blog; business to business (B2B); business to consumer (B2C); consumer to consumer (C2C); e-commerce; email; internet; newsletter; social media; social networks

Aims
To evaluate the opportunities and threats of e-commerce to business and consumers (3.3.5)

Skills practised

AO1: Knowledge and understanding	
AO2: Application	
AO3: Analysis	
AO4: Evaluation	✓

Preparation
Create enough copies of Activity sheet 3.3.5 to give one set of cards to groups of three within the class. It is preferable to photocopy the sheet onto good-quality card. Cut up the cards before the lesson. Also make one intact (not cut up) copy of Activity sheet 3.3.5 for each group of three students.

Procedure

1. Split the class into groups of three.
2. Explain that two students in each group will carry out the activity, while one will act as 'judge'.
3. Give a pack of cards to each group. Ask students to shuffle the cards before starting the activity.

Note: The pack does not need to include the Opportunity, Threat and Neutral headings.

4. Give a complete copy of Activity sheet 3.3.5 to the judge in each group. The judge should not show this sheet to the other two students in the group.
5. With the cards face down on the table, the two 'players' take turns to draw a card from the pack.
6. On their turn, the student should read the situation aloud and then make a judgement as to whether e-commerce presents an opportunity, a threat or is neutral in that context.
7. If their evaluation corresponds with the answer on Activity sheet 3.3.5, they keep the card. If not, the other player can try to 'steal' the card by offering another answer. If correct, they win the card.
8. The winner is the student holding the most cards at the end of the game.

Teacher tip: The key to this game is to encourage students to evaluate and justify their answer. Simply stating 'opportunity', 'threat' or 'neutral' is not enough. Encourage students to debate the validity of the suggested answers on the activity sheet.

You might find it useful to talk the class through an example before starting the activity.

Variation: If you feel this activity will be challenging for the students, consider running it as a teacher-led whole-group task.

Extension: If you feel the students are capable, you can set a task before starting the activity.

- Ask students to write on the blank cards examples of situations where e-commerce presents an opportunity, a threat or is neutral.
- Distribute these cards among the groups so that students can use them alongside the ready-made cards.

3.4 Marketing strategy

3.4.1 APPROPRIATE MARKETING STRATEGIES

Aims (3.4.1)

Knowledge
By the end of this section, students will understand:
• the importance of different elements of the marketing mix in influencing consumer decisions in given circumstances
• how to recommend and justify an appropriate marketing strategy in given circumstances.

Resources
• Student's Book pages 221–224
• Activity sheet 3.4.1
• Presentation software (optional)

Key business terms
cost leadership; differentiation; market challenger; marketing mix; marketing strategy; mass marketing; niche marketing; place; price; product; promotion

Lesson ideas

You should aim to cover the materials in 3.4.1 in a single one-hour lesson, plus, as appropriate, a homework assignment. To achieve the Aims for this topic, we recommend doing some of the following activities over the course of the lesson.

Some of the lesson time should be devoted to preparing for Activity 3.4.1 or Skills activity 1.

Starter suggestion

Elevator revision: Organise students into pairs. Recap the marketing section by asking students to stand up and imagine they have the length of an elevator ride (two minutes) to tell a partner everything they can remember about the marketing topic so far. As the (imaginary) lift goes back down (another two minutes), the partner writes down the key points they heard (without help). Repeat the 'lift rides' until students have covered sufficient material.

Main lesson activities

Discussion and note-taking (whole class): Talk students through the various aspects of marketing strategies. They should take notes as appropriate. Focus on recommending appropriate marketing strategies in given circumstances.

Activity: Ask students to complete Activity 3.3.1. They should identify the marketing strategy of a product they know well – this will help them understand the importance of the different elements of the marketing mix in influencing consumer decisions.

Skills activity: Using the details in the Skills activity on page 223 of the Student's Book, ask students to compare and contrast the marketing strategies of two different products/firms.

Knowledge check: Ask students to answer the Knowledge check questions on page 224 of the Student's Book. You may wish to focus on Question 3 in particular.

Plenary suggestion

Group exercise: As a summary of this topic, ask students to investigate and evaluate the marketing mix of Red Bull. Give them the following questions to consider:

- Does the marketing strategy for Red Bull focus on one element of the marketing mix or does it use a blend of all elements?

- How successful do you think Red Bull marketing is?
- Recommend and justify one change Red Bull might make to its marketing strategy.

A wide range of responses and approaches to this task is possible. Make sure students do not just describe the marketing activities for Red Bull; reward critical analysis and evaluation of the suitability of the marketing.

Ask students to consider why Red Bull has such a strong presence in Formula 1 motorsport. How does this link to the marketing strategy for Red Bull?

Tip: A useful way to start this exercise is to show students some examples of Red Bull marketing. These are readily available on the internet or in any extreme sports magazine.

Answers to Student's Book activities

Skills activity (page 223): possible outcomes

A wide range of responses and approaches to this task is possible. Make sure students do not just describe the marketing activities for their chosen products. Reward students' critical comparison and evaluation of the success and appropriateness of the marketing strategies.

Knowledge check (page 224)

1 **Identify** two examples of marketing objectives.

   Any two from: increase market share; increase product awareness/brand recognition; increase product usage; expand into new market segments; develop new products.

2 **Outline**, using appropriate examples, two factors that might affect choice of marketing strategy.

   Any two from: corporate objectives; stage of product life cycle; competition; type of product; type/state of market; availability of finance.

3 **Justify** the element or elements of the marketing mix that might be most appropriate for:

   a) a new magazine aimed at teenagers: price, promotion

   b) a laptop aimed at graphic designers: product

   c) a plain chocolate bar: promotion, place

   d) a new book in a popular series: place, promotion.

3.4.1 Appropriate marketing strategies: Activity

Activity type

Investigation

Content

Marketing strategy

Time

45 minutes

Key terms

cost leadership; differentiation; market challenger; marketing mix; marketing strategy; mass marketing; niche marketing; place; price; product; promotion

Skills practised

AO1: Knowledge and understanding	
AO2: Application	✓
AO3: Analysis	✓
AO4: Evaluation	

Preparation

Make one copy of Activity sheet 3.4.1 for each student in the class.

Aims

To identify the marketing strategy of a firm and understand the importance of the different elements of the marketing mix in influencing consumer decisions (3.4.1)

Procedure

1. Students are going to work in small groups to analyse the marketing strategy of a product of their choice, but first they look at an example as a whole class.

2. Using some of the questions below, ask students to give you details about the different elements of the marketing mix used by Kit Kat. Write them on the board.

   Product:
   - What differentiates Kit Kat from its competitors' products?
   - What is its USP?
   - How is Kit Kat packaged and sold?
   - How have Kit Kat products changed over time?
   - Where is Kit Kat in its product life cycle?

   Price:
   - Which products are Kit Kat's main competitors?
   - How much does Kit Kat cost?
   - How does this compare to the prices of competitors?
   - What pricing strategies does Kit Kat use?

   Place:
   - Where are Kit Kats sold?
   - What distribution channels are used to get Kit Kat to the customer?

   Promotion:
   - What methods does Kit Kat use to promote its products?
   - How effective are they?

3. Ask students which they think is the most important element of Kit Kat's marketing mix and why. Then give them each a copy of Activity sheet 3.4.1. They should read the information about Kit Kat's marketing strategy and compare the main points with those that they identified in their discussion (which are displayed on the whiteboard).

4. Working in groups of three, students create a poster outlining the marketing mix of a product of their choice. Later they will present this to the class. They will need to use their own knowledge of the product, combined with information they find online. Explain that the posters may be used for a classroom display, so the information must be well organised and well presented. Some products students might like to research are:
   - flights by Air Asia
   - a particular model of car
   - a service provided by HSBC
   - a stay at an IBIS hotel
   - an Apple iPhone.

5. Put students into groups of three and allow them enough time to decide on a product and to prepare an outline for their poster. Encourage students to use their tablets and laptop to find information to include in their presentation.

6. If they run out of time in class, ask students to complete their poster for homework. Tell them that each group will have three to four minutes to present their analysis to the class in the next lesson. They will be assessed on the following criteria:
   - detail of analysis
   - visual appeal of the poster
   - clarity of explanations
   - teamwork.

Teacher tips:
You could choose another example if students are not familiar with Kit Kat.

Presenting information to the class can be challenging for EAL and non-EAL learners alike. To help their confidence, it is a good idea to give students an opportunity to practise their presentations in their groups before asking them to speak in front of the class.

Variation: Instead of producing a poster, you could ask groups to prepare a PowerPoint presentation. The advantage of posters, however, is that they can be used to create a wall display of students' work after they have completed the activity.

3.4.2 Legal controls related to marketing

Aims (3.4.2)

Knowledge

By the end of this section, students will understand:

- the impact of legal controls on marketing strategy, for example, misleading promotion, faulty and dangerous goods.

Resources

- Student's Book pages 225–226
- Activity sheet 3.4.2

Key business terms

fit for purpose; marketing strategy; misleading; quality

Lesson ideas

You should aim to cover the materials in 3.4.2 in a single one-hour lesson, plus, as appropriate, a homework assignment. To achieve the Aims for this topic, we recommend doing some of the following activities over the course of the lesson.

Starter suggestion

Start the lesson by asking students to come up with the most outrageous marketing promises they can think of. You may need to give an example to start them off. For example: 'I used a new moisturiser last night, the marketing said it would make me the most attractive person on the planet!'

Discuss why laws exist in most countries to protect against false promotion and dangerous/faulty goods.

Main lesson activities

Discussion and note-taking (whole class): Talk students through the nature and impact of legal controls on marketing activities, telling them to take notes as appropriate. Focus on the impact on marketing strategy.

Group task: Split the class into small groups and assign one legal control on marketing activities (misleading promotion, faulty goods, and so on) to each group. Ask each group to:

- define the relevant legal control
- describe a related case study
- discuss the implications for a firm's marketing strategy of that control.

They should present their findings to the rest of the class.

Student activity: Ask students to complete Activity 3.4.2, either individually or in small groups. They will evaluate a variety of marketing strategies and discuss what legal controls might be relevant in each case.

Skills activity: Ask students to work individually or in small groups to identify which legal controls might be most relevant for the products listed in the Skills activity on page 226 of the Student's Book. They should feed back their findings via teacher-led questions and answers.

Tip: Alternatively, you could give this activity as homework, with students feeding back at the start of the next lesson.

Plenary suggestion

Rephrase it: Referring back to the starter activity, ask students to rephrase their outrageous marketing promise into something that is both legally and ethically acceptable. Encourage other students to challenge on the basis of points of law where relevant.

Answers to Student's Book activities

Skills activity (page 226): possible outcomes

- A car: laws relating to safety, product description, faulty goods.
- A fizzy drink: laws relating to food safety, product description.
- A computer game: laws relating to faulty goods.

Knowledge check (page 226)

1 **Identify** two ways in which a business might mislead customers in its marketing campaign.

Any two from: misleading prices; misleading features; misleading benefit claim(s); misleading/unclear terms and conditions.

2 **Explain** why there are laws to protect consumers when buying a product.

Accept any from: to prevent firms from making false or misleading claims about products; to protect consumers from harm caused by products; to prevent firms selling products that are illegal; to prevent exposure to inappropriate material (particularly for products aimed at young people); to protect consumers from unfair sales/pricing tactics.

Students should demonstrate basic/good understanding of legal controls on marketing activities and suitable explanation with supporting reference to appropriate laws/legal controls (and the implications of no legal control).

3 **Explain** two possible impacts of a business selling faulty or dangerous goods.

Customer complaints; threat of legal action if faulty product causes harm; damage to reputation; cost of refunds.

3.4.2 Legal controls related to marketing: Activity

Activity type

Evaluation activity

Content

The nature and impact of legal controls on marketing

Time

20 minutes (or at teacher's discretion)

Key terms

fit for purpose; marketing strategy; misleading; quality

Aims

To evaluate the types and impact of legal controls on marketing strategy

Skills practised

AO1: Knowledge and understanding	✓
AO2: Application	
AO3: Analysis	
AO4: Evaluation	✓

Preparation

Make enough copies of Activity sheet 3.4.2 for each student or group.

Procedure

1 Students could do this activity individually or in small groups.
2 Tell students that they are going to undertake the work of the legal body responsible for consumer protection. Their task is to discuss a variety of situations in which consumers have made complaints and to decide what, if any, action should be taken.
3 As part of their role, they are also required to advise the business on possible changes to (or restrictions on) its marketing strategy for the future.
4 Students should write their responses in the boxes provided under each case study.

Teacher tip: This exercise could be given as an individual homework. The starter activity for the following lesson would then be small group discussions where students could compare their responses.

Extension: Ask students to research (using the internet or other sources of information) other examples of legal cases related to marketing activities. Searches for 'advertising standards' or 'consumer protection' are useful starting points.

3.4.3 Entering foreign markets

Aims (3.4.3)

Knowledge

By the end of this section, students will understand:

- the growth potential of new markets in other countries
- the problems of entering foreign markets, for example, cultural differences and lack of knowledge
- the benefits and limitations of methods to overcome such problems, for example, joint ventures, licensing.

Resources

- Student's Book pages 227–232
- Activity sheet 3.4.3
- Good-quality card; dice

Key business terms

culture; economic growth; gross domestic product (GDP); language; laws/regulation; market research

Lesson ideas

You should aim to cover the materials in 3.4.3 in a single one-hour lesson, plus, as appropriate, a homework assignment. To achieve the Aims for this topic, we recommend doing some of the following activities over the course of the one-hour lesson.

Skills activity: Students should work individually or in small groups to complete the research exercise described in Skills activity 1 on page 228 of the Student's Book. They will investigate a business that has expanded into new markets. This makes a useful pre-lesson homework.

Starter suggestions

List race: Split the class into groups of about six students. Split these groups into two, with three students in each. Ask one half of each group to think of as many opportunities of entering new markets as they can and the other half to think of as many problems as they can. The winning group is the one with the longest (and most accurate) list.

Tip: This exercise works best if you give students a tight timescale.

Main lesson activities

Discussion and note-taking (whole class): Talk students through the opportunities and problems of entering new markets abroad, telling them to take notes as appropriate. Focus on the methods for overcoming the problems of entering new markets, as well as the limitations and benefits of these methods.

Second guess: After a basic introduction to the opportunities and problems and an overview of methods to overcome these problems, put students into the same groups as for the starter activity.

- Ask one half of each group to think of as many problems of entering foreign markets as they can.
- Tell the other half they must anticipate these problems and think of solutions to each problem.
- They must be prepared to debate why their proposed solutions are appropriate.
- Give the two halves time to prepare their problems and solutions.

Bring the exercise to a close with a class discussion of the problems, and of the benefits and limitations of the solutions.

Skills activity: Ask students to work in pairs to complete Skills activity 2 on page 232 of the Student's Book. They will consider the benefits of a joint venture as one possible way of entering a new market. Students will report their findings in a short presentation.

Plenary suggestion

Student activity: Activity 3.4.3, a snakes and ladders game that reinforces key topic knowledge, is designed as a fun plenary to this lesson.

Answers to Student's Book activities

Skills activities: possible outcomes

Skills activity 1 (page 228)

A wide range of responses is possible here. You may need to provide students with examples of businesses and, if possible, access to research material (newspaper or internet articles, financial accounts, and so on) for these firms.

Skills activity 2 (page 232)

Benefits: access to foreign market at only 40 per cent of cost; support and expertise of the larger firm.

Drawbacks: retain only 30 per cent of the profit; larger firm may control activities (decision-making power).

The large firm may have approached the smaller firm to access a particular expertise (product or market knowledge).

Knowledge check (page 232)

1 **Define** the term cultural difference.

   Cultural difference can mean: a difference in attitude, values, beliefs, norms, routines and expectations between individuals and groups of differing nationalities (or geographic locations).

2 **Identify** two potential reasons why a business would want to expand into a new market.

   Any two from: spread the risk of operating in one market; increase sales/profits; benefit from lower labour costs; prestige; increased customer base; opportunity to create culture-specific products.

3 **Explain** two reasons why a business might not succeed when moving into a new market.

   Any two from: cultural differences; language barriers/differences; legal barriers; lack of knowledge/expertise; competition; unfavourable economic conditions in new market.

4 **Explain** one way in which a business may overcome problems when entering a new market.

   Any one from: joint venture; use of agent; develop local expertise.

5 **Explain** one potential benefit and one potential limitation of a joint venture for a business.

   Benefits: spreads risk across more than one firm; shared expertise; lower investment requirement.

   Limitations: shared profit; potential for disagreement.

   Students need to demonstrate knowledge of the benefits and limitations of a joint venture, with suitable examples and appropriate explanation.

3.4.3 Entering foreign markets: Activity

Activity type

Snakes and ladders game

Time

20 minutes (or at teacher's discretion)

Content

Opportunities and problems of entering new markets abroad

Key terms

culture; economic growth; gross domestic product (GDP); language; laws/regulation; market research

Skills practised

AO1: Knowledge and understanding	✓
AO2: Application	
AO3: Analysis	
AO4: Evaluation	

Preparation

Make enough copies of Activity sheet 3.4.3 for each pair or group of 3–4 students. Ideally, photocopy the sheet onto good-quality card. You will also need a dice for each pair/group.

Aims

To understand the opportunities and problems of entering new markets abroad (3.4.3)

Procedure

1. Split the class into pairs or small groups. Tell them they are going to play a game that will help them learn the opportunities and problems of entering new markets abroad.
2. Ask them to choose a small playing piece from their pencil case (an eraser, a pen lid, and so on). Each student should have a different playing piece.
3. Give each group a dice.
4. Students should take turns to roll the dice and move their piece on the board.
5. If they land on a ladder (an opportunity), they move their piece up the ladder to the appropriate square. If they land on a snake (a problem of entering markets abroad), they move the piece down to the square where the snake's head is pointing. They **do not** get a follow-on go if they land on a snake or a ladder.
6. The winner is the student who reaches the finish square first.

Teacher tips: The game can last an indefinite amount of time, so it is a good idea to use this activity as a plenary up to the end of a lesson.

To reinforce learning, you could ask students to explain to the group WHY a snake or ladder is a problem or benefit BEFORE allowing them to move their piece.

Extension: Before students start playing, ask them to write additional opportunities and threats in the blank squares and to add snakes and/or ladders as appropriate.

3 Marketing: Key terms revision

Define each term and give an example or explanation. There are 2 marks per definition.

Term	Description/Definition
brand loyalty	
differentiation	
e-commerce	
first mover advantage	
market segment	
marketing mix	
niche marketing	
penetration pricing	
price inelastic	
primary data	
product life cycle	
relationship marketing	
unique selling point (USP)	

4 Operations management

Introduction

The best way to teach Operations Management is to get students to see the topic in action.
If possible, arrange a trip to a local factory. This is an excellent way to introduce the various concepts and to provide real and relevant examples to refer to back in the classroom. If time and location allow, visiting two different factories would give students the chance to compare methods and issues. If a factory visit is not possible, the internet offers access to video clips of the various production methods and quality systems in action.

The activities in this section aim to make the focus on the topics as practical as possible. Several of the suggested tasks involve hands-on activities that require students to role play production processes – this can be a fun and engaging way to enhance learning. Other activities include:

- a dominoes activity on the **meaning of production**
- the **methods of production** examined through small group discussion
- a gap-reading activity on **how technology has changed production methods**
- a practical group activity to examine **classification of costs**
- pair-work discussion of **economies and diseconomies of scale**
- an investigation of **break-even analysis** through a pair-work sharing activity
- a role-play activity examining methods of **achieving quality production**
- a ranking exercise on **factors influencing location and relocation**.

To introduce students to the concepts they will study and to help you assess students' knowledge, a useful starter activity might be:

Plan it, build it, break it

Ask students to imagine they are going to open a business that manufactures and sells pencil cases within the school. Instruct them to brainstorm in small groups:

- What they will need in order to produce the pencil cases?
- How they will produce them?
- How they will ensure that the pencil cases are good enough (i.e. of a high enough quality) to sell to fellow students?

You could ask more able students to estimate costs and to consider issues related to break-even.

Ask students to group their ideas together under headings such as:

- Costs
- Production method
- Efficiency
- Quality.

These responses could be presented as concept maps on A3 paper.

Use students' responses to give an overview of the various Operations Management topics.

At this stage of the course, students should be starting to become familiar with the skills of analysis and (for more able students) evaluation. Use the **Skills Builder** at the end of Section 4 in the Student's Book to remind students what is required to demonstrate these skills:

- recommending, for example, which production method is *most* suitable for a given firm
- justifying, with well explained reasons relevant to the case, *why* this method is most suitable.

4.1 Production of goods and services

4.1.1 THE MEANING OF PRODUCTION

Aims (4.1.1)

Knowledge

By the end of this section, students will understand:

- how to manage resources effectively to produce goods and services
- the difference between production and productivity
- the benefits of increasing efficiency and how to increase it, for example, increasing productivity by automation and technology, improved labour skills
- why businesses hold inventories
- the concept of lean production and how to achieve it.

Resources

- Student's Book pages 244–249
- Activity sheet 4.1.1
- A4 card
- Flashcards or mini-whiteboards with key terms from the topic (made by the teacher)

Key business terms

automation; division of labour; capital; capital intensive production; costs of production; efficiency; enterprise; factor inputs; inventory; kaizen; just-in-time (JIT); labour; labour intensive production; labour productivity; land; lean production; mass production; output; production; revenue; specialisation

Lesson ideas

You should aim to cover the materials in 4.1.1 in a single one-hour lesson, plus, as appropriate, a homework assignment. To achieve the Aims for this topic, we recommend doing some of the following activities over the course of the lesson.

Starter suggestion

Terminology talk: Write the words 'output' and 'efficiency' on the board. Ask students to discuss with a partner how these words might relate to their school work (class work, home learning, and so on). Ask them to record language they associate with these terms (speed, volume, and so on).

Use students' responses to introduce the terminology of this topic.

Main lesson activities

Discussion and note-taking (whole class): Talk students through efficiency, production and productivity, including methods to improve efficiency. Instruct them to take notes as relevant.

Skills activity: Ask students to carry out the investigation in the Skills activity on page 247 of the Student's Book. They will calculate employee productivity and write a short report on how it might be improved.

Discussion and note-taking (whole class): Talk students through stock-holding and lean production, including methods to implement lean production. Tell them to take notes as relevant.

Case study: Using the case study on page 249 of the Student's Book, ask students to:

- identify what makes Toyota's production system 'lean'
- state the advantages of the system.

Student activity: Ask students to complete Activity 4.1.1. This dominoes game will get them to review and understand key vocabulary for this topic.

Teacher tip: Students must be able to provide concise, accurate definitions for key business terms in the examinations. So it is a good idea to give students word lists for each section. Encourage them to keep a glossary of key terms, in a notebook or electronically, by writing the definitions for the key terms in the word list as they come across them in lessons. Doing this electronically gives them additional flexibility – they can return to the terms later on and add more information, such as examples, if they want to.

The lean school: Ask students to discuss the following questions in small groups: 'How might the school/institution adopt lean production methods?' 'What might be the advantages of this?'

Ask them to think of as many ways as they can.

Knowledge check: Ask students to answer the Knowledge check questions on page 249 of the Student's Book.

Tip: This could be given as a homework exercise.

Plenary suggestion

Write and wipe: Make and laminate flashcards (or, if possible, use mini-whiteboards) with one of the key terms from this topic written on each. Hand out a card/whiteboard to each student and ask them to use a wipeable pen to write a definition of the term they have been given. They should pass their definition to a classmate for checking, amendment and discussion.

Answers to Student's Book activities

Skills activity (page 247): possible outcomes

Current situation:

Cost per unit: $1

Productivity per employee: 15 bars per day

After training course:

Cost per unit: $0.50

Productivity per employee: 30 bars per day

After investment in technology (from original data):

Cost per unit: $0.58

Productivity per employee: 90 bars per day

Encourage students to refer to the data in their reports. If the ability profile of the class allows, draw out the simplification in the calculation of the investment in technology. (It assumes no purchasing economies of scale and no change to average wage.)

Knowledge check (page 249)

1 RM Sweets Ltd has the following production data available for two weeks' production of sweets.

	Week 1	Week 2
Number of employees	40	50
Output of sweets	30 000	35 000

   a) Calculate the productivity per employee for week 1 and week 2.

   Week 1: 750 sweets per employee

   Week 2: 700 sweets per emplpyee

   b) With reference to your answers in part (a), **explain** the difference between production and productivity.

   Production simply refers to the number of sweets produced (30 000 and 35 000); productivity refers to the efficiency with which they are produced (the measure of labour input to output).

   c) **Explain** two ways in which RM Sweets Ltd could improve their efficiency.

   Any two from: invest in automation/technology; improve employee motivation; improve employee skills (training); effective management (better coordination of resources); introduce lean production.

2 **Identify** and **explain** two benefits of RM Sweets Ltd making their production process more automated.

  Any two from: potentially faster; fewer quality issues; can produce for longer periods without a break; costs of use may be predominantly fixed rather than variable; reduce overall labour costs.

3 **Identify** two ways in which a business can manage resources to produce goods.

  Better stock holding (freeing up capital and capacity to increase production); lean production (increasing productive efficiency).

4 Define the following terms?

   a) Just-in-time

   Ordering or manufacturing only the exact amount of stock required by the customers; timing the order so stock arrives when it is needed and not before (reducing stock-holding costs).

   b) Kaizen

   Meaning (in Japanese) 'improvement' or 'change for the better': small changes to the production process on a continual basis.

4.1.1 The meaning of production: Activity

Activity type
Dominoes

Time
30 minutes

Content
Key vocabulary items in the production of goods and services.

Key terms
automation; division of labour; capital; capital intensive production; costs of production; efficiency; enterprise; factor inputs; inventory; kaizen; just-in-time (JIT); labour; labour intensive production; labour productivity; land; lean production; mass production; output; production; revenue; specialisation

Skills practised

AO1: Knowledge and understanding	✓
AO2: Application	
AO3: Analysis	
AO4: Evaluation	

Preparation
Photocopy Activity sheet 4.1.1 onto sheets of A4 card and cut up two sets of the 20 domino cards for each group of three or four students in the class.

Aims
To understand key business terms and concepts related to production, including the difference between production and productivity and the concept of lean production (4.1.1)

Procedure

1. Tell students they are going to revise the vocabulary from Topic 4.1.1 by playing a game of dominoes.

2. Check that students are clear about the differences between the following concepts:
   - production, productivity and efficiency
   - division of labour and specialisation
   - lean production, just-in-time (JIT) and kaizen.

3. Divide students into groups of three or four and give two sets of domino cards (from Activity sheet 4.1.1) to each group. Ask students to shuffle the cards and distribute five cards to each player. They should place the remaining cards face down in the centre of the table.

4. Demonstrate the activity using one of the groups. Tell students to place the cards in their hand face up on the table in front of them. (It doesn't matter if the other players in the group can see their cards.) Next, ask a member of the group to take the first card from the top of the pile and place it face up on the table.

5. Select a student to start. Explain that each card has a definition and a key business term.

   Students must find a card in their hand that links with the card(s) on the table. For example, if the card on the table reads 'The output of the business' and 'Productivity', the student could place either a card with the correct key term ('Production') to its left or the correct definition ('The output per employee') to its right.

   If they have neither card, they must draw a card from the pile and add it to their hand.

   Make sure students understand that they can only place cards at either end of the row of dominoes.

6. Explain that the winner is the first player to get rid of all of the cards in their hand.

7. Point out that a player may place consecutive cards from their hand in one turn if they are able to do so. Also, if a player takes a card from the pile that links with a card on the table, they are allowed to place that card immediately without waiting for their next turn.

8. Tell students that when placing a card, they should read the key word and matching definition aloud to the group. All students should then decide if the key word matches the definition. If they cannot agree, they can ask the teacher.

9. Allow students 15 minutes to play the game. Move around the room, making sure students are playing correctly.
10. Round off the activity by reading a few definitions to the class and nominating individual students to identify the key term.

Variation: Give one domino card to each member of the class. (If there are more than 20 students, allocate some cards to pairs of students.) Tell students that they must move around the room, stopping classmates at random and reading them their key word and definition. They must not show their card to anyone while they are doing this. If possible, ask students to memorise the word and definition on their card.

Once they find the student with the word or definition that matches their own, they must 'link' together by organising themselves in a line. At the end of the activity, ask each student to say their definition and key word aloud to the class in turn down the line to ensure that the key words and definitions are in matching order.

Extension: For homework, you could ask students to record the definitions of these words in the form of a personal glossary of key terms. Throughout Section 4.1, encourage students to add new words to their personal glossaries as they encounter them.

4.1.2 The main methods of production

Aims (4.1.2)

Knowledge

By the end of this section, students will understand:

- the features, benefits and limitations of job, batch and flow production
- how to recommend and justify an appropriate production method for a given situation.

Resources

- Student's Book pages 250–253
- Activity sheets 4.1.2A and 4.1.2B
- Examples of products made using job, batch and flow production

Key business terms

batch production; capital intensive production; flow production; job production; job satisfaction; labour intensive production; mass production; motivation; output; productivity; raw materials; standardised products; suppliers

Lesson ideas

You should aim to cover the materials in 4.1.2 in a single one-hour lesson, plus, as appropriate, a homework assignment. To achieve the Aims for this topic, we recommend doing some of the following activities over the course of the lesson.

Starter suggestion

The clothes on your back: Before the lesson, ask students (as a home learning task):

- to research job, batch and flow production
- to bring to the next class, either an example of a product produced using each method OR printed images of appropriate products.

Use their examples to lead into a discussion of the different methods.

Tip: It may be possible to cover all three methods using the clothing students wear to lessons. Job production could be covered by any tailoring done to make clothes fit.

Main lesson activities

Discussion and note-taking (whole class): Talk students through the different methods of production, telling them to take notes as relevant. Focus on recommending and justifying appropriate methods for given situations.

Case study: Using the case study on page 253 of the Student's Book, ask students to identify which method of production Lisa's crisps might have used for the new Tyrells crisps. Students should also consider why this method might have been the most appropriate.

Skills activity: Ask students to carry out the Skills activity on page 253 of the Student's Book. They will create a poster detailing the methods of production used for products familiar to them.

Student activity: Ask students to complete Activity 4.1.2. In this discussion activity they will identify the features, benefits and limitations of the three methods of production: job, batch and flow.

Plenary suggestion

Knowledge check: Ask students to answer the Knowledge Check questions on page 253 of the Student's Book.

Tip: Students could do this as a homework task.

Answers to Student's Book activities

Skills activity (page 253): possible outcomes

Encourage students to choose a wide variety of product choices across the class. Instruct students to focus on their explanation of the method of production and its appropriateness for each of their product choices.

Knowledge check (page 253)

1. **Explain** one advantage and one disadvantage to a business of using job production.

   Advantages: *Any one from:* product meets the exact requirements of the customer; the higher skill level required is more motivating for employees; premium pricing.

   Disadvantages: *Any one from:* high labour costs; long lead times for production; limited economies of scale.

2. **Identify** the main features of flow production.

   Identical products produced continuously in large quantities. Examples include televisions, cars, packed food.

3. **Explain** two advantages for ABP of using batch production.

   Any two from: the flexibility of batch production allows ABP to offer a range of different products in the same production time; ABP can adapt the product offering according to customer demand; this method offers employees a variety of tasks, which can help motivation; possible to gain some economies of scale.

4. **Outline** one limitation of using flow production.

   Any one from: flow production often requires expensive machinery and therefore high capital requirement; limited flexibility to change product type to meet customer needs; repetitive tasks for employees can lead to low motivation; machinery may break down.

4.1.2 The main methods of production: Activity

Activity type
Small group discussion

Time
25 minutes

Content
Methods of production (job, batch and flow production)

Key terms
batch production; capital intensive production; flow production; job production; job satisfaction; labour intensive production; mass production; motivation; output; productivity; raw materials; standardised products; suppliers

Objective
To understand the main features, benefits and limitations of the different methods of production (job, batch and flow) (4.1.2)

Skills practised

AO1: Knowledge and understanding	✓
AO2: Application	✓
AO3: Analysis	✓
AO4: Evaluation	✓

Preparation
Make one copy of Activity sheet 4.1.2A for each group of three to four students in the class. Photocopy and cut up one set of cards from Activity sheet 4.1.2B for each group.

Procedure

1. Tell students they are going to work in small groups to identify the features, benefits and limitations of the three methods of production: job, batch and flow production.

2. Divide the class into groups of three and give one set of the cards from Activity sheet 4.1.2B to each group. Ask each group to decide on a team name, then write the names on the board.

3. Explain that you will read a series of sentences aloud to the class. Students will have to decide in their groups which method of production each sentence is referring to. Once the group has agreed, they should hold up the relevant card: job, batch or flow.

   Emphasise that the objective of the activity is to get the right answer, not to answer as quickly as possible. Students should therefore take some time to discuss each sentence in their groups and justify their choices.

   Demonstrate the activity by reading the first sentence on Activity sheet 4.1.2A to the class. Read the sentence twice at natural speed, stressing the key words. (*Do not give students a copy of the completed Activity sheet 4.1.2A to refer to.*)

4. Allow students enough time to agree on a method of production before asking them to hold up their choice of card. If there is disagreement between groups, ask them to justify their decisions. Award one point to each group with the correct response by recording it on the board under the team's name.

5. Continue by reading each sentence in turn to the class, allowing groups sufficient time to formulate their responses.

   For a bonus point, you can select groups to provide justification for their responses. They should justify their choice of production method and say why they think it is an advantage or a disadvantage for the business.

Note: *Although suggested justifications are given on Activity sheet 4.1.2A, students may provide alternative justifications that are also acceptable.*

6. Finish the activity after about 25 minutes or when students seem to have had enough. Add up the points on the board and announce the winning group to the class.

Teacher tips: *Depending on the students' level of English, you may want to display the sentences using a PowerPoint slideshow presentation as well as reading them out to the class.*

It is important to keep the activity moving at a fairly brisk pace in order to maintain students' interest and attention. Try not to allow lengthy discussions on any particular sentence unless absolutely necessary.

Variation: Remove the 'Method of production' and 'Suggested explanation/justification' columns from Activity sheet 4.1.2A. Divide the class into groups of three or four and give each group the list of sentences from the activity sheet. Allow students 10–15 minutes to discuss each of the 25 sentences in their group. Ask students to write 'J' for job production, 'B' for batch production or 'F' for flow production next to each sentence.

Once groups have completed the activity, check the answers with the class, calling on groups to justify their choices of production method.

Extension: Allocate each student a method of production: job, batch or flow. For homework, students should search online to find a company that uses the method of production they have been allocated in its production process (YouTube is a good place to start).

They should research the company and create a poster on an A4 sheet of paper, outlining the method of production and the benefits and limitations of this method for the business.

You could ask students to present their posters to the class or discuss them in small groups in the next lesson.

4.1.3 How technology has changed production methods

Aims (4.1.3)

Knowledge

By the end of this section, students will understand:

- how technology has changed production methods, for example, using computers in manufacturing and design.

Resources

- Student's Book pages 254–255
- Activity sheets 4.1.3A and 4.1.3B

Key business terms

assembly line; automation; computer-aided design (CAD); computer-aided manufacture (CAM); division of labour; efficiency; flow production; job production; labour turnover; productivity; robotics

Lesson ideas

You should aim to cover the materials in 4.1.3 in a single one-hour lesson, plus, as appropriate, a homework assignment. To achieve the Aims for this topic, we recommend doing some of the following activities over the course of the lesson.

Starter suggestion

What you know: Ask students to choose an object in the classroom and write a brief 'story' of its design and manufacture. (Do not mention technology to students at this stage.) Then split the class into pairs. Each student should share their story with their partner. If the student has not identified it already, the partner should suggest how technology might have been used in the production process.

Main lesson suggestions

Discussion and note-taking (whole class): Talk students through how companies use computers in manufacturing and design. Tell them to take notes as relevant.

Business in practice: Using the case study on page 255 of the Student's Book, ask students to identify the benefits of using technology in production.

Skills activity: Ask students to conduct the investigation in the Skills activity on page 255 of the Student's Book. They will research a piece of CAD computer software and recommend whether a firm of architects should use the software or not.

Student activity: Ask students to complete Activity 4.1.3. They will read a passage on technology used in car manufacture and then question each other to complete the gaps in the text.

Plenary suggestion

Knowledge check: Ask students to answer the Knowledge check questions on page 255 of the Student's Book.

Tip: This could be given as a homework exercise.

Answers to Student's Book activities

Skills activity (page 255): possible outcomes

Focus students' attention on the potential benefits and drawbacks of using this software and on making a recommendation about its adoption. If students struggle to find information on suitable CAD software, instruct them to consider the use of software (i.e. technology) in general.

Knowledge check (page 255)

1. **Explain** two benefits of using robotics to help production.

   Any two from: tasks can be carried out with 100 per cent accuracy; although expensive to buy, robotics are often cheaper to run than employees are to pay; robots can work long hours (without breaks) and so increase productivity; they can often be retooled to new tasks (producing new types of products).

2. **Identify** two products that might use robotics in their manufacture.

   Accept any appropriate response, for example, cars, electrical goods, and so on.

3. **Outline** two benefits to a business of using CAD when designing their products.

   Any two from: allows for consistent output on a large scale; increases productivity as more products can be made without the need for human involvement; exact measurements can be achieved with every production; essential where manufacturing tolerances need to be minimal (for example, products for medical sciences).

4. **Explain** two ways that technology has changed production.

   Any two from: reduction in manufacturing costs; increase in speed of production; increase in manufacturing accuracy; increase in manufacturing output.

4.1.3 How technology has changed production methods: Activity

Activity type

Information gap reading activity

Time

30 minutes

Content

Innovation and technology in the production process

Key terms

assembly line; automation; computer-aided design (CAD); computer-aided manufacture (CAM); division of labour; efficiency; flow production; job production; labour turnover; productivity; robotics

Aims

To understand how technology has changed production methods, for example, using computers in manufacturing and design (4.1.3)

Skills practised

AO1: Knowledge and understanding	✓
AO2: Application	✓
AO3: Analysis	
AO4: Evaluation	

Preparation

Make one copy of Activity sheet 4.1.3A and one copy of Activity sheet 4.1.3B for each pair of students in the class.

Procedure

Part 1

1 Tell students they are going to read a passage about the evolution of car production.

2 Prepare students (activate knowledge) for the text by asking them to predict how car production has changed between 1900 and the present day.

Draw a timeline on the board with '1900' at one end and 'Present day' at the other. Allow students a couple of minutes to discuss their ideas in small groups before asking for their responses and writing them at the relevant points on the timeline.

3 Divide the class in half and sit the students in two separate groups, A and B. Give a copy of Activity sheet 4.1.3A to each student A and Activity sheet 4.1.3B to each student B.

Ask students to read the passage. Tell them to ignore the gaps in the text for now and just to read past them.

Make sure students do not share passages across the two groups.

4 After the first reading, discuss with the whole group the changes in car production mentioned in the text and add them to the timeline.

Part 2

5 Explain that students will now attempt to fill in the gaps in their passage by questioning the other group (whose passage has different gaps). To do this, they need to write questions designed to find out the missing pieces of information in their text.

6 Demonstrate this process for students using the example provided. Read the first sentence of the passage aloud and then read the question given as the example: 'What did Henry Ford and his team of engineers design first in 1913?'

Tell students the answer is 'moving assembly line' and ask them to write the words in the gap.

7 Allow students about 10 minutes to write their questions. Then pair each student in group A with a student from group B. In each pair, students take turns to ask and answer their questions. Emphasise that students can only communicate verbally and must not show their version of the passage to their partner. They continue until they have filled in all of the gaps in their passage.

8 At the end of the activity, check the answers with the class and ask students to discuss the questions below in small groups. After a few minutes, ask them to share their ideas with the class.

Question	Points for discussion
1 What problems might there have been with Ford's moving assembly line?	Ford's assembly line was monotonous and physically exhausting for employees. This led to an extremely high labour turnover rate. In order to reduce labour turnover and increase productivity, Ford more than doubled the wage for an employee to $5 per day. Another problem was the inflexibility of the production line. Only one type of car was made for 14 years – the Model T. Ford used to say 'You can have any colour you like, as long as it's black.'
2 How was Ford able to reduce the price per car by so much?	This is an opportunity to introduce the concept of economies of scale – as output increases, the cost per unit decreases.
3 What are the advantages and disadvantages for car manufacturers of introducing technology such as CAD, CAM and robotics into their production process?	Advantages: increased productivity and efficiency; lower unit cost; increased competitiveness (competitive advantage); increased profit margins; improved precision, consistency and quality; increased barriers to entry into the industry which limits competition.
	Disadvantages: expensive (requires significant capital investment); specialists may need to be hired to operate and maintain equipment and machinery, which may also be expensive.

Teacher tip: When asking students to read an extended passage, it is important to prepare them for the task by activating their prior knowledge on the subject matter and giving them a purpose for reading (steps 2–4 in the activity procedure above). This helps students to make links with what they already know and construct meaning from the text.

Extension: Ask students to answer this exam-style question below for homework:

Discuss the benefits and drawbacks for Ford of using new technology such as CAD, CAM and robotics in its car manufacturing process.

Suggested answers to Activity sheets A and B

1 How long did it take to make a car using job production? – several weeks
2 What did Ford need to produce an affordable car for the general public? – automation
3 How many cars was the Ford Motor Company producing per day two years after 1903? – 25
4 How many Model Ts were produced per day on Ford's moving assembly line? – 1000
5 How much did a Model T cost as productivity and efficiency continued to improve? – $260
6 How frequently were cars leaving the production line when production was at its peak? – every 10 seconds
7 How many vehicles does Ford produce today per day? – about 15 000
8 What is used to create 3D images of cars for designers? – computer-aided design (CAD)
9 What system is used to control giant robotic arms in the production of cars? – computer-aided manufacture (CAM)
10 What is improved by robots working continuously at low cost? – productivity

4.2 Costs, scale of production and break-even analysis

4.2.1 IDENTIFY AND CLASSIFY COSTS

Aims (4.2.1)

Knowledge
By the end of this section, students will understand:
• how to use cost data to help make simple cost-based decisions, for example, to stop production or continue
• how to classify costs using examples, for example, fixed, variable, average, total.

Resources
• Student's Book pages 256–260
• Activity sheet 4.2.1
• A large packet of small marshmallows
• Toothpicks (2 packs)
• One 30 cm ruler per group

Key business terms
average cost; component parts; fixed costs; raw materials; suppliers; total cost; variable costs

Lesson ideas

You should aim to cover the materials in 4.2.1 in a single one-hour lesson, plus, ideally, a homework assignment. To achieve the Aims for this topic, we recommend doing some of the following activities over the course of the lesson.

Starter suggestion

Listing the costs of production: Divide the class into small groups and ask students to imagine they are going to use the classroom as a base for producing jewellery boxes. Ask them to list all of the different costs they imagine might be involved.

If time and student ability allow, ask them to group the costs into similar types.

Use students' responses to introduce key terminology for this topic.

Main lesson activities

Discussion and note-taking (whole class): Talk students through the types of cost, including how to use cost data to make simple cost-based decisions. Tell them to take notes as relevant.

Tip: It is a good idea to use worked examples of calculations where possible.

Skills activity: Ask students to carry out the Skills activity on pages 257–258 of the Student's Book. They will calculate costs for a manufacturing firm using given data.

Worked example: Photocopy the two tables from the Worked example on page 259 of the Student's Book. Blank out some of the data and photocopy the tables again. Give students copies of the tables with blanks and ask them to calculate the missing data. This will help them to use data to make cost-based decisions.

Student activity: Ask students to complete Activity 4.2.1. In this practical group work activity, students identify the costs associated with building a marshmallow (or paper and card) tower.

Plenary suggestion

Knowledge check: Ask students to answer the Knowledge check questions on page 260 of the Student's Book.

Tip: This could be given as a homework exercise.

Answers to Student's Book activities

Skills activity (pages 257–258): possible outcomes

Units produced	Fixed costs	Variable costs	Total cost	Average cost
1	$6000	$4.50	$6004.50	$6004.50
100	$6000	$450.00	$6450.00	$64.50
250	$6000	$1125.00	$7125.00	$28.50
500	$6000	$2250.00	$8250.00	$16.50
1000	$6000	$4500.00	$10 500.00	$10.50
2000	$6000	$9000.00	$15 000.00	$7.50
5000	$6000	$22 500.00	$28 500.00	$5.70
10000	$6000	$45 000.00	$51 000.00	$5.10
15000	$6000	$67 500.00	$73 500.00	$4.90

Knowledge check (page 260)

1 **Identify** one example of a variable cost and one example of a fixed cost.

   Variable costs: *Any one from*: direct labour; raw materials; packaging; power (electricity).

   Fixed costs: *Any one from*: rent; salaries; marketing costs; heating/lighting costs.

2 Using examples, **explain** the difference between fixed costs and variable costs.

   Variable costs increase with output, whereas fixed costs remain the same regardless of output.

3 **Calculate** the total cost at Factory 1 of producing the following numbers of bikes:

   a) 500: $70 000

   b) 1000: $120 000

   c) 2500: $370 000

4 **Calculate** the average cost at Factory 2 of producing the following numbers of bikes:

   a) 500: $159.00

   b) 1000: $129.50

   c) 4000: $107.37

5 **Explain** why the average cost falls as Factory 2 makes more bikes.

   The greater the number of units produced, the more units over which total costs are shared. Therefore, the average cost of each unit falls.

6. If Factory 1 makes 2600 bikes and Factory 2 makes 3000 bikes, **consider** which factory produces the most profitable bikes. Use average cost data to **justify** your answer.

	Factory 1	Factory 2
Revenue per bike	$150	$150
Total costs	$280 000	$329 500
Units produced	2600	3000
Average cost	**$108**	**$110**

4.2.1 Identify and classify costs: Activity

Activity type

Group-based practical activity

Time

40 minutes

Content

Calculating fixed, variable, average and total costs

Key terms

average cost; component parts; fixed costs; raw materials; suppliers; total cost; variable costs

Aims

Skills practised

AO1: Knowledge and understanding	✓
AO2: Application	✓
AO3: Analysis	✓
AO4: Evaluation	✓

Preparation

Make one copy of Activity sheet 4.2.1 for each student in the class and bring to the lesson: one large packet of small marshmallows; toothpicks (2 packs); one 30 cm ruler for each group.

To identify and classify costs (fixed, variable, average, total) and to use cost data to help make simple cost-based decisions (4.2.1)

Procedure

1. Tell students they are going to work in small groups to make a tower using only marshmallows and toothpicks.

2. Divide the class into teams of three and give a copy of Activity sheet 4.2.1 to each student.

3. Explain that the objective of the activity is to build the tallest possible tower using the fewest possible resources. They will therefore have to minimise their costs of production. The team with the lowest average cost of production at the end of the activity will be the winner. Tell students they will have about 10 minutes to build their tower. Give each group an A4 sheet of paper as 'rental space', explaining that the tower's base must remain on that sheet.

4. Allocate each student in each group one of the roles outlined on the activity sheet. Explain each role and tell students that you will be the quality control inspector and supplier of raw materials.

5. Direct students' attention to the 'Costs of production' section of the activity sheet.
   - Explain that in order to build their tower, teams will have to incur various costs.
   - Ask students to work in groups to classify the costs provided into fixed and variable by writing them in the correct column of the table on the activity sheet.
   - Once they have completed this, check answers with the class.
   - Point out that marshmallows and toothpicks are the only costs that vary with output (i.e. the height of the tower). All other costs are therefore fixed.

6. Explain that groups now have five minutes to plan their tower. After this time, the purchaser may buy raw materials from you. However, before they can do this, they must first record the quantities and costs of the items they wish to buy in the purchase order form, which you will check.
   - There is no limit on the quantity of marshmallows and toothpicks a team can buy. However, they must remember that their main objective is to minimise the average cost of production.
   - Teams are allowed to make multiple purchases throughout the activity. However, no refunds will be given.

7. Begin the activity and move around the room checking quality standards. Ask students questions to check their understanding of costs and other business concepts.

8. After about 10–15 minutes, stop the activity and ask students to measure the height of their tower. Point out that their tower must be able to stand alone for at least 10 seconds before its height can be measured.

9. Allow students a few minutes to calculate their fixed, variable, total and average costs and record their calculations in the table at the bottom of the activity sheet. Move around the room making sure they are doing this correctly.

10 Take in the final calculations from each group and announce the winning team to the class (i.e. the team with the lowest unit cost of production). Award them the left-over marshmallows as a prize!

Teacher tip: *Use the activity as a context to revise previous topics, such as job production, and to anticipate future ones, such as quality control. You can do this during the activity by questioning individual students or after the activity in the class feedback stage.*

Variation: If marshmallows are not available or might be too distracting, use A4 paper instead of marshmallows and A4 card instead of toothpicks. Also, replace the A4 'rental space' with a sheet of A3 paper. Students can then build the tower with a combination of card and paper.

Extension: If appropriate, ask students to take a photo of their tower on their mobile phone/tablet. For homework, instruct them to prepare a brief report on the production process. In their report, they should discuss the method of production they used, the problems they encountered and what they would do differently next time to increase efficiency. They should include the photo of their tower.

4.2.2 Economies and diseconomies of scale

Aims (4.2.2)

Knowledge

By the end of this section, students will understand:

- the concept of economies of scale with examples, for example, purchasing, marketing, financial, managerial, technical
- the concept of diseconomies of scale with examples, for example, poor communication, lack of commitment from employees, weak coordination.

Resources

- Student's Book pages 261–263
- Activity sheet 4.2.2
- Average cost curve diagram with labelled axes (prepared by the teacher)

Key business terms

average cost; diseconomies of scale; economies of scale; financial economies; managerial economies; marketing economies; purchasing economies; technical economies

Lesson ideas

You should aim to cover the materials in 4.2.2 in a single one-hour lesson, plus, as appropriate, a homework assignment. To achieve the Aims for this topic, we recommend doing some of the following activities over the course of the lesson.

Starter suggestions

Explain it: Give students a copy of an average cost curve diagram (as on page 262 of the Student's Book). Make sure that the axes are labelled, but give no other explanation. Ask students to work in pairs to try to explain the downward (economies) portion of the graph. Give them a suitable context to help them, such as a clothing manufacturer.

If time and group ability allow, ask students to explain the upward (diseconomies) portion of the graph.

Main lesson activities

Discussion and note-taking (whole class): Talk students through the concepts of economies and diseconomies of scale. Tell them to take notes as relevant.

Skills activity: Ask students to conduct the investigation in the Skills activity on page 263 of the Student's Book. Students will research the economies of scale affecting a business known to them.

Tip: This could be given as a homework exercise.

Big school – big problems?: Ask students to work in pairs to list all of the problems they think the school would suffer if it doubled in size. Encourage them to think in terms of the school as a business. Use their responses to introduce the concept of diseconomies of scale.

Student activity: Ask students to complete Activity 4.2.2. This pair-work discussion requires them to understand different types of economies/diseconomies of scale.

Plenary suggestion

Knowledge check: Ask students to answer the Knowledge check questions on page 263 of the Student's Book.

Tip: This could be given as a homework exercise.

Answers to Student's Book activities

Skills activity (page 263): possible outcomes

Encourage students to calculate the cost per unit and use this as the basis for their discussion. Their presentation could be in the form of small tables comparing data across the different products.

Knowledge check (page 263)

1 **Define** the term economies of scale.

   The benefits a business gains as it grows in size; the fall in unit cost as scale increases.

2 **Explain** which of the economies of scale CACL is benefiting from.

   Purchasing economies of scale.

3 **Outline** two other economies of scale that CACL might benefit from now the business has grown.

   Any two from: technical; managerial; financial.

4 **Define** the term diseconomies of scale.

   The disadvantages a business suffers as it grows in size; an increase in unit cost as scale increases.

5 As CACL continues to grow, **explain** one possible diseconomy of scale that might affect the company.

   Any one from: poor communication; lower (poor) employee motivation; increased need for delegation (and loss of control); poor coordination.

4.2.2 Understand economies and diseconomies of scale: Activity

Activity type

Pair discussion

Time

20 minutes

Content

Economies and diseconomies of scale

Key terms

average cost; diseconomies of scale; economies of scale; financial economies; managerial economies; marketing economies; purchasing economies; technical economies

Skills practised

AO1: Knowledge and understanding	✓
AO2: Application	
AO3: Analysis	✓
AO4: Evaluation	

Preparation

Make one copy of Activity Sheet 4.2.2 for each student in the class.

Aims

To recap the various types of economies and diseconomies of scale (to add depth to the exercise, this activity also includes marketing economies, not covered in the Student's Book) (4.2.2)

Procedure

1. Tell students they are going to work in pairs to identify the different types of economies and diseconomies of scale.
2. Ensure that students are familiar with the various types of economies and diseconomies of scale by asking them to read the information on pages 261–262 of the Student's Book and to write a definition for each type. As an example, explain the concept of 'marketing economies' to the class. (This will help add depth to their knowledge from the Student's Book.)
3. Organise students into pairs and give a copy of Activity sheet 4.2.2 to each student.
4. Tell students they will work with their partner to identify the types of economies or diseconomies of scale described in each of the sentences in the activity sheet.
5. They should write the type of economy or diseconomy of scale next to each sentence in the space provided. They should also be able to justify their answers by explaining how each economy/diseconomy of scale affects the average costs of the business. Demonstrate the activity using the first sentence on the activity sheet.
6. Allow students 5–10 minutes to complete the task. In that time, move around the room asking students to justify their classifications with reference to average costs.
7. Once students have completed the activity sheet, ask each pair to compare their answers with another pair in the class. Where there are differences in their responses, students should justify their choices to each other with reference to average costs and come to a consensus on the best classification.
8. Check answers with the whole group. Nominate students to justify their classifications to the class.

Teacher tip: Try pairing students of similar ability so that neither one dominates the activity. This will make it easier for students to complete the task collaboratively.

Variation: To get students moving, you could cut up the sentences and stick them to the walls around the classroom. Students move around the room in pairs, reading the sentences and jointly deciding which economy/diseconomy of scale each sentence refers to. They write their answers next to the number of the sentence in their notebook. Once they have responded to all of the sentences, they return to their seats.

Then give each student a copy of Activity sheet 4.2.2 and ask them to discuss their answers in groups of three or four, justifying their chosen classifications.

Extension: For homework, ask students to apply their knowledge of economies/diseconomies of scale to a business of their choice, for example, Coca-Cola, Tesco, Toyota.

They should identify three potential economies of scale and three potential diseconomies of scale and explain how these might affect the business.

They should be ready to share their analysis with the class in the next lesson.

Suggested answers to Activity 4.2.2

Description	Type of economy/ diseconomy of scale	Suggested explanations for the effect on average cost (AC)
1 Large businesses are able to negotiate lower prices with suppliers.	Purchasing economies	AC falls because large firms have the power to negotiate bulk discounts on purchases from suppliers.
2 Large businesses are more likely to have problems maintaining employee morale, motivation and job satisfaction.	Poor motivation	AC increases because monotonous, repetitive jobs tend to lead to lower motivation, more sick days and hence lower productivity.
3 Large businesses are able to spread their marketing costs across a larger output.	Marketing economies	AC falls because the larger the output, the lower the marketing cost per unit sold.
4 Large businesses are able to negotiate lower interest rates on bank loans.	Financial economies	AC falls because large businesses are less risky for banks to lend to as they have assets that can be used as security on loans.
5 It can take a long time for decisions to be made in large organisations.	Poor communication	AC increases as the long chain of command in most larger companies means that decisions take more time, decreasing efficiency. Large firms may also be slow to respond to changes in the market.
6 Managers in large companies often have a wide span of control, so it is difficult to monitor all employees closely.	Poor coordination	AC increases as it is difficult to monitor all employees and some may be 'shirking' (avoiding) their duties, reducing productivity.
7 Large businesses are able to employ specialist managers who are experts in their areas.	Managerial economies	AC falls because specialisation leads to greater productivity and increased output.
8 Large businesses can afford to pay high salaries to attract the most talented and experienced employees in the industry.	Managerial economics	AC falls because talented and experienced employees work more efficiently and productively.
9 Large businesses have the capital to invest in the latest technology, equipment and machinery.	Technical economies	AC falls because the latest technology and machinery will increase productivity.
10 Within large organisations, communication problems are more likely between individuals and/or departments.	Poor communication	AC increases due to increased incidence of miscommunication and possible conflict between individuals or departments.
11 Large businesses are able to finance expansion in a variety of ways, for example, shareholders' funds and retained profits.	Financial economies	AC falls because firms are able to expand output more cheaply, i.e. they do not have to repay shareholders or pay interest on shares.

Description	Type of economy/diseconomy of scale	Suggested explanations for the effect on average cost (AC)
12 Large businesses can afford methods of advertising, such as TV commercials, which may be too expensive for smaller businesses.	Marketing economies	AC falls as this enables large firms to increase sales. The business can therefore spread its fixed costs across a larger output.
13 Employees in larger businesses often belong to trade unions.	Poor motivation/Poor coordination	AC increases because trade unions may demand higher wages. If employees go on strike, output will fall and productivity will decrease.
14 Large businesses can operate their machinery continuously (day and night) because they produce for a mass market.	Technical economies	AC falls because machinery is used at full capacity. The fixed cost can therefore be spread across a larger output.
15 There is greater need for managers in large firms to delegate tasks to subordinates, who may take longer to complete them or may not make the right decisions.	Increased need for delegation	AC increases because subordinates may lack the experience and skills needed to make decisions quickly and to complete tasks efficiently.

4.2.3 Break-even analysis

Aims (4.2.3)

Knowledge

By the end of this section, students will understand:

- the concept of break-even
- the limitations of break-even analysis.
- how to construct, complete or amend a simple break-even chart
- how to interpret a given chart and use it to analyse a situation
- how to calculate break-even output from given data
- how to define, calculate and interpret the margin of safety
- how to use break-even analysis to help make simple decisions, for example, impact of higher price.

Resources

- Student's Book pages 264–270
- Activity sheets 4.2.3A and 4.2.3B
- Presentation of how to create a break-even chart (from the internet)
- Graph paper
- A simple example of a break-even chart (prepared by the teacher)
- A break-even chart with all labels removed (prepared by the teacher)
- Spreadsheet software (optional)

Key business terms

average cost; break-even point; fixed costs; loss; margin of safety; profit; profit margin; revenue; total cost; variable costs

Lesson ideas

You should aim to cover the materials in 4.2.3 in two one-hour lessons, plus, as appropriate, a homework assignment. To achieve the Aims for this topic, we recommend doing some of the following activities over the course of the lessons.

Note: Given the nature of this topic, it will need to be teacher-led, at least at the beginning.

Starter suggestion

Core concept: Find out from students their conceptual (i.e. non-numeric) understanding of 'break-even'. Avoid introducing too many terms at this stage.

If students have limited understanding of the term, refer back to business objectives (survival) and to types of costs (and the need to cover these costs).

Main lesson activities

Present IT: Using page 264 of the Student's Book, explain to students how to calculate the break-even point.

- If electronic resources allow, talk students through the creation of a break-even chart.
- Focus on one line at a time (referring back to types of cost), building up to break-even.
- Illustrate what happens to the break-even point if different variables (price, variable costs, and so on) are changed.

Tip: There is a wide range of presentations available on the internet designed for this purpose.

Skills activity: Ask students to carry out the Skills activity on page 269 of the Student's Book. They will construct a break-even chart and use it to help make simple decisions.

Tip: Provide graph paper for students to draw their charts.

Student activity: Ask students to complete Activity 4.2.3. They answer questions based on a case study to develop their:

- understanding of break-even charts
- ability to use break-even charts to make decisions on business strategy.

Spot the problem: Give students a simple break-even chart and list on the board terms such as 'economies of scale' and 'price discounting'. Ask students to reflect on these terms and to consider how accurately break-even charts reflect reality.

Knowledge check: Students answer the Knowledge check questions on page 270 of the Student's Book.

Tip: This could be given as a homework exercise.

Plenary suggestion

Label it: Hand out a break-even chart with all labels removed. Ask students to add appropriate labels and to identify the break-even point.

Also ask students to list two limitations of break-even charts.

Tip: Use peer-to-peer marking to confirm the labels, break-even point and limitations are correct.

Answers to Student's Book activities

Skills activity (page 269): possible outcomes

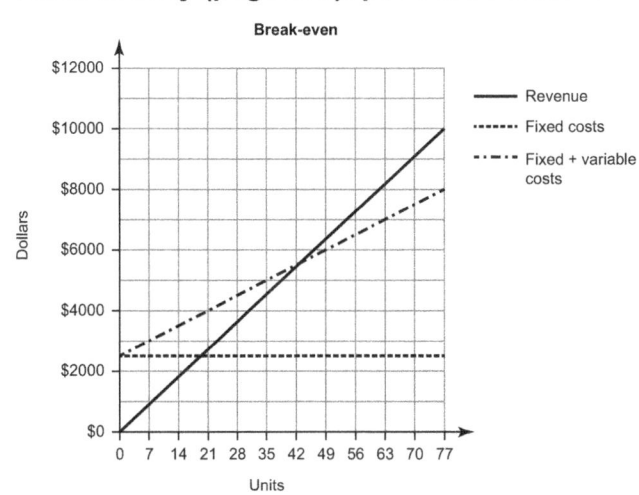

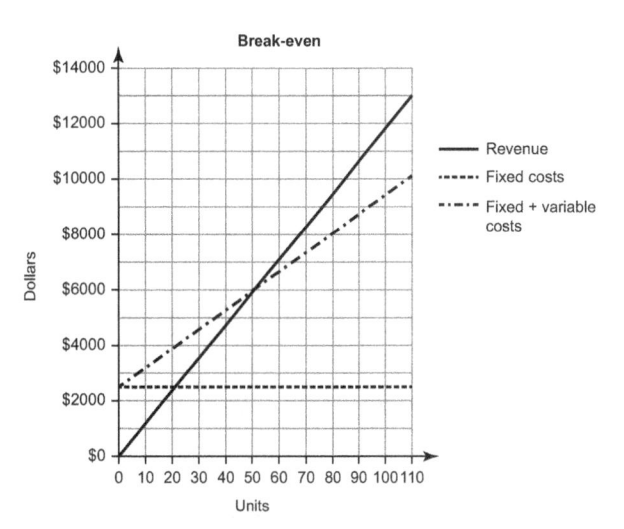

Increase of price to $130, shown here as a new graph. (Students are asked to add a new revenue line to the same graph.) At the new price, break-even falls to 42 units (41.6).

Advantages: reduces break-even point; increases profit per unit.

Disadvantages: may reduce consumer demand; depends on price of competing products.

On the basis of the limited data, a price rise is recommended, but encourage students to consider the implications of demand.

Knowledge check (page 270)

1 A business selling handbags has the following information:

Selling price $4   Variable costs $2   Fixed costs $2000

a) **Define** the term break-even.

The point at which total costs are equal to total revenue; the business makes neither a profit nor a loss.

b) **Calculate** the break-even point based on the above data. Show your working.

Contribution per unit: $40 − $25 = $15

Break-even: 2000/15 = 134 units (accept 133.3 recurring)

c) **Calculate** the break-even point if the selling price was to increase to $50.

Break-even: 2000/25 = 80 units

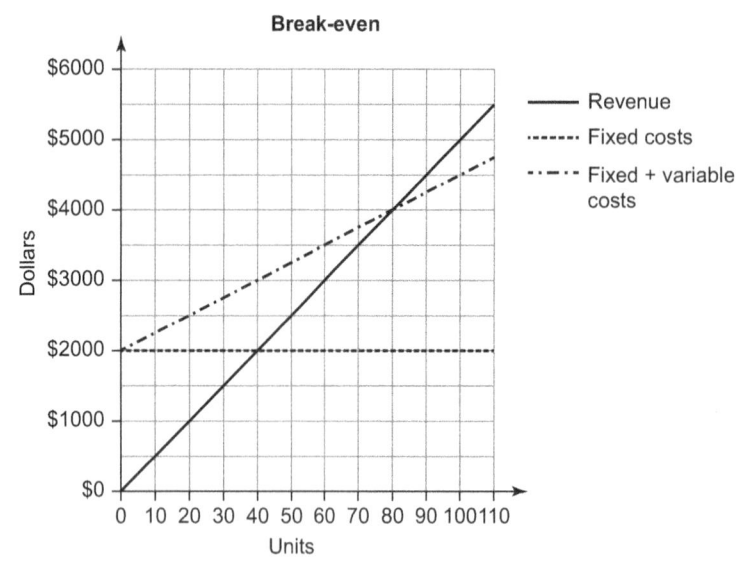

Break-even

(Graph showing Revenue, Fixed costs, and Fixed + variable costs lines; y-axis Dollars $0–$6000, x-axis Units 0–110)

2. Irum Hussain, a sole trader selling jewellery, has produced a break-even chart for her business. Her fixed costs are $200.

   a) Using the graph, **identify** the break-even point.

   26 units

   b) Using the graph, **calculate** the margin of safety if sales are 30 units.

   20 units

   c) Using the graph, **calculate** the following:

   i) the selling price per bag: $20

   ii) the average cost per bag at 14 units: $26.80

   iii) the average cost per bag at 24 units: $20.83

   d) Amend the graph to show an increase in fixed costs to $250. **Outline** the impact on the break-even point if the fixed costs increase.

   Break-even point shifts to 33 units.

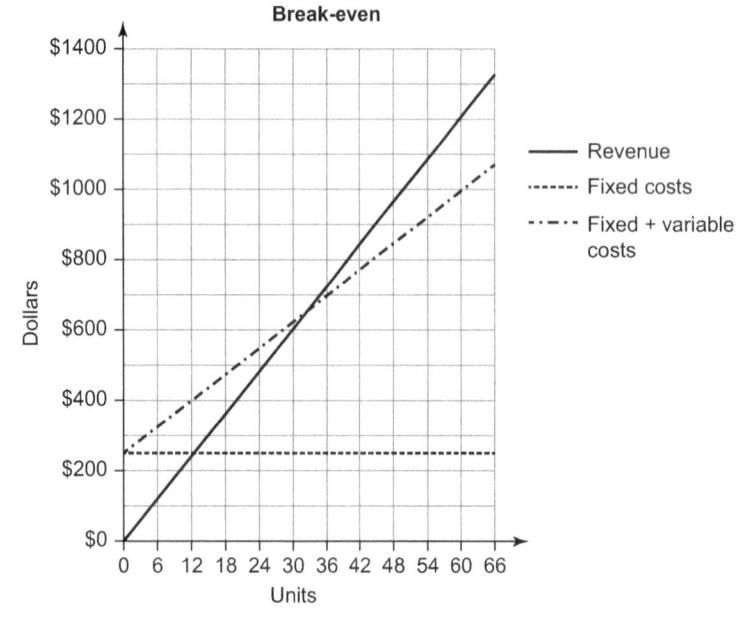

   Break-even

   (Graph showing Revenue, Fixed costs, and Fixed + variable costs lines; y-axis Dollars $0–$1400, x-axis Units 0–66)

3. **Explain** two limitations of a break-even chart to someone like Irum.

   Assumes variable costs stay the same (no economies of scale); assumes selling price remains the same (no bulk buying discounts for customers); assumes only one type of product sold at fixed price.

4.2.3 Break-even analysis: Activity

Activity type

Information sharing activity

Time

40 minutes

Content

Break-even charts

Key terms

average cost; break-even point; fixed costs; loss; margin of safety; profit; profit margin; revenue; total cost; variable costs

Skills practised

AO1: Knowledge and understanding	✓
AO2: Application	✓
AO3: Analysis	✓
AO4: Evaluation	✓

Preparation

Make one copy of Activity sheets 4.2.3A and 4.2.3B for every pair of students in the class. Make one copy of Activity sheet 4.2.3C for every student in the class.

Aims

To explain, interpret and use a simple break-even chart (4.2.3)

Procedure

1 Tell students they are going to use break-even charts to help decide on the best strategy for a business.

2 Divide the class into two groups, A and B. Hand a copy of Activity sheet 4.2.3A to each student in group A and a copy of Activity sheet 4.2.3B to each student in group B.

3 Read the case study scenario about Speedster Bikes at the top of the activity sheet to the class. Explain that students in group A will construct a break-even chart for the Avalanche mountain bike, while students in group B will construct one for the Hurricane racing bike. Students will then be paired with a member of the other group and will have to use their charts to decide on the best bicycle for Anton to produce.

4 Allow students a few minutes to complete Question 1 on their activity sheet before checking the answers as a class. It is important that students have classified the fixed and variable costs correctly before proceeding.

5 Tell students they have about 10 minutes to complete Questions 2–4 on their activity sheet. Move round the room checking that students are completing the questions correctly.

6 Once students have completed the activity sheet, ask them to check their answers against those of other students in their group. Briefly move round the groups, checking the accuracy of students' charts and ensuring that their break-even levels of output are correct.

7 Now, pair up one student from group A with one student from group B and give a copy of Activity sheet 4.2.3C to every student in the class. Explain that they must work together to complete Questions 5–9.

8 Again, move round the room, listening in on students' discussions and offering guidance when necessary.

9 Discuss students' answers with the class. Make sure they offer justification for their responses.

Teacher tip: Make sure students back up their opinions with evidence from the stimulus material and justify their opinions. You can do this by questioning the students, but backing up their opinions should become a habit for students as they move through the course.

Variation: Ask students to complete the calculations and chart using an Excel spreadsheet. You could then ask them to explain the effects of changes in selling price and costs by manipulating the data in their spreadsheets.

Extension: For homework, students write an essay discussing the usefulness of cost-benefit analysis for Speedster Bikes.

Answers to Activity Sheets 4.2.3A and 4.2.3B

Part 1

1 The completed table is as follows:

Fixed costs	Amount (per month)	Variable costs	Amount (per bicycle) Avalanche	Amount (per bicycle) Hurricane
Rent	$1500	Wages	$40	$50
Electricity	$100	Component parts	$65	$70
Capital equipment and machinery (leased)	$500	Paint	$10	$10
Interest on loan	$250	Raw materials	$25	$45
Salaries	$2000	Tyres	$20	$30
Telephone	$50			
Marketing	$600			

2 The completed tables are as follows:

Avalanche mountain bikes

Output	Fixed costs ($)	Variable costs ($)	Total cost ($)	Total revenue ($)
20	5000	3200	8200	500
40	5000	6400	11 400	10 000
60	5000	9600	14 600	15 000
80	5000	12 800	17 800	20 000
100	5000	16 000	21 000	25 000

Hurricane racing bikes

Output	Fixed costs ($)	Variable costs ($)	Total cost ($)	Total revenue ($)
20	5000	4100	9100	5600
40	5000	8200	13 200	11 200
60	5000	12 300	17 300	16 800
80	5000	16 400	21 400	22 400
100	5000	20 500	25 500	28 000

3 The completed graphs are as follows:

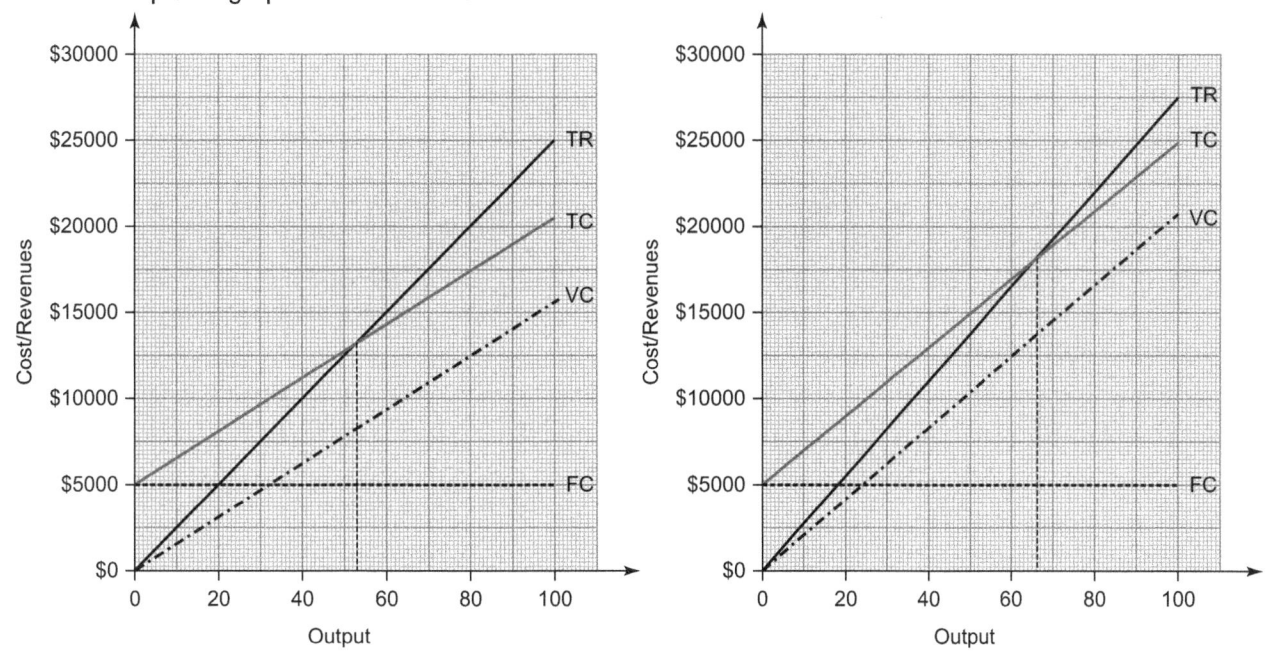

4 Avalanche: break-even level of output = 56 (rounded up from 55.57)

Hurricane: break-even level of output = 67 (rounded up from 66.67)

Part 2

5 The completed table is as follows:

	Avalanche mountain bike	Hurricane racing bike
Break-even level of output	56 units	67 units
Total profit	5000	1000
Margin of safety	24	13
Selling price	$250.00	$280.00
Average cost	$222.50	$267.50
Profit margin per unit	$27.50	$12.50

6 Anton should produce Avalanche mountain bikes for the following reasons:
- the break-even level of output is lower
- the total profits are higher
- the margin of safety is higher
- the profit margin is higher.

7 The completed table is as follows:

	Hurricane racing bike
Break-even level of output	53 units
Total profit	6800
Margin of safety	27
Selling price	$300.00
Average cost	$267.50
Profit margin per unit	$32.50

8 Anton should now produce the Hurricane racing bike, as at the new price of $300, the total profit, margin of safety and unit profit margins are higher in comparison with the Avalanche mountain bike, while the break-even level of output is lower.

9 Limitations could include:
- The break-even chart is based on the assumption that Anton will be able to sell every bicycle he produces. If there is a change in market conditions, such as an economic recession or increased competition, he may not be able to sell all his bicycles, which will reduce his revenue and may increase his costs (for example, storage costs).
- The accuracy of the break-even chart depends on the accuracy of Anton's forecasted figures for costs and revenues, for example, if costs rise or revenue is lower than expected, the break-even level of output will be higher.
- As Anton's business grows, he may benefit from economies of scale that will lower the average cost per bicycle and reduce his break-even level of output. This is not shown in the break-even chart.

4.3 Achieving quality production

4.3.1 THE IMPORTANCE OF QUALITY AND HOW TO ACHIEVE QUALITY PRODUCTION

Aims (4.3.1)

Knowledge	Resources
By the end of this section, students will understand: • what quality means and why it is important for all businesses • the concept of quality control and how businesses implement quality control • the concept of quality assurance and how this can be implemented.	• Student's Book pages 271–273 • Activity sheets 4.3.1A and 4.3.1B • Card; paper; scissors; coloured pencils

Key business terms

customer satisfaction; quality, quality assurance; quality checkers/inspectors; quality control; spot checking

Lesson ideas

You should aim to cover the materials in 4.3.1 in a single one-hour lesson, plus, as appropriate, a homework assignment. To achieve the Aims for this topic, we recommend doing some of the following activities over the course of the lesson.

Starter suggestion

Bad experience: Ask students to discuss with a classmate a product they have bought that they think was of bad quality.

Ask them to list the reasons they think the quality was poor. They should use business studies language where possible.

Ask them to consider the implications of their opinion for the business (they may not buy the product again; negative publicity – they are telling their classmate about it).

Main lesson activities

Discussion and note-taking (whole class): Talk students through quality assurance, quality control and why quality is important for all businesses. Tell them to take notes as relevant.

Student activity: Ask students to complete Activity 4.3.1. They will work in small groups to produce aeroplanes. The aim is to reinforce students' understanding of quality control versus quality assurance.

Skills activity: Ask students to carry out the investigation in the Skills activity on page 273 of the Student's Book. They will consider how a soft toy manufacturer might improve quality.

Business in practice: Using the case study on page 273 of the Student's Book, ask students to identify the problems a firm may face if the quality of its products is poor.

Knowledge check: Ask students to answer the Knowledge check questions on page 273 of the Student's Book.

Tip: This could be given as a homework exercise.

Plenary suggestion

Cut and paste: Copy the advantage and disadvantage tables from page 272–273 of the Student's Book.

- Cut out and mix up the advantages/disadvantages for quality control and quality assurance.
- Give sets of the mixed-up advantages/disadvantages to pairs or small groups of students.
- Ask them to place them under the appropriate heading: quality assurance or quality control.

Answers to Student's Book activities

Skills activity (page 273): possible outcomes

Encourage students to refer to methods of ensuring high quality introduced in the Student's Book: quality assurance, quality control.

Develop students' knowledge of international trade by covering communication barriers, distance and cultural differences as barriers to achieving quality.

Knowledge check (page 273)

1. **Identify** two reasons why quality is important for a business.

    Any two from: ability to charge higher prices; reputation benefits and associated marketing advantages; higher sales; lower rework (the repair/remanufacture of faulty goods), returned goods and customer complaints.

2. **Outline** two benefits to a business of using a quality control system.

    Any two from: helps ensure that products meet customers' requirements; generates more sales; better reputation; can identify poor-quality products before they become finished goods, which reduces the chances of selling poor-quality products to customers (lowering complaints).

3. **Identify** two differences between a quality control system and quality assurance.

    Quality control checks that products meet quality standards; quality assurance attempts to ensure that quality is not 'inspected in' to the product but 'built in' through the efforts of all employees.

    Quality control occurs at set points in the production process; quality assurance in inherent in the whole process.

4. **Analyse** one benefit for a business of implementing a quality assurance system.

    Any one from: better-quality products, lower rework (the repair/remanufacture of faulty goods); lower costs (less rework and no need to employ quality control checkers); higher prices; generates more sales; better reputation; can identify poor-quality products before they become finished goods, which would mean it could reduce the chances of selling poor-quality products to customers (lowering complaints), which could also then mean a higher chance of customer loyalty and repeat custom.

4.3.1 The importance of quality and how to achieve quality production: Activity

Activity type

Role play

Time

30 minutes

Content

Production, quality control and quality assurance

Key terms

customer satisfaction; quality, quality assurance; quality checkers/inspectors; quality control; spot checking

Aims

To understand the concept of quality control and how businesses implement quality control, and to understand the concept of quality assurance (4.3.1)

Skills practised

AO1: Knowledge and understanding	✓
AO2: Application	✓
AO3: Analysis	✓
AO4: Evaluation	✓

Preparation

Make one copy of Activity sheet 4.3.1A for each group of four or five students in the class and cut out the cards. Make one copy of the aeroplane template on Activity sheet 4.3.1B for each group. Paste each template onto thick card and carefully cut out around the outline of the aeroplane (or you could ask students to do this). Each group will also need about 20 pieces of blank paper (each big enough for one aeroplane), one pair of scissors and one set of coloured pencils.

Procedure

1. Tell students that they are going to work in a small group as a business producing aeroplanes. They will use division of labour to produce the planes. Each student will take on the role of a production employee specialising in a particular stage of the production process.

2. Divide the class into groups of four or five and give each group a set of role cards from Activity sheet 4.3.1A and one aeroplane template from Activity sheet 4.3.1B. If there are more than five students in a group, allocate the additional student(s) the role of aircraft painter (along with students 4 and 5). If there are only four students in a group, remove one of the aircraft painter roles.

3. Tell students to take a role card each and read it aloud to their group. Once students are clear on their roles, give them the appropriate equipment:
   - the aeroplane template and blank paper to Student 1
   - scissors to Student 2
   - coloured pencils to Students 3, 4 and 5.

4. Ask groups to organise themselves into a production line, from 1 to 5.

5. When students are ready to begin, tell them they will have 10 minutes in which to continuously produce as many aeroplanes as possible. Also let them know that you will be taking on the role of quality inspector and walking around the room checking the quality of their work. You will reject any components or finished products that do not satisfy quality standards. Remind students that the safety of future passengers depends on the quality of their work.

6. Move around the room monitoring students' progress and checking quality standards.

7. Stop the activity after 10 minutes. Display or write on the board the questions in the table below and ask students to discuss them in their groups. After about five minutes, ask students to share their ideas with the class and discuss some of the points in the right-hand column of the table with the class.

8 Finish by asking students to identify links between this activity and other business concepts they have learned, for example, flow production, motivation, productivity, and so on.

Question	Points for whole class discussion
1. Would your customers be satisfied with all of the completed aeroplanes? Why or why not?	Accept students' responses. Point out that this question is asking them to inspect their work for defects after it has been completed and is therefore an example of quality control.
2. What quality control procedures did your business have in place?	Quality control is carried out by a quality inspector and occurs after a component or product has already been produced. It is concerned with detecting and rejecting components and final products that are not up to a certain standard. In this activity, the quality inspector was the teacher.
3. What quality assurance procedures did your business have in place?	Quality assurance is about achieving 'zero defects'. It is concerned with preventing faults from occurring. In order for quality assurance to be effective, employees must 'self-check' the quality of their own work. Discuss with students the extent to which they monitored the quality of their own work during the activity.
4. How could the quality of your aeroplanes be improved?	Accept students' responses before pointing out that quality can always be improved. This is known as 'continuous improvement'. Businesses must encourage individual employees to continuously look for ways to improve the quality of their work.
5. Why is quality important for your business?	Accept answers in the context of the airline industry. These may include: • customer satisfaction • competitive advantage (for example, Boeing and Airbus) • reputation for excellence • higher sales and profits • passenger safety (moral responsibility).

Teacher tip: During the production stage of the activity, move around the room asking individual students (particularly the less able members of the group) questions to help them make connections with different parts of the course syllabus. For example:

- *How could this process be made more productive?*
- *What method of production are you using here?*
- *How might quality assurance differ from quality control in this context?*

Variation: You could assign the roles of 'quality inspector' and 'production manager' to two students in each group in addition to their roles as outlined on the role cards. This could lead to further discussion on quality control versus quality assurance and possibly on management style during the class feedback stage of the activity.

Extension: Students could use the internet (or other information sources) to research situations in which businesses have sold defective products to customers.

Students could write a newspaper article saying what the defect was, why it occurred and the consequences it had for the business.

Students may want to research one of the following companies: Toyota, Tesco or Kellogg's.

4.4 Location decisions

4.4.1 FACTORS INFLUENCING LOCATION AND RELOCATION DECISIONS

Aims (4.4.1)

Knowledge

By the end of this section, students will understand:

- factors relevant to the location decision of manufacturing businesses and service businesses
- factors that a business could consider when deciding which country to locate operations in
- the role of legal controls on location decisions
- how to recommend and justify an appropriate location for a business in given circumstances.

Resources

- Student's Book pages 274–278
- Activity sheets 4.4.1A and 4.4.1B
- Map of the local town/area

Key business terms

capital intensive; customers; grants; infrastructure; labour intensive; legislation; location; manufacturing industry; market; minimum wage; raw materials; relocation; saturated market; scale of production; services industry; subsidies; suppliers; taxes; trade barriers

Lesson ideas

You should aim to cover the materials in 4.4.1 in a single one-hour lesson, plus, as appropriate, a homework assignment. To achieve the Aims for this topic, we recommend doing some of the following activities over the course of the lesson.

Starter suggestion

Discussion: Ask students to consider the advantages and disadvantages of the school's/institution's location. Ask them to consider the location in relation to other schools nearby:

- Why did the schools locate where they are?
- What factors might have influenced the decision?

Use students' responses to generate a list of factors affecting location on the board.

Main lesson activities

Discussion and note-taking (whole class): Talk students through the factors influencing location. Tell them to take notes as relevant. Make sure you cover factors that a business could look at when considering overseas locations.

Case study: Ask students to read the case study on page 276 of the Student's Book. They will identify:

- which of the factors affecting overseas location is represented in the case study
- which other(s) may have been significant.

Student activity: Ask students to complete Activity 4.4.1. They will evaluate factors affecting location decisions.

Skills activity: Ask students to carry out the investigation described in the Skills activity on page 278 of the Student's Book. They will analyse the suitability of two different options (either in their local area or in two different countries) for the location of a business of their choice.

Group think: Ask students in small groups to brainstorm all the legal factors they can think of that might affect where a firm locates. They should share their ideas with other groups and add at least three new ideas to their own list.

Use students' responses to cover the key legal controls on location.

Knowledge check: Students answer the Knowledge check questions on page 278 of the Student's Book.

Tip: This could be given as a homework exercise.

Plenary suggestion

Paper share: Ask each student to write one example of a business on a small piece of paper. It must be a business that their classmates will know, but try to encourage variety. Collect in the papers and redistribute them at random among the class.

Ask each student to write on the piece of paper they have been given one factor that would be significant for the location of that firm. If time allows, repeat this for a factor that would not be significant.

Ask students to state the company name and factor(s) to the whole group. Use students' responses to prompt reinforcement of the key factors.

Answers to Student's Book activities

Skills activity (page 278): possible outcomes

Encourage students to refer directly to the factors affecting location decisions when creating their maps.

If possible, source a map of the local town/area before the lesson and mark possible sites on the map. These sites need not be vacant; simply mark on the map as many possible sites for students to choose.

Knowledge check (page 278)

1   **Consider** two factors that might be important when deciding where to relocate.

    Any two from: proximity to raw materials; proximity to suitable infrastructure; price of land; government influence; size of available land; availability of sufficient numbers of skilled labour.

2   **Consider** two factors that might influence a business thinking of relocating overseas.

    Any two from: saturated domestic market; lower labour costs; lower rental/expenses; proximity to/ availability of raw materials; government influence (favourable business taxes, and so on).

3   **Explain** why a country with a low minimum wage might influence a business's decision to relocate.

    As labour is the largest component of total costs, cheaper labour has significant cost advantages; a lower minimum wage reduces labour costs and increases profitability.

4   Other than minimum wage, **identify** three legal issues that might influence a business's decision to relocate overseas.

    Tax; legal considerations (legislation); trade barriers.

5   **Explain** two factors that are important when relocating a manufacturing business.

    Any two from: space; access to raw materials; access to suitable infrastructure (depending on size of raw materials/finished products).

4.4.1 Factors influencing location and relocation decisions: Activity

Activity type

Ranking on a continuum

Time

40 minutes

Content

Factors affecting a business's location decisions

Key terms

capital intensive; customers; grants; infrastructure; labour intensive; legislation; location; manufacturing industry; market; minimum wage; raw materials; relocation; saturated market; scale of production; services industry; subsidies; suppliers; taxes; trade barriers

Skills practised

AO1: Knowledge and understanding	✓
AO2: Application	✓
AO3: Analysis	✓
AO4: Evaluation	✓

Preparation

Make one copy of Activity sheet 4.4.1A for each group of three or four students in the class. Photocopy and cut out one set of cards from Activity sheet 4.4.1B for each group.

Aims

To understand the main factors influencing the location and relocation decisions of a business (4.4.1)

Procedure

1 Using real-world examples of businesses, ask students what factors determine where a business chooses to locate. Write students' responses on the board in the form of a spider diagram.

2 Tell students that they are going to look at a range of businesses and identify the most important factors affecting their location decisions.

3 Divide the class into groups of three and give each group a copy of Activity sheet 4.4.1A and a set of the cut-up cards from Activity sheet 4.4.1B.

4 Explain to students that they are going to identify and then rank the factors affecting the location decisions of particular businesses in order of importance. They will do this by placing each factor on a scale from 'most important' to 'least important'.

5 Demonstrate the activity using Situation 1.

6 Read the situation aloud to the class and ask students to identify which factors the business should consider using the cut-up cards from Activity sheet 4.4.1B.

7 Students will suggest the relevant factors. Make sure they justify their choices.

8 Ask students to rank the relevant factors in order of importance using the continuum provided. Allow students a few minutes to do this before asking them to justify their decisions briefly to the class. Encourage debate and discussion if there is disagreement between students.

9 Next, allocate two or three situations to each group. For example, group 1 discusses Situations 2 and 3, group 2 Situations 4 and 5, and so on. It doesn't matter if two groups are discussing the same situation.

10 Explain that students should complete the ranking activity for their allocated situations. They should also note down the three most important factors affecting each business. If they can think of any other important factors that are not included on the cards, they should note these down as well.

11 Allow students enough time to complete their discussions. To round off the activity, ask each group to feed back to the class on the most important factor affecting the location decision of one of the businesses they discussed. Make sure each group justifies its decision.

Teacher tip: *Make sure EAL students in particular are familiar with the vocabulary they need to complete the activity successfully. Words like 'proximity' and 'premises' are not specific business terms, but they can act as a barrier to EAL students' understanding. It can therefore be beneficial for these students if you teach vocabulary items such as these to the class before the start of the activity.*

Variation: You could also organise this activity as a jigsaw speaking task.

- Instruct half of the groups in the class to discuss Situations 2 to 4 (half A) and the other half to discuss Situations 5 to 7 (half B).
- Allow students sufficient time to complete the activity for at least two of their situations.
- Following this, pair one student from half A with a student from half B and ask them to outline for each other the most important factors affecting the location decisions of the businesses they discussed in their group.

This has the advantage of maximising student talking time, although it will require more class time.

Extension: Students choose one situation from Activity sheet A and write a response to the following exam-style question:

Discuss three factors affecting the business's location decision.

4 Operations management: Key terms revision

Define each term and provide an example or explanation. There are 2 marks per definition.

Term	Description/Definition
average cost	
break-even	
computer aided manufacture (CAM)	
diseconomies of scale	
efficiency	
fixed cost	
flow production	
infrastructure	
job production	
lean production	
productivity	
quality assurance	

5 Financial information and decisions

Introduction

Finance is arguably the most important Business Studies subject and often the most difficult for students to grasp. The concepts behind the financial management of a business nearly all involve numbers, therefore it is imperative that students are used to working with numbers and feel confident doing so.

The case material in this section gives students plenty of opportunities to:

- develop their understanding of the concepts behind the financial management of a business
- put theory into practice by working with data.

Grasping the difference between cash and profit is central to understanding finance and financial management. Students generally assume that a business has profit, but this is not the case. Correct use of the terms cash and profit will help them achieve the higher mark bands with questions aimed at the finance section of the syllabus.

Use the early activity below to get students working with numbers and looking at the difference between cash and profit. Once they have discussed the various points, you can link to the topics they will learn about.

Rent a Bike Sightseeing Tours

A business that organises tours of a local palace and gardens offers tourists the opportunity to cycle around the palace grounds on a hire bike.

Bike hire for the day costs $50 per bike.

Each month the business has to pay the palace $1000 in costs.

The business has the following numbers of customers each month:

Jan	Feb	Mar	Apr	May	June	July	Aug	Sept	Oct	Nov	Dec
13	12	20	20	35	50	60	80	70	22	10	6

Points for discussion (with links to topics shown in brackets):

- How much profit did the business make by the end of the year? (Profit/income statements)
- Using a percentage, how much of its sales did it turn into profit? (Profitability/profit margins)
- Are there any months when the business might struggle to pay its costs? (Working capital/liquidity)
- What costs might the business have to pay each month? (Gross and net profit)
- What are the problems in not being able to pay those costs? (Working capital/liquidity)
- How could the business solve these problems? (Cash flow/cash flow forecasting)
- Who might be interested in the information you have calculated? (Users of accounts)

5.1 Business finance: needs and sources

5.1.1 THE NEED FOR BUSINESS FINANCE

Aims (5.1.1)

Knowledge	Resources
By the end of this section, students will understand: • the main reasons why businesses need finance, for example, start-up capital, capital for expansion and additional working capital • the difference between short-term and long-term finance needs.	• Student's Book pages 292–294 • Activity sheets 5.1.1A and 5.1.1B • Access to ICT for research tasks • Mini whiteboards and pens

Key business terms

business expansion; capital expenditure; long term; revenue expenditure; short term; takeover; working capital

Lesson ideas

You should aim to cover the materials in 5.1.1 in a single one-hour lesson, plus, as appropriate, a homework assignment. To achieve the Aims for this topic, we recommend doing some of the following activities over the course of the lesson.

Starter suggestion

Discussion: Ask the class: 'What is finance?' 'Why/when might a business need finance?' 'Where might a firm find financing?' 'How might time affect the amount and type of finance needed?'

Give students a few minutes to discuss these questions in small groups and collate their answers (on individual whiteboards or a class whiteboard) so that they are available for the next exercise.

Main lesson activities

Discussion and note-taking (whole class): Ask students to read about the various reasons why businesses might need finance on pages 292–294 of the Student's Book.

Discuss these with the class and add any new points to the list on the board.

Link these reasons to short-term and long-term finance needs and make sure students take basic notes.

Student activity: Ask students to complete Activity 5.1.1A. They will identify the short- and long-term finance needs of four example businesses.

Discussion (whole class): Ask students what is meant by short-term and long-term finance.

Explain that the type of finance used depends on what the business is using it for. For example, a restaurant that needs funds to buy fresh ingredients is likely to use a short-term method of finance. But if the business wants to open another restaurant, it will need to use a long-term method.

Student activity: Ask students to complete Activity 5.1.1B, a memory game. They will match a business situation with the correct term of finance.

Skills activity: Ask students to complete the Skills activity on page 294 of the Student's Book. They will identify firms in their country that have recently raised funds.

Knowledge check: Students should answer the Knowledge check questions on page 294 of the Student's Book.

Plenary suggestion

Lesson review: Put students in groups to brainstorm reasons why businesses might need finance. Nominate one student from each group to write one reason on the board. Then point to each reason in turn and ask students to say whether short- or long-term financing would be most appropriate and why.

Answers to Student's Book activities

Skills activity (page 294): possible outcomes

Students should present their findings in a table. They will give examples of expenditure and timeframes. You could also ask them to define capital and revenue expenditure. Example answers:

Example	Capital or revenue expenditure	Short or long term
Local farm	Revenue expenditure (animal feed)	Short term (monthly)

Knowledge check (page 294)

1 **Using examples, outline** two reasons why a firm needs finance.

   Any two from: to pay the costs of starting up, e.g. new premises; to pay for the day-to-day running of the business, e.g. purchase of inventory, payment of wages; to expand output, e.g. purchase of capital equipment; to expand the business, e.g. opening a new store; to develop new products; to increase efficiency, e.g. new machinery, training for employees; to fund R&D, e.g. for new product development.

2 **Justify** appropriate financial timeframes (short or long term) for the following business activities:

   a) Nike builds a new retail store in India.

   Long term. Purchasing the land and paying for construction is very expensive, so Nike will have to borrow funds over a long period of time (more than 5 years).

   b) TGP Capital's (a financial investment company) takeover of Billabong Clothing.

   Long term. TGP Capital needs a large sum of money to purchase 51 per cent of the shares in Billabong clothing. It will take many years to pay this money back.

   c) A small firm needs funds to pay salaries.

   Short term. This firm needs quick access to money as it has to pay employees in the near future. The firm can repay this short-term loan when its cash flow situation improves.

   d) A factory in Vietnam installs a new production line system.

   Long term. Savings from increased productivity and efficiency could be used to pay off the new system in 1 to 5 years.

   e) An African firm buys a new delivery vehicle.

   Long term. A delivery vehicle should take between 1 and 5 years for the business to pay off.

   f) The fashion retailer Zara buys material from Bangladesh.

   Short term. Zara should be able to repay the loan within 1 year using revenue from the sale of its clothing.

5.1.1 The need for business finance: Activity A

Activity type
Jigsaw reading

Content
Reasons why businesses need funds

Time
30 minutes

Key business terms
business expansion; capital expenditure; long term; revenue expenditure; short term; takeover; working capital

Aims
To identify reasons why businesses need funds (5.1.1)

Skills practised

AO1: Knowledge and understanding	✓
AO2: Application	✓
AO3: Analysis	✓
AO4: Evaluation	✓

Preparation
Make one copy of Activity sheet 5.1.1A for each student in the class.

Procedure

1 Students are going to work in small groups to complete a jigsaw reading task. They will identify the main reasons why certain businesses need funds.

2 Divide the class into two equal groups, A and B. Give a copy of Activity Sheet 5.1.1A to each student in the class.

3 Explain that group A is going to read and discuss the case studies for Businesses 1 and 2 and make notes under the headings provided. Group B will read the case studies for Businesses 3 and 4 and make notes under the headings.

Emphasise that students should only read and discuss their allocated business case studies.

4 Tell students they will have about 10 minutes to do this. Then they will be paired up with a student from the other group to explain why the businesses they analysed need funds. They will justify their reasons.

5 Give students enough time to discuss their business case studies in sufficient depth and to make notes.

6 Next, arrange students into pairs, one student from group A with one student from group B.

Students will have about 10 minutes to explain each case study to their partner and feed back on the reasons why each business needs funds.

Students should listen to each other and make notes in the spaces provided.

They may contribute additional points or ask questions.

7 Round up the activity by nominating students to summarise their reasons for one or more of the businesses to the whole class.

Teacher tip: *Group students of mixed abilities. That way the more able students will scaffold the weaker ones in terms of subject knowledge and language. This will help the weaker students to communicate more confidently and effectively in the pair-work task.*

Variation: This activity could also be done as a four-way jigsaw activity. Divide the class into four groups and allocate just one situation to each group.

Extension: Students choose one business and write a response to the following exam question:

Identify and explain three reasons why this business may need funds.

Suggested answers to Activity 5.1.1

Profitability

1 Using the measure of profitability, last year's profitability is better, although only slightly:

	Last year	This year
Gross profit margin	22%	21%
Profit margin	7%	6%

However, this year, sales were $500 000 better than last year (22 per cent increase), although Premier Fashions Ltd is turning less of those sales into profit. This is likely to be because of the discounts they have been offering customers.

The increase in minimum wage and energy costs will also reduce the company's profitability. Its overheads have increased by $75 000 over the year (21 per cent increase).

Liquidity

2 Again, last year appears to be the better year:

	Last year	This year
Current ratio	1.82 : 1	1.5 : 1
Acid test ratio	1.14 : 1	0.5 : 1

The current ratio is better: for every $1 of short-term debt, the company has $1.82 to cover it, whereas in this year it has only $1.50 to cover it.

What is more worrying is the acid test. Last year the company had an acid test ratio of 1.14 : 1, which is quite healthy. This year they have an acid test ratio that is very poor and which suggests liquidity problems. The reasons for this could be that they are holding too much inventory. With 15–20 mini seasons there is a good chance they will not be able to sell 'last season's stock', which means that any spare garments are wasted – along with the money used up in producing them.

In addition, this year the company has an overdraft. This appears to have been used to pay for the inventory and a $100 000 increase in non-current assets. Using short-term sources of finance to pay for long-term assets is a very poor decision.

Return on capital employed

3 Despite the company's poor liquidity, this year has a better ROCE than last year:

	Last year	This year
ROCE	15%	16%

Judgement

4 The company's financial performance depends on how it is measured. Which is more important, profitability or liquidity? Shareholders would view profitability as more important, whereas management might consider liquidity to be more important.

Given the poor acid test ratio for this year, liquidity should be viewed as the best measure of performance, so last year is a much better year. However, although last year is better than this year, we do not know how Premier Fashions Ltd's competitors performed. The information provided is not enough on its own for us to make a definitive judgement.

5.1.1 The need for business finance: Activity B

Activity type
Matching and memory card game

Content
Short-, medium- and long-term financing

Time
20 minutes

Key business terms
business expansion; capital expenditure; long term; medium term; revenue expenditure; short term; takeover; working capital

Aims
To identify the appropriate term of financing for a business's situation (5.1.1)

Skills practised

AO1: Knowledge and understanding	✓
AO2: Application	✓
AO3: Analysis	✓
AO4: Evaluation	✓

Preparation
Photocopy the two sets of cards on Activity sheet B onto different coloured card, one colour for Set A and another colour for Set B. Make enough complete sets for every group of two or three students in the class. Cut up the cards and mix them up before distributing them to students.

Procedure

1. Tell students that they are going to play a memory game, in which they will have to match a business situation with the correct term of finance (short, medium or long term).
2. Divide students into groups of two or three.
3. Give each group a set of cards. Students should work together to match the business situations (set A) with the appropriate term of finance (set B).
4. Discuss the answers with students. Nominate individual students to justify their choices.
5. Ask students to shuffle the cards and arrange them in a regular pattern face down on the table.
6. One student turns over a business situation card (one colour) and then turns over a term of finance card (another colour). If the term of finance matches the business situation, the student keeps the matching pair. If students cannot agree on whether the cards match, the teacher can arbitrate.
7. If the situation does not match, students should return both cards face down to their previous positions. Students must attempt to remember where the cards are positioned and pick up the appropriate matching cards in future rounds.
8. The game continues until all the cards have been claimed. The student with the most matching cards is the winner.

Teacher tip: You do not need to distinguish between long-term (greater than five years) and medium-term (1–5 years) finance. Knowledge of medium-term finance is useful, however, in helping to distinguish between sources of finance and appropriate timeframes – therefore medium-term finance is included in this exercise. Remind students that medium-term sources of finance should be treated as long term.

When students are matching up the cards in the first part of the activity, ask them to pick up one business situation card at a time and discuss it as a group rather than dividing up the task between them. Although this is more time-consuming, it will promote discussion and analysis of the various situations. Remind students that the objective is to discuss each business situation in depth, not to finish as quickly as possible.

5.1.2 The main sources of finance

Aims (5.1.2)

Knowledge

By the end of this section, students will understand:

- internal sources and external sources, with examples
- short-term and long-term sources with examples, for example, overdraft for short-term finance and debt or equity for long-term finance
- the importance of alternative sources of capital, for example, micro-finance, crowd-funding
- the main factors considered in making the financial choice, for example, size and legal form of business, amount required, length of time, existing loans
- how to recommend and justify appropriate source(s) of finance in given circumstances.

Resources

- Student's Book pages 295–307
- Activity sheets 5.1.2A, 5.1.2B and 5.1.2C
- Scissors
- Information on overdrafts available at local banks: leaflets, website information, and so on, (for the Skills activity on page 299 of the Student's Book)

Key business terms

crowdfunding, capital expenditure; cash flow; debentures; debt; debt factoring; dividends; economy of scale; equity; external finance (bank loan; leasing; overdraft; trade credit); franchising; gearing; gearing ratio; grants; hire purchase; internal finance (owners' funds; retained profit; sale of assets; working capital); joint venture; long-term finance; micro-finance; sale and leaseback; revenue expenditure; share issue; short-term finance; venture capital

Lesson ideas

You should aim to cover the materials in 5.1.2 in two one-hour lessons, plus, as appropriate, a homework assignment. To achieve the Aims for this topic, we recommend doing some of the following activities over the course of the lessons.

Starter suggestion

Recap: Ask students to suggest why a business might need funds. Write their suggestions on the board. Students should discuss in small groups where (types, sources, and so on) a business might get financing for each of the situations on the board. Allow them to feed back their ideas to the class. Ask questions to prompt responses, such as:

- Where could the business obtain funds from inside the business?
- What about from outside the business?

Main lesson activities

Discussion and note-taking (whole class): Present the various sources of internal and external financing discussed on pages 295–307 of the Student's Book. Discuss them with the class.

Make sure you cover the advantages and disadvantages of each source. Tell students to make notes as necessary.

Skills activity: Ask students the meaning of the term 'venture capitalist'. Tell them to do the related Skills activity on page 303 of the Student's Book. Give them a few minutes to discuss their understanding of venture capital in groups of three or four before presenting their ideas to the class. Choose two or three groups to share their recommendation with the class.

Pair-work: One student in each pair should read the Debt and equity section on pages 295–296 of the Student's Book. The other student should read the Micro-financing section on page 305. The students should then explain the concepts to each other, making brief notes.

If time allows, you could repeat this exercise in reverse, with students adding to their notes any points they missed in the first run-through.

For a final check, ask one or more pairs to explain the concepts to the whole class.

Discussion and note-taking (whole class): Present the factors affecting choice of finance on pages 305–307 of the Student's Book. Discuss them with the class. Tell students to make notes as necessary.

Skills activity: Ask students to complete the final Skills activity on page 307 of the Student's Book. They should evaluate the most appropriate factors affecting the choice of finance in a number of situations.

They should work in pairs or small groups to produce a concept map of their recommendations. They then evaluate another group's responses.

Discussion (whole class): Lead a class discussion on the factors affecting choice of finance using the final Skills activity as a guide.

Student activity: Ask students to complete Activity 5.1.2C. They will choose and justify the best sources of finance for a start-up business from the sources offered.

Tip: This would make a useful homework exercise.

Further student activities: To support fuller development of the Aims, you could ask students to carry out Activity 5.1.2A (to consolidate their understanding of key terms) and Activity 5.1.2B (recommending and ranking sources of finance for different businesses).

Plenary suggestion

Concept map: Students should work in small groups to prepare a concept map linking the key business concepts and terms presented in Section 5.1 Business finance: needs and sources. Students begin with the main idea in the middle of the page and use arrows to link the various concepts covered throughout the section. They should annotate their map by noting the relationship between concepts next to each arrow. For example, 'Businesses need finance in order to expand'.

Answers to Student's Book activities

Skills activities: possible outcomes

Skills activity 1 (page 299)

Students may find it difficult to interpret complex overdraft terms. Accept 'headline' overdraft figures (i.e. published interest rate rather than a more complex breakdown of total cost) and a basic summary of features (for example, a comparison of overdraft fees and limits).

Risks might include: interest rate changes; the risk of increasing fees; the dangers of trading on debt (students may mention overtrading).

In their reasons for using an overdraft, students should refer to short-term cash flow management.

Skills activity 2 (page 303)

Advantages:

- It may be one of the few sources of finance available to a start-up business.
- Venture capitalists often offer management advice and consultancy as part of the loan.

Disadvantages:

- The firm will need to share ownership and profit with the venture capitalists.
- Venture capital is usually available only to high-potential businesses with strong growth prospects.

The recommendation depends on the owner's willingness to accept further share of ownership (and the extent to which the venture capitalist wants a say in how the business is run). As this is a small family firm, venture capital may not be the *most* appropriate source of finance – a bank loan or similar may be more appropriate.

Skills activity 3 (page 307)

Accept any reasonable answer with appropriate justification. For example:

Situation	Source of finance	Justification
A highly geared and very profitable manufacturer needs funds to build a new factory.	Depends on ownership type: share issue or convert to limited status	May be reluctant to take on further debt (increasing gearing), therefore equity finance more appropriate.
A firm, such as Apple Inc, with significant cash reserves wants to invest in research and development of new products.	Cash	Risk and cost free (able students may draw attention to opportunity cost).
A writer (sole trader) who publishes exercise books needs funds for a larger than usual print run; she is unwilling to use personal assets as security.	Overdraft or bank loan	Overdraft appropriate if revenue from book sales is likely to be received in the short term. Can secure a loan against personal assets.
A partnership of lawyers needs additional funds to expand the business; the current partners are reluctant to further share ownership.	Bank loan	Conversion to limited status or taking on an additional partner is not possible because of the current partners' reluctance to share ownership.
A profitable and well-established public limited company seeks financing for an expensive project at a time when interest rates are high.	Shares issue; retained profit; debenture	Bank loan unfavourable because of high interest rates. If retained profits are sufficient, this is the cheapest method. Share issue is slow and expensive but is appropriate for a long-term project. Debenture, although this is expensive because of high interest rates.

Knowledge check (page 307)

1 **Explain** when a business might prefer to use a bank overdraft rather than a bank loan.

   An overdraft is when a bank allows the business to overdraw its savings or cheque account by a certain amount. It is a short-term method of finance. It is quicker to arrange than a bank loan. *Example:* to overcome cash flow problems or other relevant example.

2 **Explain** the differences between equity and debt.

   Equity is the capital in the business that is raised from the sale of shares; debt is the capital in the business that is borrowed from an external source, such as a bank. Debt must be paid back with interest; equity does not need to be repaid – shareholders may receive a dividend or sell their shares to a third party.

3 **Define** the term debt factoring.

   Any two from: Debt factoring is when a business sells its debt to a debt factoring company. Debt is sold for an amount less than its full value. It is a method of solving short-term cash flow problems.

4 **Define** the term venture capital.

   A venture capitalist invests funds in a start-up business in exchange for a share of the business ownership or an agreed profit share.

5. **Explain** the difference between leasing and hire purchase.

   Leasing is when a business pays a weekly or monthly fee in return for the use of an asset such as a vehicle or piece of machinery. Hire purchase is when a business pays for an asset over time by weekly or monthly instalments rather than paying the full price on purchase. The business eventually takes ownership of the asset if hire purchase is used, but not when leasing is used.

6. **Outline** an example of when micro-finance may be an appropriate source of finance.

   Any two from: Micro-finance is most common in developing countries. It is suitable for small businesses or entrepreneurs. Businesses are able to borrow small amounts, usually without needing to provide security.

7. **Identify** three factors a business might consider when deciding on sources of finance.

   Any three from: availability of internal funds; timeframe (short or long term); cost (interest rate); type of business; loss of control; current gearing ratio; need to provide security.

5.1.2 The main sources of finance: Activity A

Activity type

Dominoes

Content

Sources of finance available to businesses

Time

40 minutes

Key terms

bank loan; capital expenditure; debentures; debt factoring; external finance; grant; hire purchase; internal finance; leasing; long-term finance; micro-finance; overdraft; owners' funds; retained profit; revenue expenditure; sale of assets; share issue; short-term finance; trade credit; working capital

Aims

To understand the main sources of financing available to businesses (5.1.2)

Skills practised

AO1: Knowledge and understanding	✓
AO2: Application	
AO3: Analysis	
AO4: Evaluation	

Preparation

Make one copy of Activity sheet 5.1.2A for each student in the class. Students will need scissors to cut out their dominoes.

Procedure

1. Tell students they are going to write definitions for a range of business terms related to sources of finance and then play a game of dominoes.
2. Hand out Activity sheet 5.1.2A to each student.
3. Students have 15 minutes to write definitions for the business terms on the sheets. The first few have been done as examples. Point out that term 1A matches with definition 1B, term 2A matches with definition 2B, and so on. Give students time to compare their definitions with a classmate and make changes if necessary.
4. Tell students to cut out each individual domino card, removing the numbers and letters.
5. Divide the class into groups of three. Students should combine their cut-up cards and shuffle them.
6. Demonstrate the game. Each student in the group starts with five cards in their hand. They should lay these out on the table in front of them. (It doesn't matter that team members can see each other's cards.)
7. Students take one card from the top of the pile and place it face up on the table. They then take turns to match a card in their hand with the card(s) on the table. They may place their card at either end of the chain of dominoes.
8. If a student is not able to place a card, they must take a new card from the pile and add it to their hand. The first student to get rid of all their cards is the winner.

Teacher tip: To save time, students could complete steps 3 and 4 for homework and you could play the game at the beginning of the next lesson.

Extension: For homework, students could paste their dominoes into their exercise books, matching the business terms with the definitions, as a permanent record. Alternatively, you could put the cards away to play again in a later lesson.

5.1.2 The main sources of finance: Activity B

Activity type

Ranking sources of finance on a continuum

Content

Factors affecting choice of finance and the sources of finance available to businesses

Time

30 minutes

Key business terms

bank loan; debentures; debt factoring; franchising; grant; hire purchase; leasing; overdraft; owners' funds; retained profit; sale of assets; share issue; trade credit; venture capital; working capital

Skills practised

AO1: Knowledge and understanding	✓
AO2: Application	✓
AO3: Analysis	✓
AO4: Evaluation	✓

Preparation

Photocopy and cut out one set of the activity cards and the continuum arrow from Activity sheets 5.1.2B (1) and 5.1.2B (2) for each group of three or four students in the class.

Aims

To recommend and justify appropriate method/s of finance for a given business situation (5.1.2)

Procedure

1 Tell students that they are going to work in groups of three or four to discuss the various sources of finance available to different businesses. Their objective is to decide on the most appropriate sources for each business.

2 Students place the situation cards in a pile face down on the table in front of them. One student should take one card from the pile and read it aloud to their group.

3 Students should then consider each source of finance in turn, placing the relevant cards on the continuum from 'very appropriate source of funds' to 'not at all appropriate source of funds'.

For example, if a group decides that a source of finance is appropriate for a particular situation, they should place the card on the left of the continuum. The further left they place the card, the more appropriate the source of finance for the given situation.

4 Demonstrate the activity to the class. Remind students that they must use their business knowledge to discuss and justify why each source of finance is either appropriate or not appropriate for the business.

5 Once the group has considered all possible sources of finance for a particular situation, they should take another situation card from the pile and repeat the process for the new business.

6 As a rounding-off activity, you could ask each group to recommend the most appropriate source of finance for one of the businesses and justify their decision to the class. Encourage debate if there is disagreement between groups.

Teacher tip: Create class sets of the activity cards for later use by photocopying them onto coloured card and laminating them.

Variation: This activity could also be done as a jigsaw task. Give half of the groups in the class Situations 1 to 4 and the other half Situations 5 to 8 to complete in their small groups. Following this, pair up one student from each half. Ask students to feed back to each other on the sources of financing they recommended for each of their situations. They should justify their choice.

Extension: Students choose one situation card and write a response to the following question:

Discuss three methods the business could use to finance its expenditure.

5.2 Cash flow forecasting and working capital

5.2.1 THE IMPORTANCE OF CASH AND OF CASH FLOW FORECASTING

Aims (5.2.1)

Knowledge

By the end of this section, students will understand:

- why cash is important to a business
- how to explain what a cash-flow forecast is, how a simple one is constructed and the importance of it
- how to amend or complete a simple cash-flow forecast
- how to interpret a simple cash flow forecast
- how short-term cash flow problems might be overcome, for example, increasing loans, delaying payments, asking debtors to pay more quickly.

Resources

- Student's Book pages 308–313
- Activity sheets 5.2.1A and 5.2.1B
- Two multi-packs of small chocolate bars or sweets (or other 'commodity' to sell for Activity 5.2.1A)

Key business terms

cash flow forecast; cash inflows; cash outflows; net cash flow

Lesson ideas

You should aim to cover the materials in 5.2.1 in two one-hour lessons, plus, as appropriate, a homework assignment. To achieve the Aims for this topic, we recommend doing some of the following activities over the course of the lessons.

Starter suggestion

Business simulation: Use Activity 5.2.1A to set up a simulation of a new business and introduce the concept of cash flow forecasts. Students act as customers in your new business and keep a record of the cash flow using a table.

Main lesson activities

Discussion and note-taking (whole class): Develop the starter activity into a class discussion. Explain the importance of managing cash flow for a business, outlining the difference between profit and cash.

- Profit is simply a figure that is calculated after a period of trading.
- Cash is the 'real' money that a business has on a day-to-day basis to pay its bills.

Using pages 308–309 of the Student's Book, students should make brief notes on cash flows, cash inflows and cash outflows.

Constructing a cash flow forecast: Use the worked example on pages 310–311 of the Student's Book to explain how to construct a cash flow forecast. Refer to the starter activity to consolidate students' learning.

Skills activity: Ask students to complete the Skills activity on page 313 of the Student's Book. They will construct a cash flow forecast based on the information given for Al-Rashid Clothing Ltd. You may need to provide a template for this. When they have completed the cash flow forecast, they will identify the business's cash flow problems and recommend how to improve the cash flow.

Knowledge check: Ask students to make notes on the importance of cash flow forecasting and then answer the Knowledge check questions on page 313 of the Student's Book.

Tip: This could be given as a homework task.

Plenary suggestion

Activity review: Ask students to peer assess the cash flow forecast they constructed in the Skills activity. Then ask them to share with the class their recommendations for how to improve Al-Rashid Clothing Ltd's cash flow.

Answers to Student's Book activities

Skills activity (page 313): Possible outcomes

Application: Students should produce the following cash flow forecast. You may need to provide a template for this.

$m	January	February	March	April	May	June
Cash flow forecast for Al-Rashid Clothing Ltd						
Inflows						
Sales	4.0	4.0	4.0	5.0	6.0	7.0
Total	4.0	4.0	4.0	5.0	6.0	7.0
Outflows						
Labour	2.0	2.0	2.0	2.5	3.0	3.5
Rent	1.5	1.5	1.5	1.5	1.5	1.5
Electricity			0.5			0.5
Marketing	1.2	1.2	1.2	7.2	1.2	1.2
Total	4.7	4.7	5.2	11.2	5.7	6.7
Net cash flow	(0.7)	(0.7)	(1.2)	(6.2)	0.3	0.3
Opening balance	0.0	(0.7)	(1.4)	(2.6)	(8.8)	(8.5)
Closing balance	(0.7)	(1.4)	(2.6)	(8.8)	(8.5)	(8.2)

Analysis: Students should identify cash flow problems throughout the six-month period:

- Negative net cash flows for January to April, especially in April when the business has a negative net cash flow of $6.2m.
- Net cash flow is improving in May and June with a positive cash flow of $0.3m. However, it will take about 30 months (8.8/0.3) to achieve a positive closing balance.

If the business does not have an overdraft facility, it will face severe liquidity problems from April onwards and could potentially be forced to close unless sales increase significantly.

Evaluation: Recommendations might include:

- Find cheaper rent.
- Reduce the workforce, as their wages are consistently the business's highest cost.
- Take out a bank loan to cover the cost of the advertising campaign. This will prevent the negative cash flow. Although the business will have to make repayments on the loan, the sales are predicted to increase after the advertising so the business should be able to make the repayments.

Knowledge check (page 313)

1 **Define** the following terms:

   a) Cash inflow

   Money that a business receives/money coming into a business that can come from a variety of sources such as sales/a bank loan.

   b) Cash outflow

   Money that a business spends/going out of a business that can be spent on paying bills.

2 **Identify** two possible inflows and two possible outflows that a business might have.

   Any two inflows from: revenue/sales; loan; grant from the government; share capital.

   Any two outflows from: bills/overheads; stock/inventory/suppliers; wages/salaries; loan repayments; mortgage repayments; investment opportunities.

3 **Explain** two reasons why it is important to produce a cash flow forecast.

   It can help a business predict the timings of future cash flows. This will help the business ensure that it has sufficient funds to make the payments/prevent any potential liquidity/cash flow problems.

   It can help a business plan for the future. This can help a business decide when it might be ready for possible investment or growth opportunities.

4 **Calculate** the net cash flow for the month of March.

   $140 000 – $130 000 = $10 000

5 **Calculate** the closing balance for the month of April.

	April
Inflows	$140 000
Outflows	$143 000
Net cash flow	($3000)
Opening balance	$15 000
Closing balance	$12 000

   Students should show the working out in their answer and give the currency.

6 **Explain** two ways a business could improve its cash flow.

   Increase its inflows:
   - Generate more sales; this could be done by increasing the selling price of its products. However, this may reduce the demand for the product.
   - Get a bank loan. This would only be a short-term method as the loan would have to be repaid.
   - Ask suppliers for credit. This would allow the business more time to pay its bills, improving the cash flow in the short term.

   Decrease its outflows:
   - The business could reduce the number of employees. However, this may reduce its ability to produce/supply.
   - Find cheaper suppliers. However, this may affect the quality of the supplies.

   Ask the bank for an overdraft. This would allow the business more cash in the short term. However, the overdraft would have to be paid back, often with interest.

5.2.1 The importance of cash and of cash flow forecasting: Activity

Activity type

Class simulation/student worksheet

Content

The need to cash flow forecasting

Time

30 minutes

Key terms

cash inflows; cash outflows; closing balance; liquidity; net cash flow; opening balance

Aims

To understand the purpose and construction of a cash-flow forecast (5.2.1)

Skills practised

AO1: Knowledge and understanding	✓
AO2: Application	✓
AO3: Analysis	✓
AO4: Evaluation	

Preparation

Photocopy and cut out enough of the currency (Activity sheet 5.2.1B) for every student in the class to have a selection of dollar notes. Make one copy of the cash flow table template (Activity sheet 5.2.1A) for every student in the class. Bring into the lesson a commodity of your choice to 'sell' to students; sweets or mini-chocolate bars work well (two multi-packs should be enough).

Procedure

1. Explain to the class that you are starting a business trading a commodity of your choice. Assign the following roles to students (in pairs, small groups or individually): Electricity provider; Rent (landlord); Suppliers (the number of suppliers will depend on how many different products you wish to sell); Bank.
2. Explain that all students are also potential customers.
3. Distribute money (from Activity sheet 5.2.1B) around the class. Give each student $15 to spend as a customer. Give some additional money to the suppliers, landlord and electricity provider for them to use as change. Give the rest of the money (a minimum of $200) to the bank.
4. Give the products you wish to sell to the suppliers.
5. Choose an accountant from the group to complete the cash flow table on Activity sheet 5.2.1A as the game develops. They will need to record all inflows and outflows as each 'day' is played out.

Playing the game

6. Follow the procedure for each 'day' of trading described in the table below. (Of course, each 'day' of trading does not have to take place on a different day, they could all be completed within the same lesson. Make it clear to students when each 'day' starts and finishes.)
7. Before completing the cash flow for each day, count out the money so the students can see where the inflow/outflows have come from. Use the accountant's record of the inflows and outflows to produce a class version on the board for all students to see.

Day 1	• Ask students how you can start trading without any money. Prompt them to suggest a bank loan. Obtain a loan of $100 from the bank (inflow). Agree to start $20 repayments from the next day. (Suggest to the students in charge of the bank that they charge a weekly interest rate of 10 per cent.)
	• Use the money to buy some stock from your suppliers (outflow) and sell on to any students who wish to buy (inflow). It is important to sell on to the students at cost price to encourage cash flow problems.
	• Finish the day's trading and calculate the net cash flow and balances.

Day 2	• Make a repayment to the bank of $20 plus any interest that students add (outflow).
	• Purchase some more stock from your suppliers (outflow).
	• Sell the products to students who wish to buy. Remember to keep the selling price low to encourage cash flow problems later in the week.
	• Finish the day's trading and calculate the net cash flow and balances.
Day 3	• Make a repayment to the bank of $20 plus any interest that the students add (outflow).
	• You will need to pay the landlord $80 rent for the last three days (outflow).
	• Purchase some more stock. Try to purchase more stock than you have the money for to introduce the concept of trade credit. (Note: do not put an entry on your cash flow forecast as no transaction has taken place.) Agree to pay the suppliers back tomorrow.
	• Sell your stock, again keeping a low selling price (inflow).
	• Finish the day's trading and calculate the net cash flow and balances.
Day 4	• Make a repayment to the bank of $20 plus any interest that the students add (outflow).
	• Pay back the suppliers (outflow).
	• Pay the electricity bill of $60 for the week (outflow).
	• Ideally, you will no longer have enough cash flow to make the payment. Ask students to suggest the problems of not being able to pay bills on time. Agree an overdraft with the bank.
	• Purchase more stock (if possible).
	• Sell your stock, again keeping a low selling price (inflow).
	• Finish the day's trading and calculate the net cash flow and balances.
Day 5	• Make a repayment to the bank of $20 plus any interest that the students add (outflow).
	• Pay your accountant $50 for their services (outflow).
	• Complete the balances, explaining the importance of managing cash flow.
	Note: *Aim to be in negative net cash flow every day, with the exception of Day 1.*

Discussion

8 When you have finished the simulation, discuss with students the importance of managing cash flow, emphasising that the closing balance is the working capital (how much capital 'money' the business has to work with on a day-to-day basis). Emphasise the importance of timings of cash flows and the problems that can result from not having enough cash.

9 Ask students to recommend ways to improve the business's cash position. Their ideas might include:

- allow more credit time with their suppliers
- agree a bigger loan to cover all upcoming expenses
- find cheaper accommodation
- increase the inflows.

Teacher tip: *As you work through the simulation, make sure you buy too much stock from the suppliers and sell it to the customers for too low a price. This should ensure that you run into cash flow problems halfway through the simulation.*

Variation: Rather than have one student act as accountant, ask all students to complete the cash flow forecast as you go through the simulation.

5.2.2 Working capital and liquidity

Aims (5.2.2, 5.5.2)

Knowledge
By the end of this section, students will understand:
- the concept and importance of working capital
- the concept and importance of liquidity.

Resources
- Student's Book pages 314–316
- Activity sheet 5.2.2
- Image of a bathtub
- News websites for research tasks

Key business terms
capital; cash; inventory (stock); liabilities; liquidity; trade credit; trade payables; trade receivables; working capital

Lesson ideas

You should aim to cover the materials in 5.2.2 in a single one-hour lesson, plus, as appropriate, a homework assignment. To achieve the Aims for this topic, we recommend doing some of the following activities over the course of the lesson.

Starter suggestion

Bath time! To help students to understand the concept of 'working capital' (cash), use the metaphor of water (liquid).

Draw or display an image of a bathtub on the board. The taps represent the inflows of cash and the plug represents the outflows. Ask students to draw the bathtub and label it. Explain that the water (or cash) in the bathtub represents the business's **liquidity**. If the business runs out of water (cash) and the bathtub runs dry, the business will not be able to pay its bills.

Ask students: 'In what circumstance might this happen?' (Answer: when the outflows (bills) are more than the inflows.)

Main lesson activities

Discussion and note-taking (whole class): Discuss the concept of credit, which means allowing customers a period of time before they have to pay for their goods or services. Introduce the importance of customers paying promptly – if there is a delay before they pay, the business will have to wait to receive the money and will not be able to pay bills in the meantime.

Many short-term cash flow problems are either caused by credit or can be solved by negotiating a credit period. Students need to understand the difference between 'cash sales' and 'credit sales' and how they affect a business's cash flow.

Student activity: Once students understand the concept of credit, ask them to attempt Activity 5.2.2. They will read a series of scenarios and explain how each situation will affect the business's working capital/liquidity.

Skills activity: Ask students to attempt the Skills activity on page 316 of the Student's Book. They can work in pairs to search for a business that has working capital/cash-flow problems. Students could start by finding a relevant news site and then search for cash flow problems.

Knowledge check: Ask students to answer the Knowledge check questions on page 316 of the Student's Book.

Tip: This could be given as a homework task.

Plenary suggestion

Feedback: Students discuss the business they researched in the Skills activity with the rest of the group. Each pair should outline one reason why the business in question is having cash flow problems and one recommendation for improving the business's cash flow.

Answers to Student's Book activities

Skills activity (page 316): Possible outcomes

Students might suggest any of the following solutions to the business's working capital problem:

- Increase the inflows: increase demand through advertising or increase the selling price to receive more inflows. Customers might not notice a small increase in selling price.
- Lower the outflows: cut back on any unnecessary expenditure or make some employees part-time or redundant. However, this might affect the business's ability to produce.
- Request a longer credit period from the trade payables (suppliers): this will give the business more time to sell its product before it has to pay the trade payables, which will give it more chance of receiving sufficient money to pay for the supplies.

Knowledge check (page 316)

1 **Define** the following terms:

   a) Cash payment

   When a customer pays with cash, which means the business receives its money straightaway.

   b) Credit period

   When a business allows a customer a certain period of time before the customer has to pay for goods/services.

2 **Explain** the meaning and importance of working capital.

   Working capital is the money a business currently has to pay for everyday expenses such as bills and suppliers.

   Also accept the formula: working capital = current assets – current liabilities

3 **Explain** one reason why working capital is important to a business.

   Working capital is important because a business has to pay bills. If the business has insufficient working capital, it will not be able to make payments on time. This may mean having to pay late payment fees or not being allowed future credit.

4 **Explain** why it is so important for a business to manage liquidity.

   Liquidity is a business's ability to pay its short-term liabilities/debts/bills.

5 **Explain** two potential short-term methods of improving liquidity.

   Negotiating a longer credit period with the business's trade payables will give the business more time to sell its product in order to generate the sales (revenue) to pay the bill.

   Asking customers to pay for their products promptly will mean that the business does not have to wait to receive the cash from its customers.

5.2.2 Working capital and liquidity: Activity

Activity type
Mini case studies

Content
Identifying whether business situations are good or bad for working capital

Time
20 minutes

Key terms
credit; liquidity; trade payables; trade receivables; working capital

Aims
To understand the concepts of working capital and liquidity (5.2.2, 5.5.2)

Skills practised

AO1: Knowledge and understanding	✓
AO2: Application	✓
AO3: Analysis	✓
AO4: Evaluation	

Preparation
Make a copy of Activity sheet 5.2.2 for every student in the class.

Procedure

1. Explain to students that they will be reading a series of scenarios and identifying whether the situation is good or bad for the business's working capital and liquidity.
2. Give each student a copy of Activity sheet 5.2.2.
3. Ask students to read through the scenarios and to highlight any information they consider to be important.
4. Students should complete the first column in the table by simply stating whether or not each scenario is likely to benefit working capital and liquidity or to be a problem.
5. They should explain their answer in the third column, using pages 314–315 of the Student's Book to help them.
6. Students can then discuss their answers, either in small groups or as a whole class.
7. Hand out the solution sheet for students to peer assess each other's work.

Teacher tip: When justifying their choices, students need to explain how each scenario will affect the business's working capital/liquidity, rather than simply explaining why they think the scenario will have a positive/negative effect on cash flow.

Extension: Ask students to choose one of the scenarios and write a brief report on how to improve the business's liquidity.

Suggested answers for Activity 5.2.2

Scenario	Is this good or bad for working capital and liquidity?	Explain your answer
François de Gould is a sole trader based in South Africa. He arranges flowers for weddings and summer balls. François normally allows customers two months' credit when paying for their flowers. However, François has to pay his suppliers within a week of buying the flowers.	This is bad for working capital.	As François allows customers two months' credit, he will have to wait two months until he receives any payment. As he has only one week to pay his suppliers, this could mean that he has to wait seven weeks until he has the cash to purchase more flowers. This might mean he is unable to buy as much inventory (stock) as he needs.
Charlie and Jack started C&J Male Clothing two years ago. They have designed a new range of summer clothing. However, there are only two weeks left of the summer period and they still have 85 per cent of their stock.	This is bad for working capital.	A business needs to ensure that it has the right amount of inventory to meet demand. If it has too much inventory (as in this scenario), it will have money tied up in inventory that it will not be able to sell.
Fanchi Construction PLC is an Italian construction firm. It has just negotiated a new six-month credit period with its suppliers, as customers are now demanding a two-month credit period before they pay Fanchi for jobs.	This is good for working capital.	Large businesses are able to negotiate longer credit periods as they place such large orders. As Fanchi has six months' credit, it can add value to the raw materials and receive payment for them before it has to pay its own suppliers (trade payables).
Exoniture is an antique furniture retailer based in Abu Dhabi, United Arab Emirates. When the business started, it took out a large loan with a very high interest rate in order to pay for the shop furnishings and to buy inventory. The business now has to pay large monthly repayments as well as expensive rent for a shop in Abu Dhabi's new shopping mall. New competition within the mall has resulted in a decrease in sales for Exoniture. For the last three months, the business's sales have not covered its monthly bills.	This is bad for working capital.	Because of the high repayments, especially to the bank, Exoniture will need to ensure that its sales are more than its bills. If it cannot make repayments to the bank, the business may have to close down. It is also unlikely that banks will lend Exoniture any more money to make up for the fall in revenue, as the business already has a loan that it is struggling to repay.

5.3 Income statements

5.3.1 WHAT PROFIT IS AND WHY IT IS IMPORTANT

Aims (5.3.1)

Knowledge

By the end of this section, students will understand:

- how a profit is made
- the importance of profit to private sector businesses, for example, reward for risk taking/enterprise, source of finance
- how to explain the difference between profit and cash.

Resources

- Student's Book pages 317–320
- Activity sheets 5.3.1A, 5.3.1B and 5.3.1C
- Access to ICT for research activity

Key business terms

business objectives; costs; dividends; gross profit; profit; overheads; raw materials; revenue expenditure; sales revenue; turnover

Lesson ideas

You should aim to cover the materials in 5.3.1 in two one-hour lessons, plus, as appropriate, a homework assignment. To achieve the Aims for this topic, we recommend doing some of the following activities over the course of the lessons.

Starter suggestion

What is profit? Explain the terms 'sales revenue', 'costs' and 'profit'. Show students a simple worked example, as on page 319 of the Student's Book.

Main lesson ideas

Student activity: Ask students to complete Activity 5.3.1A. They will calculate the profit made by the business in each scenario.

Discussion and note-taking (whole class): Once students have calculated their answers, explain the terms 'gross profit' and 'profit'. You may want to explain the difference using the term 'net profit' to make the differences clear to students. Tell them to make notes as necessary.

Student activity: Ask students to attempt Activity 5.3.1B. This will introduce the concepts of sales revenue, costs and profit and allow students to calculate how profit is made, using some basic numeracy skills.

Cash and profit: Clear up the common misconception that cash and profit is the same thing. It is important that students can differentiate between these terms. To illustrate the point, recap a business's inflows: loans, share capital and sales revenue. Stress the point that it is only sales revenue that is included when calculating profit.

Student activity: Ask students to attempt Activity 5.3.1C. They will answer questions on a case study to help them understand how cash and profit are different.

Skills activity: Ask students to carry out the Skills activity on page 320 of the Student's Book. The emphasis is on improving their application and evaluation skills. They should enter 'increase in profit' into an internet search engine to research four businesses that have seen an improvement in profit.

Tip: This would make a useful homework exercise.

Plenary suggestion

Knowledge check: Ask students to answer the Knowledge check questions on page 320 of the Student's Book. Go through the answers and use this opportunity to emphasise the aims.

Answers to Student's Book activities

Knowledge check (page 320)

1 **Define** the following terms:

   a) Revenue

   The money a business receives from customers.

   Alternatively: selling price × quantity sold

   b) Cost of sales

   The cost of the raw materials needed to make the product.

   c) Overheads

   Costs that are not associated with making a product but that are still essential for a business to operate.

2 **Identify** four overheads that the business might have to pay.

   Any four from: rent; salaries (not wages); electricity; rates; power; marketing; transport costs; administration costs; interest/finance costs.

3 **Calculate** the business's revenue.

   40 000 × $240 = $9 600 000

   Student answers should show working and include the currency.

4 If each unit cost Al Hasawi International $200 to make, **calculate** the business's gross profit for the year.

Sales	$9 600 000
Costs of sales = 40 000 × $200	$8 000 000
Gross profit	$1 600 000

5 Student answers should show working and include the currency.

6 **Calculate** the business's profit for the year.

   $1 600 000 − $1 400 000 = $200 000

   Student answers should show working and include the currency.

5.3.1 What profit is and why it is important: Activity A

Activity type

Calculation activity

Content

Calculating profit

Time

15 minutes

Key terms

costs; profit; sales revenue

Aims

To understand how to calculate profit (5.3.1)

Skills practised

AO1: Knowledge and understanding	✓
AO2: Application	
AO3: Analysis	
AO4: Evaluation	

Preparation

Make one copy of Activity sheet 5.3.1A for each student in the class.

Procedure

1. Make sure students understand the terms 'sales revenue', 'costs' and 'profit'.
2. Give each student a copy of Activity sheet 5.3.1A.
3. Ask students to read the scenarios and work out each business's profit for the year. They can work individually or in pairs depending on their ability.
4. Advise students to lay out their workings using the headings Sales, Costs and Profit.

Teacher tip: Scenario 2 is more difficult than Scenario 1 as it requires more advanced numeracy skills. You may wish to give students either Scenario 1 or Scenario 2 depending on their mathematical ability.

Extension: Change the numbers involved in the scenarios to make the maths more challenging. Alternatively, display more numbers as percentages, which students will have to work out before they can calculate the profit.

Answers to Activity 5.3.1A

Scenario 1

	$
Sales	200 000
Cost of materials	100 000
Other costs	70 000
Profit	30 000

Scenario 2

	$
Sales	
Kitchen stools	40 000
Dining room chairs	200 000
Beds	150 000
	390 000
Cost of materials	
Kitchen stools	20 000
Dining room chairs	100 000
Beds	75 000
	195 000
Other costs	
Rent	25 000
Salaries	70 000
Bills	24 000
Marketing	30 000
	149 000
Profit	46 000

5.3.1 What profit is and why it is important: Activity B

Activity type
Case study and questions

Content
Calculating profit

Time
30 minutes

Key terms
gross profit; profit; sales revenue

Aims
To understand how profit is made (sales revenue, gross profit and profit) (5.3.1)

Skills practised

AO1: Knowledge and understanding	✓
AO2: Application	✓
AO3: Analysis	
AO4: Evaluation	

Preparation
Make one copy of Activity Sheet 5.3.1B for each student.

Procedure

1. Hand out Activity sheet 5.3.1B to each student.

   Note: The questions are differentiated to meet different ability levels: Questions 7, 8 and 9 are designed to stretch more able mathematicians.

2. Read the case study to the class. Alternatively, before they start work on the questions, ask students to read the case study and questions in small groups and to identify the key points.

3. Students should work on the questions individually.

4. When students have finished, discuss the answers with the class and ask students to explain their workings. Alternatively, mark the students' answers as an assessment of their understanding of this topic.

Teacher tip: There are a number of percentages included within the questions. Depending on the group's ability, you may have to explain to students how to read simple pie charts and calculate percentages. For example:

19% of $210 900

$210 900 × 0.19 = $40 071

Or:

210 900/100 × 19 = $40 071

Extension: Students should work out which factory has been more profitable. They will need to calculate the profitability margins. This would be a good introduction to analysing accounts.

Answers to Activity 5.3.1B

1. 105 450 × $2 = $210 900

2. Answers to Question 2

   a) UK   43% $210 900 × 0.43 = $90 687
   b) France 19% $210 900 × 0.19 = $40 071
   c) Austria 7% $210 900 × 0.07 = $14 763

3. Sales revenue $210 900
   Cost of sales $94 905 (105 450 × 0.90)
   Gross profit $115 995
4. Overheads $26 000
   Profit $89 995
5. Number of sales 105 450 increases by 8%.
   105 450 × 1.08 = 113 886
   Cost of sales increases by 10% per unit
   $0.90 × 1.10 = $0.99 per unit
   Overheads increase by 12%
   $26 000 × 1.12 = $29 120
   Sales revenue $227 772
   Cost of sales $112 747 (113 886 × 0.99)
   Gross profit $115 025
   Overheads $29 120
   Profit $85 905
   Profit for the year will fall from $89 995 to $85 905 which is a decrease of $4090.
6. Answers to Question 6

Product	Units sold	Selling price	Sales revenue
Mini chocolate eggs	135 000	$1.25	$168 750
Chocolate pears	270 000	$2.75	$742 500
Total			**$911 250**

7. Answers to Question 7

Product	Units sold	Cost of production	Cost of sales
Mini chocolate eggs	135 000	$0.50	$67 500
Chocolate pears	270 000	$1.10	$297 000
Total			**$364 500**

Gross profit $546 750
Overheads $350 000
Profit $196 750

8. Answers to Question 8

Product	Units sold	Selling price	Sales revenue
Mini chocolate eggs	128 250	$1.25	$160 313
Chocolate pears	256 500	$2.75	$705 375
Total			$865 688

Product	Units sold	Cost of production	Cost of sales
Mini chocolate eggs	128 250	$0.50	$64 125
Chocolate pears	256 500	$1.10	$282 150
Total			$346 275

Gross profit $519 413
Overheads $400 000
Profit $19 413

9 Answers to Question 9

	Europe	Middle East	Total
Sales revenue	$227 772	$865 688	$1 093 460
Cost of sales	$112 747	$346 275	$459 022
Gross profit			$634 438
Overheads	$29 120	$400 000	$429 120
Profit			$205 318

Extension

Which factory has been more profitable?

	Europe	Middle East
Sales revenue	$227 772	$865 688
Profit	$85 905	$119 413
Profitability margin	38%	14%

Even if the sales revenue of the Europe factory is less, it is more profitable as it is turning more of its sales revenue into profit.

5.3.1 What profit is and why it is important: Activity C

Activity type

Case study and questions

Content

Interpreting a cash flow forecast

Time

30 minutes

Key terms

cash flow; cash inflow; cash outflow costs, profit; revenue

Skills practised

AO1: Knowledge and understanding	✓
AO2: Application	✓
AO3: Analysis	✓
AO4: Evaluation	

Preparation

Make one copy of Activity sheet 5.3.1C for each student in the class.

Aims

To understand the difference between cash and profit and why profit is important to a private sector organisation (5.3.1)

Procedure

1 Read the case study to the class.
2 Ask students to look at the cash flow forecast and to read the questions. They should highlight the information in the forecast that will help them to answer the questions.
3 Students should work on the questions individually or in pairs, depending on their ability.
4 Walk around the classroom providing help where necessary by asking students questions and pointing out the information they need to use in the cash flow forecast.
5 When students have finished, discuss the answers with the class and ask students to explain their workings. Alternatively, mark the students' answers as an assessment of their understanding of this topic.

Teacher tip: You may need to recap on cash flow before the activity, as the case study questions require students to have knowledge of both cash and profit.

Extension: Students should calculate the gross profit and profit per month. They should use profit margins to make a judgement on which month is the most profitable for Cardsplus PLC.

Answers to Activity 5.3.1C

1 Inflows: Sales revenue

Outflows: Suppliers; Electricity; Marketing; Salaries; Rent

2 Answers to Question 2

Sales revenue	$10.8
Cost of sales	$7.0
Gross profit	**$3.8**
Overheads	$2.8
Profit	**$1.0**

3 Profit only concerns the inflows from customers and the costs associated with generating that income. For example, although a loan is an income, it is not received from selling a product or service so is not considered when calculating profit. The same applies to the loan repayment and the purchasing of new machinery. Although they are outflows that have to be paid, they are nothing to do with calculating profit for a period of time.

4 Answers to Question 4

Benefits of paying out the dividends	Drawbacks of paying out the dividends
• It will keep shareholders happy. • It might increase the value of shares, which is good if the company wants to raise more money by issuing more shares in the future.	• The company has only made $1 million over the last six months – this will leave no profit available for other things such as reinvestment. • Despite making a profit, the company's cash-flow forecast suggests cash-flow or liquidity problems. Therefore it does not have any money to pay shareholders because of loan repayments and the new machinery. • The company has already paid out $1.2 million in dividends this year; that should be enough.

Extension

Sales revenue	1.25	1.25	1.25	1.25	1.70	4.10
Cost of sales	0.60	0.60	0.60	0.70	2.50	2.00
Gross profit	0.65	0.65	0.65	0.55	−0.80	2.10
Overheads	0.40	0.30	0.70	0.30	0.40	0.70
Profit	0.25	0.35	−0.05	0.25	−1.20	1.40
Profit margin	20%	28%		20%		34%

Therefore, December is the most profitable month as the company turns more of its sales into profit.

5.3.2 Income statements

Aims (5.3.2)

Knowledge

By the end of this section, students will understand:

- the main features of an income statement, for example, revenue, cost of sales, gross profit, profit and retained profit
- how to use simple income statements in decision making based on profit calculations.

Resources

- Student's Book pages 321–324
- Activity sheets 5.3.2A, 5.3.2B and 5.3.2C
- Scissors and glue sticks

Key business terms

cost of sales; dividends; income statement; operating profit; partnership; public limited company (PLC); retained profit; sales revenue; sole trader; stakeholders

Lesson ideas

You should aim to cover the materials in 5.3.2 in two one-hour lessons, plus, as appropriate, a homework assignment. To achieve the Aims for this topic, we recommend doing some of the following activities over the course of the lessons.

Starter suggestion

Student activity: Ask students to complete Activity 5.3.2A. This introduces them to the main components of an income statement. Review the answers and recap the difference between gross profit and profit.

Main lesson ideas

Discussion and note-taking (whole class): Develop students' understanding of an income statement using pages 321–324 of the Student's Book. Emphasise the common misconception (see below). Go through one or both of the worked examples on pages 321 and 322 of the Student's Book. Tell students to make notes.

Common misconception: The income statement shows how much profit a business has made over a period of time.

- It is important that students grasp that the bottom figure, the retained profit, is how much the business has made over that trading period. It is not the amount of cash flow it has to spend on paying bills.
- It is important that students understand that only costs and revenues associated with trading are included on the income statement.

Student activity: Ask students to complete Activity 5.3.2B. This matching and sorting activity will consolidate their knowledge of the key terms involved in an income statement. They may refer to the Student's Book.

Discussion and note-taking (whole class): Explain to students how businesses can use an income statement to make decisions in order to improve profit (page 323 of the Student's Book).

Skills activity: Students should complete the Skills activity on page 324 of the Student's Book. They could work individually or with a partner to complete the income statement; however, they should write the report individually.

Students should lay out the income statement in the same format as that used on page 322 of the Student's Book, itemising all of the overheads.

Knowledge check: Students should answer the Knowledge check questions on page 324 of the Student's Book.

Tip: This would make a useful homework exercise.

Plenary suggestion

Student activity: Students should complete Activity 5.3.2C. They will put the rows in an income statement into the correct order and fill in the missing figures. Finish the lesson by going through the correct layout and test students on what the figures mean.

Answers to Student's Book activities

Skills activity (page 324): possible outcomes

The income statement should be as follows:

Income statement for Taste of Asia PLC	
	£ million
Sales revenue	80
Cost of sales	45
Gross profit	35
Overheads	
Rent	4
Salaries and wages	4
Marketing	6
Insurance	1
Total	**15**
Operating profit	20
Finance costs	5
Profit before tax	15
Tax @ 20%	3
Profit after tax	12
Dividends	10
Retained profit	2

Possible content of the Finance Director's report:

- Last year the business made £2 million retained profit. This year it needs to increase profit by £3 million in order to achieve its objective.
- Marketing costs could be lowered, but this may mean that sales may fall, reducing the sales revenue.
- The business could use cheaper suppliers. However, as this is a restaurant business, the quality of the raw materials and food is its main selling point, so this would be risky.
- The business could increase the selling price of meals. However, an increase in selling price might reduce demand, lowering sales revenue.
- Taste of Asia PLC could, and ultimately should, reduce the dividend payment if it wants more retained profit. However, this may make the shareholders unhappy. This could lead to the shareholders requesting a change at the next AGM or wanting to sell their share (although this would not impact on Taste of Asia unless it wishes to raise more finance through share capital).

Knowledge check (page 324)

1 **Explain** the following terms that might appear on an income statement:

   a) Revenue

   The money received/coming into a business from customers/selling its product or service.

   b) Retained profit

   The profit earned over a period of time that is the business's to reinvest. Alternatively: The bottom figure of an income statement after all the costs have been taken off.

2 **Calculate** the year's profit.

   $4.0 million – $2.5 million = $1.5 million

   Student answers should include workings out.

3 **Define** the following terms:

   a) Gross profit

   The profit made once the cost of sales has been subtracted.

   Alternatively: sales revenue – cost of sales = gross profit.

   b) Overhead

   The costs incurred by a business that are not directly linked to producing the product.

5.3.2 Income statements: Activity A

Activity type

Sorting activity

Content

Creating an income statement

Time

15 minutes

Key terms

gross profit; profit; sales revenue

Aims

To understand the main elements of an income statement (5.3.2)

Skills practised

AO1: Knowledge and understanding	✓
AO2: Application	
AO3: Analysis	
AO4: Evaluation	

Preparation

Make one copy of Activity sheets 5.3.2A (1) and 5.3.2A (2) for every pair of students in the class. Cut out each row of the table on Activity sheet 5.3.2A (1), making sure each item and the associated figure remain on the same strip of paper. Each pair of students should have a glue stick.

Procedure

1. Explain to students that they are going to sort out some of the inflows and outflows for a business into two groups:
   - those associated with normal trading over a period of time
   - those **not** associated with normal trading over a period of time.

   They are then going to use the relevant inflows and outflows to create an income statement.

2. Divide the class into pairs and give each pair a set of the cut-out items from Activity sheet 5.3.2A (1) and a copy of Activity sheet 5.3.2A (2).

3. Students should place the two heading cards on the table in front of them. They then work with their partner to sort out the items under the two heading cards.

4. Go through the answers before students continue with the next part of the activity.

5. Students now select the inflows and outflows that they need to complete the income statement on Activity sheet 5.3.2A (2). They should discard any inflow or outflow items that are not associated with a business's normal trading over a particular period of time.

6. Students should lay the cut-out items in the correct places on the income statement. They can then calculate the gross profit and net profit and write these figures in the boxes with the bold outline. Allow students to use their Student's Book to help with this if necessary.

7. Go through the income statement with students so they can check their answers and make changes if necessary.

8. Students can then stick the items into place on the balance statement.

Teacher tip: It is important to stress that a loan and the repayment are not associated with profit as they are not linked to the customers or providing a product for customers. In addition, the purchase of machinery is not linked to a particular period of time. It is therefore not included when calculating profit.

Extension: You can extend the activity by asking students to add the following to the income statement, doing any necessary calculations:

- corporation tax at 12 per cent (students will need to calculate this)
- profit after tax (students will need to calculate this)
- dividends of $150 000
- retained profit (students will need to calculate this).

Answers to Activity 5.3.2A

Inflows (revenues)/Outflows (costs) associated with normal trading over time	
Money received from selling products to customers	$650 000
Cost of raw materials	$100 000
Electricity charge for the period	$20 000
Maintenance of machinery for the period	$35 000
Marketing costs for the period	$75 000
Finance costs (interest on loan) incurred over the period	$5000
Rent of premises	$60 000
Employees' salaries	$70 000
Inflows (revenues)/Outflows (costs) not associated with normal trading over time	
Money received from a loan	$400 000
Loan repayment	$50 000
Purchase of new machinery	$500 000

Income statement

Sales revenue	
Money received from selling products to customers	$650 000
Cost of sales	
Cost of raw materials	$100 000
Gross profit	**$550 000**
Less: Expenses (overheads)	
Electricity charge for the period	$20 000
Maintenance of machinery for the period	$35 000
Marketing costs for the period	$75 000
Finance costs (interest on loan) incurred over the period	$5000
Rent of premises	$60 000
Employees' salaries	$70 000
Profit	**$285 000**

Extension

Corporation tax at 12%	$34 200
Profit after tax	$250 800
Dividends	$150 000
Retained profit	$100 800

5.3.2 Income statements: Activity B

Activity type
Matching and sorting activity

Content
The key components of an income statement

Time
10 minutes

Key terms
corporation tax; dividends; expenses; gross profit; operating profit; profit after tax; profit before tax; retained profit; sales revenue

Aims
To identify the key components of an income statement (5.3.2)

Skills practised

AO1: Knowledge and understanding	✓
AO2: Application	
AO3: Analysis	
AO4: Evaluation	

Preparation
Make a copy of Activity sheet 5.3.2B for each pair of students in the class. Cut out the cards so that each key term and each definition is on a separate card.

Procedure

1 Tell students that they are going to consolidate their knowledge of the items on an income statement by doing a matching actvity.
2 Divide the class into pairs and give each pair a set of mixed-up cards from Activity sheet 5.3.2B.
3 Students take turns to read out a key term for their partner to find the matching definition.
4 Students should pair up each key term card and definition card as they go through the activity.
5 When they get to the end, they should read to match the correct term with the correct definition. This activity works best when students are working in pairs.
6 Go through the answers with the class.
7 Ask students to sort the cards into the order they would appear on an income statement. They can refer to the Student's Book if necessary. (The order on the activity sheet before it is cut up is the correct order.)

Teacher tip: *Keep a copy of the complete activity sheet to use as an answer sheet when checking students' answers.*

Extension: Students should complete step 7 of the activity without looking at the Student's Book.

5.3.2 Income statements: Activity C

Activity type
Sorting activity

Content
Completing an income statement

Time
10 minutes

Key terms
corporation tax; cost of sales; dividends; finance costs; overheads; profit, retained profit; sales revenue

Aims
To identify the key features of an income statement (5.3.2)

Skills practised

AO1: Knowledge and understanding	✓
AO2: Application	
AO3: Analysis	
AO4: Evaluation	

Preparation
Make a copy of Activity sheet 5.3.2C for each pair of students in the class. Cut out each row of the table on the activity sheet, making sure each item and the associated figure (or blank box) remain on the same strip of paper.

Procedure

1. Tell students that they are going to consolidate their learning from this topic by ordering and completing an income statement.
2. Divide the class into pairs and give each pair a set of the mixed-up rows from Activity sheet 5.3.2C.
3. Ask students to sort the rows into the correct order to construct an income statement.
4. They should then calculate the missing profit figures and write them in the spaces.
5. Finish the lesson by going through the correct layout and testing students on what all the figures mean.

Teacher tip: Use this as a plenary to round off work on this topic.

Answers to Activity 5.3.2C

Sales revenue	$450 000
Cost of sales	$250 000
Gross profit	$200 000
Expenses	$100 000
Operating profit	$100 000
Finance costs	$25 000
Profit before tax	$75 000
Tax	$25 000
Profit after tax	$50 000
Dividends	$45 000
Retained profit	$5000

5.4 Statement of financial position

5.4.1 THE MAIN ELEMENTS OF A STATEMENT OF FINANCIAL POSITION

Aims (5.4.1)

Knowledge

By the end of this section, students will understand:

- the main classifications of assets and liabilities, using examples.

Resources

- Student's Book pages 325–327
- Activity sheets 5.4.1A and 5.4.1B
- Access to ICT for research tasks

Key business terms

assets; current assets; current liabilities; equitable funds; equity; liabilities; non-current assets; non-current liabilities

Lesson ideas

You should aim to cover the materials in 5.4.1 in a single one-hour lesson, plus, as appropriate, a homework assignment. To achieve the Aims for this topic, we recommend doing some of the following activities over the course of the lesson.

Starter suggestions

Statement of financial position diagram: Explain that a statement of financial position lists all the assets (what a business owns) and how the business has paid for them (at any given time). Students should copy the image on page 325 of the Student's Book into their notebooks.

Student activity: Students should do Activity 5.4.1A. This will test their ability to distinguish between assets, liabilities and equity (money that has been invested that does not need to be paid back).

Main lesson activities

Concept map: Ask students to create a concept map of assets and liabilities, using pages 325–326 of the Student's Book to help them.

They should use the concept map to distinguish between:

- current and non-current assets
- current and non-current liabilities.

Definitions: Using pages 326–327 of the Student's Book, ask students to write definitions of all the assets and liabilities covered:

- property, machinery, technology, fixtures and fittings, vehicles, inventory, trade receivables, bank balance, mortgage, long-term loan, debenture, overdraft trade payables.

They should also write a definition of equitable funds and share capital.

Statement of financial position layout: Tell students how a simple statement of financial position is laid out, using the example on page 327 of the Student's Book. Students should make a note of the correct layout using the headings from the book.

Student activity: Students should complete Activity 5.4.1B. This will help them learn how the statement of financial position is laid out and understand, in more detail, how equity and liabilities fund a business's assets.

Skills activity: Students should attempt the Skills activity on page 327 of the Student's Book. They should copy the half-completed statement of financial position and then explain which business is performing better.

To answer the final bullet point, they should consider what else they might need to know in order to make a better judgement.

Teacher tip: This activity would make a good homework task.

Plenary suggestion

Knowledge check: Students should answer the Knowledge check questions on page 327 of the Student's Book. They can then peer assess each other's work.

Answers to Student's Book activities

Skills activity (page 327): possible outcomes

	Business A	Business B
Non-current assets	$	$
Machinery	100	10
IT	30	100
Premises	70	40
	200	150
Current assets		
Inventory	15	2
Trade receivables	15	4
Cash	5	20
	35	26
Current liabilities		
Trade payables	(40)	(20)
Net current assets	(5)	6
Total	195	156

The statement of financial position shows us that Business A is more likely to be a manufacturing business, as it has more machinery and a larger amount of unsold stock (inventory). In contrast, Business B has more technological assets, which implies it might be a service business such as a bank or insurance company.

Business A has a greater amount of assets, i.e. it owns more. However, Business A also has more short-term debt as it has current liabilities of 40, compared with 20 for Business B.

For either reason, students can select Business A or B. It would be useful to know:

- How long has each business been in operation? (The longer they have been operating, the more assets they are likely to have.)
- How does this compare with their competitors?
- How much profit did they make over the year?
- For the manufacturing business, when was the statement of financial position recorded? How much of the $15 of inventory does the business anticipate selling?

Knowledge check (page 327)

1 **Explain** the following terms using examples:

   a) Non-current asset

   An item a business owns that they intend to keep/use for longer than a year.

   Examples include (any one): property; vehicles; technology; machinery; fixtures and fittings.

   b) Current asset

   An item a business owns that it intends to use within a period of a year.

   Examples include (any one): money in the bank; cash in hand; trade receivables; inventory (stock).

2 Using an example, **explain** the term current liability.

   Current liability is a debt that needs to be paid within the period of a year.

   Examples include (any one): trade payables; overdrafts.

5.4.1 The main elements of a statement of financial position: Activity A

Activity type
Matching activity

Content
Assets and liabilities

Time
15 minutes

Key terms
asset; equity; liabilities

Aims
To identify the difference between assets and liabilities (5.4.1)

Skills practised

AO1: Knowledge and understanding	✓
AO2: Application	
AO3: Analysis	
AO4: Evaluation	

Preparation
Make one copy of the definition cards on Activity sheet 5.4.1A (1) and one copy of the answer table on Activity sheet 5.4.1A (2) for each pair or small group of students in the class. Cut out the definition cards around the dotted lines, so that each card contains the key term and the matching definition.

Procedure
1. Explain that students are going to sort out a number of assets, liabilities and equity into the correct categories.
2. Divide the class into pairs or small groups and give each pair/group a set of definition cards and a copy of the table from Activity sheets 5.4.1A (1) and 5.4.1A (2).
3. Students take turns to pick a definition card and read it to their partner/group. They must discuss each card and decide where it goes in the assets, liabilities and equity table.
4. They may refer to pages 325–327 of the Student's Book if they need help.
5. Go through the answers as a class and ask students to either write the key terms in the correct places on the table or stick the definition cards into place.

Teacher tip: Write or display a definition of an asset, a liability and equity on the whiteboard – this will help students make the correct choices.

Extension: Students should sort the liabilities and assets into current (less than a year) and non-current (more than a year).

Variation: For a more challenging activity, you could separate the terms from the definitions. Then students could match the correct definition with each term before they classify each item as an asset, a liability or equity.

Activity 5.4.1A: Answers

Definitions: As on Activity sheet 5.4.1A (1)

Assets: *Non-current:* Machinery; Premises; Vehicles

Current: Inventory; Trade receivables; Bank balance

Liabilities: *Non-current:* Loan

Current: Overdraft; Trade payables

Equity: Share capital; Retained profit

5.4.1 The main elements of a statement of financial position: Activity B

Activity type

Constructing a statement of financial position

Content

The key components of a statement of financial position

Time

30 minutes

Key terms

assets; cash; inventory; liabilities, trade payables; trade receivables

Aims

Skills practised

AO1: Knowledge and understanding	✓
AO2: Application	✓
AO3: Analysis	✓
AO4: Evaluation	✓

Preparation

Make one copy of Activity sheet 5.4.1B (1) and one copy of the statement of financial position template (either Activity sheet 5.4.1B (2) or (3)) for every student in the class.

To understand the key components of a statement of financial position and how they are constructed (5.4.1)

Procedure

1. Explain the layout of the statement of financial position on Activity sheet 5.4.1B (2), which lists:
   - non-current assets
   - current assets
   - current liabilities
   - capital employed (equity and non-current liabilities).
2. Students should read through the case material on Activity sheet 5.4.1B (1).
3. Explain that the statement of financial position gives an historical look at what the business has bought and how it has been paid for. Students should highlight the key terms in the text and identify whether these are assets or liabilities.
4. Students complete the statement of financial position on either Activity sheet 5.4.1B (2) or Activity sheet 5.4.1B (3) using the information in the case material.
5. They then answer Questions 2 and 3 on Activity sheet 5.4.1B (1).

Teacher tip: Students should use their statement of financial position (Question 1) when answering Questions 2 and 3. Therefore, it might be suitable to peer assess students' answers to Question 1 before they attempt Questions 2 and 3.

Variation: Two versions of the statement of financial position template have been provided to allow for differentiation.

- Activity sheet 5.4.1B (2) includes definitions and can be used with EAL or for less able students.
- Activity sheet 5.4.1B (3) doesn't include the definitions.

Extension: Once students have completed the statement of financial position, you could ask them to calculate the ratio of current assets to current liabilities.

Suggested answers to Activity 5.4.1B

1 Answers to question 1

Non-current assets	Items that are owned by a business for more than one year	$
	Property	100 000
	Machinery	10 000
	(A) Total	110 000
Current assets	Items the business owns, but is expected to use within the year	
	Stock (Inventory)	3000
	Trade receivables	2000
	Bank	2000
	(B) Total	7000
Current liabilities	Debts that the business will have to pay within the year	
	Creditors	3000
	(C) Total	3000
Net current assets	The working capital the business has in the short term after its debts are taken into account	
	(B – C) Total	4000
Net assets	The total amount a business is worth, all of the assets minus the short-term debt. This should be a balancing figure.	
	(A + B – C) Total	114 000
Financed by:	Long-term debt and equity used to fund the business	
	Long-term loan	10 000
	Mortgage	60 000
	Share capital	40 000
	Reserves	4000
Capital employed:	Long-term loans + equity	
	The other balancing figure	
	Total	114 000

2 Answers could include: At the moment the business does not have enough money to pay for the stock. They only have $2000 in the bank when their short-term debt (trade payables) are $3000. However, they will be capable of paying the debt on the provision that they are either paid by their trade receivables or they sell some more stock

3 Answers could include
   a) Sell stock.

Advantages	Disadvantages
Turn inventory in cash that can be used to pay bills	None

   b) Sell more stock by having a sale.

Advantages	Disadvantages
Gain cash quickly to pay the bills	Will not receive the full amount for their inventory. This will lower their potential profit.

   c) Ask trade receivables to pay quicker.

Advantages	Disadvantages
Customers pay quicker meaning they have the cash to pay the trade payables.	

   d) Offer a discount to trade receivables as an incentive to pay quicker.

Advantages	Disadvantages
Gain cash quickly to pay the bills	Will not receive the full amount from the customers. This will lower their potential profit.

5.4.2 Interpreting a statement of financial position

Aims (5.4.2)

Skills

By the end of this section, students will be able to:

- interpret a simple statement of financial position and make deductions from it, for example, how a business is financing its activities and what assets it owns, sale of inventories to raise finance.

Resources

- Student's Book pages 328–330
- Activity sheet 5.4.2
- Access to ICT for research task

Key business terms

assets; capital employed; equity; liabilities; liquidity; sources of finance

Lesson ideas

You should aim to cover the materials in 5.4.2 in a single one-hour lesson, plus, as appropriate, a homework assignment. To achieve the Aims for this topic, we recommend doing some of the following activities over the course of the lesson.

Starter suggestion

Review of sources of finance: To understand the statement of financial position and make deductions from it, students will need to understand how the business has paid for its assets (items that the business owns). So they will need an understanding of sources of finance.

Recap on the key sources by asking students how they would pay for the following types of assets:

- Property – students might suggest a mortgage or loan.
- Machinery – students might suggest a loan, share capital and/or retained profit.
- Vehicles – students might suggest a loan, share capital and/or retained profit.
- Inventory – students might suggest trade credit.

Main lesson activities

Discussion and note-taking (whole class): Go through the layout of a statement of financial position and the worked example on pages 328–329 of the Student's Book.

It is important that students understand that a statement of financial position does not show how much profit a business has made over a year. However, it does show how much of the business's profit has been reinvested into the business. This will be shown on the statement of financial position as 'reserves'.

Student activity: Once students understand that a statement of financial position is a list of assets (what a business owns) and a list of how they have paid for the assets, they should be able to attempt Activity 5.4.2.

They can use the worked example on page 329 of the Student's Book to help them answer the questions based on the three statements of financial position.

Skills activity: Students should work in pairs to do the Skills activity on page 330 of the Student's Book. They will prepare a forecast statement of financial position for a business they would like to start up.

Knowledge check: Students should answer the Knowledge check questions on page 330 of the Student's Book.

Tip: This could be given as a homework task.

Plenary

Feedback: Ask students to share their findings from the Skills activity with a larger group or with the whole class. Each pair should state the benefits and disadvantages of using either equity or liabilities to pay for the assets for their business.

Answers to Student's Book activities

Skills activity (page 330): Possible outcomes

Students could use a table like the one below to help them list the assets they will need and how they will be paid for.

Potential assets	How will they be paid for?	Liability or equity?

Students can then use the worked example on page 329 to help them compile their forecast statement of financial position. For example, a restaurant might require the following assets:

Assets	$	Liabilities (how they will pay for them)	$
Premises	150 000	Mortgage	150 000
Oven	10 000	Loan	55 000
Furnishings and equipment	45 000	Trade payables	5000
Inventory	5000		

Knowledge check (page 330)

1 **Identify** and **explain** two stakeholders that might be interested in a business's statement of financial position.
   - The bank will be interested, as it will want to see how much existing debt the business has. This will influence the bank's decision whether to lend the business any more money.
   - Suppliers will be interested, as they will want to see that the business has sufficient current assets to cover its existing current liabilities. This will influence their decision whether to allow any credit to the business for future orders.

2 **Explain** the difference between equity and non-current liabilities.
   - Equity is money that has been invested in the business and that does not have to be paid back. It comes from shareholders' or owners' funds or retained profit.
   - Non-current liabilities are debts that have to be paid back over a period longer than one year, for example, a bank loan.

   Students must explain the difference between the two terms.

3 **Explain** how a statement of financial position can show how a business has funded its assets.

   A statement of financial position will show:
   - how much liability (debt) a business has
   - how much share capital it has invested
   - how much retained profit (reserves) it has invested.

5.4.2 Interpreting a statement of financial position: Activity

Activity type
Worksheet

Content
Interpreting and comparing three simple statements of financial position

Time
30 minutes

Key terms
assets; capital employed; equity; liabilities; liquidity; sources of finance

Aims
To interpret a simple statement of financial position and make deductions from it (5.4.2)

Skills practised

AO1: Knowledge and understanding	✓
AO2: Application	✓
AO3: Analysis	✓
AO4: Evaluation	

Preparation
Make a copy of Activity sheet 5.4.2 for every student in the class.

Procedure

1. Explain to students that they will be using their knowledge to interpret and compare three simple statements of financial position.
2. Give each student a copy of Activity sheet 5.4.2.
3. Ask students to look at statements of financial position A, B and C. Recap the key terms used on the statements and ask students to tell you what each of these terms means.
4. Students should work individually to answer the questions relating to the statements of financial position. Encourage them to refer to Section 5.1 (pages 292–307 of the Student's Book) to help them.
5. Go through the answers with the class. Students can complete any questions they could not answer.

Teacher tip: Encourage students to use the financial ratios covered in Topic 5.5.1 (pages 331–336 of the Student's Book) to develop their understanding of statements of financial position and ratio analysis.

Extension: Recap the concept of gearing covered in Topic 5.1.2 (see page 296 of the Student's Book). Remind students (or ask them to tell you) that this is a way of measuring how much of a business's capital employed (invested money) has been borrowed from the bank.

$$\frac{\text{Long-term loans}}{\text{Capital employed}} \times 100$$

Ask students to calculate the gearing for each of the three statements of financial position and to explain the drawbacks of borrowing large amounts of money from a bank.

Suggested answers to Activity 5.4.2

1 Business B ($650 million).

2 Retained profit does not need to be paid back. Therefore, the business does not have to make repayments in the future that can affect its cash flow.

Retained profit does not require any additional interest or dividend payments. This means that the business can retain more of its profit in the future.

3 $80 million of Business C's capital employed has been borrowed from the bank.

4 The business has to pay back the loan, which means it must ensure it has sufficient funds each month to make the repayment.

Loans have to be paid back with interest. Interest is a cost, so the business might not make as much profit.

5 One benefit of using share capital as a source of finance is that the business does not have to make any repayments with interest, which means it has lower costs than businesses with high amounts of borrowing.

One disadvantage of using share capital is the business will have to pay more dividends, which means it can reinvest less of its profit into the business in the future.

6 Business C has the worst liquidity. This is because it has more current liabilities than current assets, which means it will have to sell some of its non-current assets to pay its short-term debt.

Business B has the best liquidity, as it has net current assets of $80 million. This means that the business has sufficient cash to pay off its short-term debt.

However, much of Business B's current assets are tied up in inventory and there is no guarantee that it will ever sell the inventory.

Therefore, Business A could also claim to have the best liquidity, as this business has net current assets of $45 million but much lower levels of inventory.

	Business A	Business B	Business C
Current ratio	2.13 : 1	2.33 : 1	0.50 : 1
Acid test	1.38 : 1	0.83 : 1	0.13 : 1

Extension

Gearing

Business A	Business B	Business C
$\frac{100}{465} \times 100 = 21.5\%$	$\frac{100}{650} \times 100 = 15.4\%$	$\frac{80}{140} \times 100 = 57.1\%$

A business with high gearing is unlikely to be offered any future loans by a bank, as the business will have too much to pay back.

In addition, a highly geared business will have to pay more interest, which will lower its profit.

5.5 Analysis of accounts

5.5.1 PROFITABILITY AND FINANCIAL PERFORMANCE
Aims (5.5.1, 5.5.3)

Knowledge

By the end of this section, students will understand:

- the concept and importance of profitability.
- how to interpret the financial performance of a business by calculating and analysing profitability ratios and liquidity ratios: gross profit margin, profit margin, return on capital employed, current ratio, acid test ratio.

Resources

- Student's Book pages 331–336
- Activity sheets 5.5.1A, 5.5.1B and 5.5.1C
- Access to ICT for research tasks (company websites with company accounts)

Key business terms

acid test ratio; business performance; current ratio; evaluation of liquidity ratios; gross profit margin; liquidity; profit margin; profitability; return on capital employed (ROCE)

Lesson ideas

You should aim to cover the materials in 5.5.1 in a single one-hour lesson, plus, as appropriate, a homework assignment. To achieve the Aims for this topic, we recommend doing some of the following activities over the course of the lesson.

Starter suggestion

Concept map: Ask students to work in groups of 2–4 to create a concept map of all the different ways to analyse a business's performance. They could consider the following:

- profitability
- liquidity
- market share
- number of outlets/branches
- value of sales revenue
- number of units sold
- number of customers.

Encourage students to think about what they have learned so far from the Section 5 topics.

Main lesson activities

Discussion and note-taking (whole class): Take feedback of students' ideas from the lesson starter, with emphasis on profitability and liquidity. Ask students to make notes on profitability and liquidity ratios using pages 331–335 of the Student's Book.

Make sure you explain the following:

- The difference between profit and profitability – emphasise that profitability can be easily compared with other businesses, whereas profit is determined by the size of the business.
- A business's performance should be evaluated from the viewpoint of both its profitability and its liquidity. The more important measure, in the short term, is the business's liquidity, as the ability to pay debts is more important than making a trading profit over a particular period of time.

Student activity: Using their notes and the worked examples in the Student's Book, students should complete Activity 5.5.1. They will practise analysing accounts by calculating financial ratios based on a case study company.

Skills activity: Students can now attempt the Skills activity on page 336 of the Student's Book. They will research the accounts of three companies. They will present their findings as a formal report that includes a copy of the financial statements and their interpretation of the company's performance using relevant accounting ratios, including:

- profit and gross profit margin
- acid test
- current ratio
- ROCE.

Tip: This could be given as a homework task.

Plenary suggestion

Knowledge check: Students should answer the Knowledge check questions on page 336 of the Student's Book.

Answers to Student's Book activities

Skills activity (page 336): Possible outcomes

Students' reports should include:

- an income statement
- a statement of financial position.

Students could include the following to help them make a judgement about the business's profitability:

- profit margin
- gross profit margin
- ROCE.

Students could include the following to help them make a judgement about the business's liquidity:

- current ratio
- acid test.

Knowledge check (page 336)

1 **Explain** the following terms:

   a) Profit margin

   The amount of profit a business makes as a percentage of its sales.

   Or: The amount of the sales revenue that is turned into profit, expressed as a percentage. *Also allow the formula:* profit divided by revenue multiplied by 100.

   b) Liquidity

   The ability of a business to pay its short-term debt.

   Also allow the formula: current assets minus current liabilities.

2 **Calculate** the following ratios using this information.

   a) Gross profit margin

   $\dfrac{300\,000}{750\,000} \times 100 = 40\%$

   b) Profit margin

   $\dfrac{100\,000}{750\,000} \times 100 = 13\%$

   Students should show working out.

3 **Explain** what gross profit and profit margins will show Imran.

   The gross profit margin will show Imran how much of his sales he has turned into gross profit. This is the profit made after the cost of manufacturing the furniture has been taken off. The profit margin shows how much profit Imran has made after overheads have been taken off as a percentage of the sales revenue.

4 **Calculate** the following two ratios, using the information from the table.

   a) Current ratio

   $\dfrac{95\,000}{50\,000} = 1.9 : 1$

   b) Acid test

   $\dfrac{35\,000}{50\,000} = 0.7 : 1$

   Students should show working out.

5 **Explain** whether Imran should be concerned about his business's liquidity.

   - The current ratio shows the business's ability to pay off its short-term debt. For every $1 of debt the business has $1.90 in current assets to pay its debts. This is good, although it is $0.10 below the industry average.
   - The acid test shows the business's ability to pay off its short-term debt excluding inventory, as there is no guarantee that this will be sold. This figure is $0.40 below the industry average and shows that if the inventory is not sold then the business cannot pay its short-term debt.
   - Whether Imran should be concerned depends on how likely the business is to sell its inventory. If it cannot sell the inventory, it will have liquidity problems.

   The answer must include a judgement as to whether Imran should be concerned.

5.5.1 Profitability and financial performance: Activity

Activity type
Case study

Content
Using accounting ratios to analyse a business's performance

Time
45 minutes

Key terms
acid test; current ratio; gross profit margin; profit margin; return on capital employed

Skills practised

AO1: Knowledge and understanding	✓
AO2: Application	✓
AO3: Analysis	✓
AO4: Evaluation	✓

Preparation
Make a copy of the case study material (Activity sheets 5.5.1A and 5.5.1B) for every student. Make enough copies of the answer template (Activity sheet 5.5.1C) for all those students who will need help with structuring their answers.

Aims
To understand how to analyse accounts by calculating and interpreting the following ratios: gross profit margin, profit margin, current ratio, acid test, return on capital employed (5.5.1)

Procedure

1. Explain to students that they will be using a case study business to practise analysing a set of accounts. You could ask them to imagine they have been hired by the business to help them work out whether their performance has improved over the past year.
2. Give each student within the group a copy of the case study.
3. Ask students to read the case study and to highlight any key points they think will help them demonstrate application skills.
4. Using pages 331–335 of the Student's Book to help them, students should calculate all the possible ratios for last year and this year. Encourage students to interpret the results by asking: 'What do these ratios tell us about the business's liquidity and profitability?'

Variation: You could differentiate the activity by giving students a template (Activity sheet 5.5.1C) to complete.

Extension: Ask the more able mathematicians in the group to calculate the percentage change in the following figures:

- sales revenue
- non-current assets
- capital employed.

Teacher tip: When students are interpreting what the ratios show them, ask them why this might be the case. There are clues in the text.

5.5.4 Why and how accounts are used

Aims (5.5.4)

Knowledge

By the end of this section, students will understand:

- the needs of different users of accounts and ratio analysis
- how to explain how users of accounts and ratio results might use information to make business decisions, for example, whether to lend to or invest in the business.

Resources

- Student's Book pages 337–340
- Activity sheets 5.5.4A, 5.5.4B and 5.5.4C

Key business terms

liquidity; profitability; stakeholders

Lesson ideas

You should aim to cover the materials in 5.5.4 in a single one-hour lesson, plus, as appropriate, a homework assignment. To achieve the Aims for this topic, we recommend doing some of the following activities over the course of the lesson.

Starter suggestion

Newspaper headlines: Show students the newspaper headings on Activity sheet 5.5.4A. Ask them to make a concept map of all the stakeholders who would be interested in the information and why. They should do this for all the headlines. They can either work in pairs or in small groups.

Tip: You may need to recap on the key business stakeholders covered in Section 1.5.2 The role of stakeholder groups involved in business activity, pages 59–63 in the Student's Book.

Main lesson activities

Student activity: Following on from the starter activity, ask students to complete Activity 5.5.4B. This will help them to apply the same stakeholders (users) from the starter activity to the final accounts of a business, explaining why they might have an interest in the figures the accounts show. Students should complete the worksheet individually, using pages 338 and 339 of the Student's Book to help.

Skills activity: Students should complete the Skills activity on page 340 of the Student's Book. They should work in small groups/pairs and present their findings to the rest of the class. Make sure their presentation covers all the bullet points in the Skills activity.

Knowledge check: Students should answer the Knowledge check questions on page 340 of the Student's Book.

Tip: This could be given as a homework task.

Plenary suggestion

Student activity: Students work individually to complete Activity 5.5.4C. Provide the solutions for students to peer assess each other's work.

Answers to Student's Book activities

Skills activity (page 340): possible outcomes

A shareholder who wants long-term investment is ideally looking at a business that can grow so that they are likely to make a bigger profit in the future. Businesses that pay all of their profit as dividends have to borrow money from the bank to grow, meaning they have to pay interest.

Relevant ratios:

	Amadi Construction	ASM Buildings	Palmas & Balsas
Profit margin	47%	33%	58%
ROCE	35%	25%	23%

Choice of business to invest in:

- Amadi currently has the best return on investment and is paying $3000 in dividends each year, which is 86 per cent of their profit. However, this is not good for the long term, as the business is not reinvesting much and is having to borrow money to grow.
- ASM has the lowest profit margin so it is turning less of its sales into net profit. In addition, this business has the highest amount of debt. Its reserves of $500 indicate that it has not invested much of its previous years' profit back into the business.
- Palmas & Balsas has the highest profit margin, which shows it is turning more of its sales revenue into profit. In addition, although its ROCE is the lowest, it is reinvesting most of the profit (86%) into the business for long-term growth.

Knowledge check (page 340)

1 **Identify** and **explain** two stakeholders who might be interested in a business's income statement.
   - Government: will want to see an income statement, as the net profit figure is how corporation tax is calculated. Therefore the government will be able to see if the right amount of tax has been paid.
   - Shareholders: will want to see how much of the company's profit is being allocated to dividends. This will affect the future value of their shares.

   Also allow:
   - Lenders: potential lenders will want to ensure that the business makes sufficient profit to make the necessary repayments before they decide to offer the business any credit.
   - Competitors: competitors may want to see how their profit margins compare. They can use this information to measure their own business's performance.

2 **Explain** why potential shareholders might be interested in a business's profit margin.

   They will be interested because the net profit margin shows a business's profitability. They can use this to assess how much money the business is reinvesting to grow the business.

3 **Explain** how other businesses might make use of a competitor's gross profit margin.

   Businesses can look at competitors' gross profit margin to assess how efficiently they are using their raw materials. They can use this information to try to improve their own performance.

4 **Explain** how a bank might use a business's statement of financial position when deciding whether to lend the business money.

   A bank will want to see how much long-term debt the business already has; any more might make repayments too high. In addition, they are likely to want to see the value of assets the business holds to act as security should repayments not be made.

5.5.4 Why and how accounts are used: Activity B

Activity type
Annotation activity

Content
The users of business accounts

Time
30 minutes

Key terms
statement of financial position; income statements; stakeholders (users of accounts)

Aims
To understand the different users of business accounts (5.5.4)

Skills practised

AO1: Knowledge and understanding	✓
AO2: Application	✓
AO3: Analysis	✓
AO4: Evaluation	

Preparation
Make a copy of Activity sheet 5.5.4B for each student.

Procedure

1 Explain to students that they will be working on their own to identify which parts of an income statement and statement of financial position a number of stakeholders will be interested in. They will have to:
   - identify the stakeholder in each case
   - give a reason why the stakeholder is interested in this information.
2 Give each student a copy of Activity sheet 5.5.4B.
3 Students should annotate the income statement and statement of financial position by writing in the boxes. They should work individually, using pages 338 and 339 of the Student's Book if necessary.
4 Review students' answers in a class feedback session. Ask individual students to give their answers and ask other students to agree or disagree, justifying their opinions.

Teacher tip: You may need to review the key elements of an income statement and a statement of financial position before students complete the activity.

Extension: For a more in-depth analysis, ask students to use the accounts to calculate ratios.

Variation: For a slightly more difficult activity, erase the arrows linking the stakeholder boxes to the income statement and statement of financial position before copying the activity sheet. Students will then have to decide which parts of the income statement/statement of financial position each stakeholder will be interested in.

Answers to Activity 5.5.4B

Income statement

GROSS PROFIT:

Stakeholder: Competitors:

Interest: Would be interested to see how much profit the business makes from its raw materials. This is a measure of profitability and efficiently. Gross profit margin: 33%.

NET PROFIT:

Stakeholder: Government.

Interest: The government will use this figure to charge the business corporation tax. Profit margin: 17%.

DIVIDENDS:

Stakeholder: Shareholder

Interest: Shareholders will use the income statement to see how much of the business's profit is being allocated to dividends.

Balance sheet

CURRENT LIABILITIES:

Stakeholder: Trade payables

Interest: The trade payables may be interested to see if the business already has a high level of short-term debt before they agree to offer a credit period.

NET TOTAL ASSETS:

Stakeholder: Investors

Interest: Investors might want to see how much the business owns and how shareholders' money has been used in the past.

FINANCED BY:

Stakeholder: Lenders

Interest: Any potential lenders will want to see the balance sheet to see how much existing debt the business already has.

5.5.4 Why and how accounts are used: Activity C

Activity type
Matching activity

Content
The ways in which different stakeholders use accounts

Time
10 minutes

Key terms
statement of financial position; income statement; stakeholders (users of accounts)

Aims
To understand how different stakeholders use accounts (5.5.4)

Skills practised

AO1: Knowledge and understanding	✓
AO2: Application	
AO3: Analysis	
AO4: Evaluation	

Preparation
Make one copy of Activity sheet 5.5.4C for each student in the class.

Procedure

1. Tell students that they are going to review their knowledge of how different stakeholders use accounts by completing a matching activity. They need to match each stakeholder with what they look for in a business's accounts.
2. Give each student a copy of Activity sheet 5.5.4C.
3. Ask students to work individually to match each stakeholder group with the appropriate usage of accounts. They should draw a line between each stakeholder and the correct reason.
4. Students can then peer assess each other's work.

Teacher tip: This makes a good plenary activity to round off the topic.

Variation: You could cut out the boxes on the activity sheet to give students a set of cards to match up.

Extension: Only provide the students with the different uses of accounts. Tell them to identify the stakeholder group that they think best fits each usage.

Answers to Activity 5.5.4C

Trade payables: will want to see the level of net current assets to ensure that the business can pay its existing current liabilities.

Shareholders: will want to see the amount of profit that has been allocated to dividends.

Government: will check the profit figure in the income statement. This is the figure that is taxable.

Lenders: will check the amount of long-term liabilities in the statement of financial position before making a decision to lend the business more money.

Competitors: will want to see what margins a business is operating on and how efficiently it is using its raw materials.

Investors: will want to see the net total assets to see how much the business is worth. This will help them make their decision.

Auditors: will check to make sure that the business's accounts have been constructed in accordance with official accounting regulations.

5 Financial information and decisions: Key terms revision

Define each term and provide an example or explanation. There are 2 marks per definition.

Term	Description/Definition
assets	
cash flow	
liabilities	
profit margin	
profitability	
raw materials	
share capital	
working capital	

6 External influences on business activity

Introduction

External Influences is an exciting topic. Relevant case studies and examples can be found on television, in newspapers and online every day, so lessons can be based on real, contemporary events. Yet for many students External Influences is conceptually abstract and entirely new – many of them will never have given the economy a second thought.

The aim of the activities within this section is therefore to break down the topics into manageable chunks and to give innovative examples of how the topics may be taught. Each chapter includes a substantive activity that can be used, in a fun and engaging way, to reinforce learning.
These activities include:

- a board game activity that examines **government policy**
- an investigation of **environmental and ethical** concerns using dominoes
- a student debate on **globalisation** and **international trade**
- an examination of **multinational companies** using a jigsaw reading activity
- a categorisation exercise based on **exchange rates**.

To introduce students to the concepts they will study and to help you gauge student knowledge, a useful activity might be collage creation.

Collage creation

Bring to class a wide range of newspapers, magazines and articles that cover the topics from this section. Split your class into small groups. Each group should consider one of the following questions:

- What types of things do governments do that affect businesses?
- How do business activities affect the environment?
- What are multinational firms? Are they a positive or negative influence on the countries in which they operate?
- What are business ethics? Can you find examples of ethical business decisions and unethical business decisions?
- What are exchange rates? Why do they change?

Using the various source materials, students should choose articles that help to represent an answer to the question issued to their group. They should cut out and stick articles, images and quotes in a collage that represents their answer.

While students are involved in this activity, move around the room listening to their discussions and asking questions to assess their level of current knowledge. Don't attempt to explain topics in detail; for now a basic overview is sufficient.

By this stage of the course, students should be aware of the skills needed to make progress. That said, you can use the **Skills Builder** at the end of Section 6 in the Student's Book to remind them that external influences do not affect all firms equally (*application*) – good progress comes from showing a clear ability to apply knowledge to a *particular* situation. Similarly, use the **Skills Builder** to remind students that recommending (*evaluation*) how a firm might respond to a particular external influence is the key to excellent progress.

6.1 Economic issues

6.1.1 BUSINESS CYCLE

Aims (6.1.1)

Knowledge	Resources
By the end of this section, students will understand: • the main stages of the business cycle, for example, growth, boom, recession, slump • the impact on businesses of changes in employment levels, inflation and Gross Domestic Product (GDP).	• Student's Book pages 354–357 • Activity sheets 6.1.1A and 6.1.1B • Access to ICT (if possible)

Key business terms

boom; business cycle; bust; gross domestic product (GDP); recession; recovery; slump; taxation; value added tax (VAT)

Lesson ideas

You should aim to cover the materials in 6.1.1 in one lesson, most likely alongside 6.1.2. To achieve the Aims in this topic, we recommend doing some of the following activities.

Starter suggestions

Show students the business cycle diagram (page 354 of the Student's Book). Provide them with the names of contemporary or historic businesses (for example, Apple, Tata, Kodak) and ask students to guess what stage of the business cycle they think these businesses are at presently.

Main lesson activities

Mime: Split the class into small groups and ask students to create a mime that represents each stage of the business cycle.

Student activity: Ask students to complete Activity 6.1.1. Students should write definitions for each term and then provide examples of their impact of their impacts, with an up-to-date example.

Compare: Students should research GDP data for five countries, including recent changes in the GDP. Alternatively, you could give them the relevant data.

- Tell them to analyse the differences in each country's GDP and to suggest reasons why the GDPs may be different.
- They should suggest how the changes in the GDP for each country may impact on businesses within that country.

Tip: You may find it useful to set the Skills activity on page 361 of the Student's Book (a GDP research exercise) as a homework leading into this class-based task.

Plenary suggestions

Ask students to read the case study on page 355 of the Student's Book. Either as independent study in the classroom or as a homework activity, students should research into how Starbucks are currently operating in regards to opening new stores in their country. Encourage students to consider where in the business cycle Starbucks are now.

Answers to Student's Book activities

Skills activity (page 361): possible outcomes

Basic information on GDP (and its components) is sufficient for this activity. Students may find the relevant data but find it difficult to extract the relevant information. Anticipate short articles with relevant facts/figures but limited linkage.

Tip: After briefly introducing GDP (a concept students may have studied in Geography), use this exercise as a homework task (supported by instructions to read the relevant section of the Student's Book) This can then be used as a starter activity for the opening lesson of this topic.

6.1.1 Business cycle: Activity

Activity type

Definitions and examples

Time

30 minutes (or at teacher discretion)

Content

Causes and effects of changes in the Business Cycle

Key terms

boom; recession; slump; recovery

Aims

To understand the causes and effects of the different stages of the business cycle (6.1.1)

Skills practised

AO1: Knowledge and understanding	✓
AO2: Application	✓
AO3: Analysis	✓
AO4: Evaluation	

Preparation

Make available a copy of Activity sheet 6.1.1A and Activity sheet 6.1.1B for each student. Students will also need access to the internet and either an exercise book or word processing software.

Procedure

1. Explain to students that they are going to complete the worksheet through a combination of using their prior knowledge and researching using the internet.
2. Students can either work individually, in pairs or in small groups.
3. Each student, pair, small group is to put an entry into each box for Activity sheet 6.1.1A.
4. On completion of Activity sheet 6.1.1A, students progress onto Activity sheet 6.1.1B where they write down their findings, in their own words, and apply this to different examples of businesses.
5. Students have finished when all boxes in Activity 6.1.1A have entries and all of the questions in Activity sheet 6.1.1B have been answered.

Teacher tip: Before students begin, students can spend a few minutes discussing in groups what they already know about the business cycle and its stages.

Variation: To make the activity more accessible for less able students, you could pre-populate some of the boxes so that they have fewer to research and complete.

6.1.2 How government control over the economy affects business activity and how businesses may respond

Aims (6.1.2)

Knowledge

By the end of this section, students will understand:

- how to identify government economic objectives, for example, increasing gross domestic product (GDP)
- the impact of changes in taxes and government spending
- the impact of changes in interest rates.

Resources

- Student's Book pages 358–366
- Activity sheets 6.1.2A and 6.1.2B
- Newspapers, business magazines and/or print-outs from relevant websites
- Dice and counters

Key business terms

balance of payments; bankruptcy; central bank; corporation tax; direct taxes; disposable income; downturn; economic growth; employment; export; fringe/non-financial benefits; gearing; government spending; import; income tax; inflation; interest rate; price elastic; price inelastic; price stability; productivity; spending power; taxation; value added tax (VAT)

Lesson ideas

You should aim to cover the materials in 6.1.2 over several weeks. Depending on the ability of your group and the time available, this topic could take 3–4 weeks. To achieve the Aims for this topic, we recommend doing some of the following activities over the course of the lessons.

Starter suggestions

What do you know? As students will not be familiar with many of the concepts in this topic, start by writing various key terms on the board and ask students if they know what they mean.

What do they do? To answer the question 'What do governments do?', students should work in small groups to list as many government activities as possible. They should then consider why governments undertake these activities. Use their responses as an introduction to the broad scope of this topic.

Interested? Introduce interest rates by displaying the deposit rates offered by a local bank on the board.

- Ask students what the rates mean.
- Repeat the exercise with loan rates from the same bank.
- Now ask them to imagine they have $1 million deposited (or the equivalent local currency) at the bank. Would they be happy or unhappy if the interest rates went up or down?
- Then ask them to imagine they have borrowed $1 million from the bank. How would they feel about changes in the rates?

Use their answers to lead into the topic.

Main lesson activities

Discussion and note-taking (whole class): Talk students through the various government economic objectives and policies. Tell them to take notes as appropriate. Focus on how businesses might respond to economic changes.

Cut it out: Take into class a large selection of newspapers, business magazines or print-outs from relevant websites.

Students should create a collage of articles and images related to this topic. For example, they might find an article reporting that the central bank has raised interest rates and link this in their collage to an article discussing the impact of interest rates on business. The key to the exercise is encouraging students to develop links between economic changes and business responses.

You could allow students to link articles by topic but not necessarily by story or theme.

Discussion (Taxing times): Students should list all the different taxes they can think of. To expand the list, ask them to consider what taxes their parents pay and what taxes companies pay. Illustrate the impact of a rise or fall in taxes by asking them to consider their own spending habits if a tax on pocket money (allowances) was introduced. Use this to lead into a discussion on the impact of taxation on business.

Research activity (Interest rates): Ask students to investigate the interest rate in a country of their choice. They should consider the following:

- What is the current interest rate?
- Who controls the interest rate (the government or the central bank)?
- Has the interest rate risen or fallen recently?
- Investigate why any change in the rate has taken place. Was the aim economic growth or economic slowdown?
- What might this have meant for businesses?

Pair students with a classmate who has chosen a different country. They should compare and contrast their findings. If possible, write students' findings on the board under the following headings:

- Country
- Who controls?
- Risen/Fallen, Why?
- Impacts.

Use this summary to discuss reasons for interest rate changes and the impact on business.

Investigation: Split the class into small groups and assign each group a different topic from this section (government spending, interest rates, and so on). Each group should prepare a presentation that explains the topic to the rest of the class AND explains how businesses might respond to economic changes related to this topic.

Knowledge check: Students should complete the Knowledge check questions on page 366 of the Student's Book.

Tip: This exercise could be given as a homework task.

Plenary suggestions

Student activity: Activity 6.1.2 is designed as a fun plenary for this topic. It could be used at the end of a lesson or as a summative lesson in itself. The aim of this board game activity is to review various government economic objectives and policies and the impact of those policies.

Answers to Student's Book activities

Knowledge check (page 366)

1 **Identify** one government objective.

   Any one from: sustainable economic growth; full employment; price stability; stable balance of payments. *Accept appropriate alternatives.*

2 **Explain** how economic growth is measured.

   GDP (gross domestic product): A measure of the value of all goods and services produced within a country over a period of time.

3 **Outline** the four main stages of the business cycle.

   Growth; boom; recession; slump.

4 **Explain** two strategies a business might use to survive a recession.

Strong brand; develop essential products; reduce products' price elasticity of demand; open overseas branches; introduce lead production; ensure continual cost-efficiency.

5 **Explain** the difference between direct and indirect taxes.
- Direct taxes are those charged on income (individual or company profit).
- Indirect taxes are applied to the purchase of goods.

6 **Outline** how interest rates affect business profits.

Higher interest rates will increase the debt burden (for geared firms) and reduce profits. Lower interest rates will reduce the debt burden and increase profits. Interest rates also affect consumer spending and thus affect business profits: higher interest rates may increase saving and increase the debt burden on consumers, thus reducing their spending; lower interest rates reduce the debt burden and increase disposable income (discouraging saving).

6.1.2 How government control over the economy affects business activity and how businesses may respond: Activity

Activity type
Board game

Time
30 minutes (or at teacher discretion)

Content
Changes in taxes, government spending and interest rates

Key terms
government spending; income tax; interest rates

Aims
To understand how changes in taxes, government spending and interest rates can affect business activity (6.1.2)

Skills practised

AO1: Knowledge and understanding	✓
AO2: Application	✓
AO3: Analysis	✓
AO4: Evaluation	

Preparation
Prepare one copy of the game board (Activity sheet 6.1.2A) enlarged to A3 size and one set of cut-up cards from Activity sheet 6.1.2B for each group of three students in the class. Each group will also need one six-sided dice and each player will need a counter.

Procedure

1. Explain to students that they are going to play a board game that requires them to analyse the effects of changes in income tax, government spending and interest rates.

2. Divide the class into groups of three or four. Give each group a copy of the game board, a set of cards and a dice, plus a counter for each player.

3. Each student takes five cards and places their counter on START. They place the remaining cards in a pile face down in the centre of the game board. Students should arrange their cards on the table in front of them. It does not matter if students can see each other's cards.

4. Students take turns to roll the dice and move their counter. When they land in a square they read the situation and use any appropriate cards in their hand to respond.

   Example: A student might have the following cards in their hand: 'Prices fall', 'Consumer demand falls', 'Unemployment increases', 'GDP rises', 'Cost of borrowing falls'. If they land on 'The government cuts spending', they can put down 'Consumer demand falls', 'Unemployment increases' and 'Prices fall'.

   As the student lays down each card, they explain to their group how it affects business activity and link it to the initial policy action of a cut in government spending. If the other students are not satisfied with the explanation or link, they may challenge it.

5. A player is awarded one point for each card they successfully link to the government policy and business activity. They should put these cards to one side and replace them with cards drawn from the top of the pile, so that they always have at least five cards in their hand.

6. If a player lands on:
   - 'Miss a turn', they miss their current turn
   - 'Swap cards', they may swap any number of cards from their hand with cards drawn randomly from the pile
   - 'Policy decision' or 'START', they may choose the government policy to which they link their cards
   - 'Pick up a card', they may pick up one card from the pile and add it to their hand.

Cambridge Assessment International Education
Business Studies Teacher's Guide

7 As students play the game, move around each group and check that they are playing correctly. Also, be on hand to settle any disputes between players.

8 The game ends when there are no cards left in the centre of the board or when a predetermined time limit has been reached. The winner is the student who has accumulated the most cards.

Teacher tip: *Before they start the game, it might be a good idea for students to spend a few minutes in their groups linking as many of the cards as possible to the various government policies.*

Variation: To make the game more accessible for less able students, you could remove some cards, such as 'Employees' real wage decreases', from the pack.

6.2 Environmental and ethical issues

6.2.1 ENVIRONMENTAL CONCERNS AND ETHICAL ISSUES AS BOTH OPPORTUNITIES AND CONSTRAINTS FOR BUSINESSES

Aims (6.2.1)

Knowledge

By the end of this section, students will understand:

- how business activity can impact on the environment, for example, global warming
- the concept of externalities: possible external costs and external benefits of business decisions
- sustainable development; how business activity can contribute to this
- how and why business might respond to environmental pressures and opportunities, for example, pressure groups
- the role of legal controls over business activity affecting the environment, for example, pollution controls
- the ethical issues a business might face: conflicts between profits and ethics
- how business might react and respond to ethical issues, for example, child labour.

Resources

- Student's Book pages 367–377
- Activity sheet 6.2.1
- Scissors

Key business terms

boycotting; competitive advantage; conservation of resources; corporate social responsibility (CSR); deforestation; depletion of resources; environmental audit; ethical behaviour; exploitation of labour; fair trade; fossil fuels; global warming; infrastructure; labour turnover; legal controls and regulations; multinational company; negative externality; negative publicity; petitioning/lobbying; positive externality; pressure groups; stakeholders; shareholders; sustainable development

Lesson ideas

You should aim to cover the materials in 6.2.1 in two one-hour lessons, plus, as appropriate, a homework assignment. To achieve the Aims for this topic, we recommend doing some of the following activities over the course of the lessons.

Starter suggestion

The school's impact: Introduce the topic by asking students to consider the impact of the school's activities on its indirect stakeholders (the externalities). For example, students could work in pairs or small groups and report their ideas back to the whole class.

You could broaden this discussion to include sustainable development and ethics. For example, does the school use paper from sustainable sources?

Use students' suggestions to introduce the concept of externalities and the potential for such externalities to be both positive and negative.

Main lesson activities

Discussion and note-taking (whole class): Talk students through environmental and ethical issues. Tell them to take notes as appropriate. Focus on the impact of environmental and ethical issues on business activity.

Investigation: To introduce and prompt analysis of environmental issues, students should do Skills activity 1 on page 371 of the Student's Book. They will write a summary of an environmental issue from the point of view of particular stakeholders:

- a manager
- a member of the local community
- a politician.

Skills activity: To encourage evaluation of ethical issues, students should do Skills activity 2 on page 375 of the Student's Book. For this debate on business ethics, split the class into small groups and assign the position of 'For' or 'Against' to the students in each group.

Knowledge check: Students should complete the Knowledge check questions on page 377 of the Student's Book.

Tip: This exercise could be given as a homework task.

Situation report: To summarise key issues, students should work in groups or as individuals to list five environmental or ethical issues a business may face. You could give them a specific type of business to focus on, such as a clothing manufacturer. They should list the possible impact of each issue for business and how a business might respond.

Plenary suggestions

Activity 6.2.1 is designed as a fun plenary for this topic. Students will recap and analyse the links between various key terms from the topic. It could be used at the end of a lesson or as a summative lesson in itself.

Answers to Student's Book activities

Skills activities: possible outcomes

Skills activity 1 (page 371)

Encourage students to write their summary and analysis in prose, not as bullet points or lists. Suggest that they apply their knowledge to the context of each stakeholder.

Tip: To develop skills, give students this activity as an individual exercise (getting them to consider all three viewpoints) or ask them to complete it in a group of three and discuss the stakeholder perspectives with each other.

Skills activity 2 (page 375)

Encourage students to present balanced (and justified) views, using evidence from the scenario where possible. Challenge assumptions and extreme statements or positions. Wrap up with a class discussion on the case and use students' different views to reinforce how difficult it is to judge what is 'ethical'.

Knowledge check (page 377)

1 **Define** the term externalities.

   The positive or negative impacts a firm can have on society and the environment around it.

2 **Identify** three constraints a government may place on a firm's activities to reduce its environmental impact.

   Any three from: building/planning regulations (i.e. location); pollution controls; congestion charges; waste management charges/taxes; requiring businesses to use a proportion of energy from renewable sources; controlling materials used for new buildings.

3 **Explain**, using a suitable example, the phrase sustainable development.

   Economic/business development that meets today's needs without damaging the ability of future generations to meet their needs – what we do today should not harm our future.

4 **Explain** two possible ways in which a business might respond to environmental pressures.

   Any two from: lower waste/pollution; offset pollution, waste or land use with investment in environmental initiatives; promote environmental consciousness as a way to improve brand/increase sales.

   Accept any other appropriate response.

5 **Outline** what is meant by the term business ethics.

A business acting in ethical (right/fair) ways in countries where it operates; conducting business morally.

6 **Explain**, using an example, two possible impacts of pressure group activity on a business.

Any two from: reduction in sales; damage to brand image/company reputation; legal requirement/consumer pressure to change operations.

Accept any other appropriate response.

6.2.1 Environmental concerns and ethical issues as both opportunities and constraints for businesses: Activity

Activity type

Dominoes

Time

40 minutes

Content

Environmental concerns and ethical issues

Key terms

boycotting; conservation of resources; corporate social responsibility (CSR); environmental audit; ethical behaviour; exploitation of labour; fair trade; legal controls and regulations; negative externality; negative publicity; petitioning/ lobbying; positive externality; pressure groups; shareholders; stakeholders; sustainable development

Skills practised

AO1: Knowledge and understanding	✓
AO2: Application	
AO3: Analysis	
AO4: Evaluation	

Preparation

Make one copy of the dominoes on Activity sheet 6.2.1 for each student in the class. Students will need scissors to cut out their dominoes.

Aims

To understand the key terms related to environmental concerns and ethical issues (6.2.1)

Procedure

1. Tell students that they are going to write definitions for a range of business terms related to environmental concerns and ethical issues and then play a game of dominoes.
2. Give a copy of the activity sheet to each student.
3. Working individually, students have 15 minutes to write definitions for the business terms on the activity sheets. The first three have been done as examples. Point out that term 1A matches definition 1B, term 2A matches definition 2B and so on.
4. After they have completed the activity sheet, allow students time to compare their definitions with a classmate and make changes if necessary.
5. Students should cut out the domino cards around the dotted lines so that they remove numbers and letters.
6. Divide the class into groups of three and ask students to combine all their cut-up cards into one pile.
7. Demonstrate the game. Each student in the group starts with five cards laid out on the table in front of them. It does not matter if group members can see each other's cards.
8. Students take one card from the top of the pile and place it face up on the table. They then take turns to match a card in their hand with the card(s) on the table. They may place their card at either end of the chain of dominoes.
9. If a student is not able to place a card, they must take a new card from the pile and add it to their hand. The first student to get rid of all their cards is the winner.

Teacher tip: For homework, students could paste their dominoes into their exercise books, matching the business terms with the definitions, as a permanent record. Alternatively, the cards could be put away to play again in a later lesson.

Teacher tip: To save time, students could complete steps 3 and 5 for homework and play the game at the beginning of the next lesson.

Note: If required, explanations of the key terms can be found on pages 367–377 of the Student's Book, as well as in the Student's Book Glossary (pages 402–408).

6.3 Business and the international economy

6.3.1 THE IMPORTANCE OF GLOBALISATION

Aims (6.3.1)

Knowledge	Resources
By the end of this section, students will understand: • the concept of globalisation and the reasons for it • the opportunities and threats of globalisation for businesses • why governments might introduce import tariffs and import quotas.	• Student's Book pages 378–382 • Activity sheets 6.3.1A and 6.3.1B • Large world map • Examples of goods and images of goods made in a variety of countries

Key business terms

communication; developing economies; disposable income; economic growth; economic trading bloc; emerging economies; export; fair trade agreements; globalisation; homogeneous; import; interdependent; international trade; labour migration; protectionism; quota; tariff

Lesson ideas

You should aim to cover the materials in 6.3.1 in two one-hour lessons, plus, as appropriate, a homework assignment. To achieve the Aims for this topic, we recommend doing some of the following activities over the course of the lessons.

Starter suggestion

How different are we? If the nationality mix of your class allows, a useful and interesting way to start this topic is to compare the similarities and differences between the spending patterns of those nationalities. Write headings on the whiteboard, such as:

- Favourite music
- Last movie watched
- Favourite food
- Type of phone owned
- Brand of trainers owned.

Tip: Choose headings that are likely to result in similar responses across the different nationalities.

Ask students to come up to the board to write their preferences/answers under each heading. Use the responses to introduce the concept of homogeneity as one reason for globalisation.

Variation: Ask students to list a variety of non-local brands that can be found in their country. Ask them to consider how many of these brands can be found in multiple countries (i.e. to identify the overwhelming popularity of global brands).

Main lesson activities

Discussion and note-taking (whole class): Talk students through the importance of globalisation, paying particular attention to the opportunities and threats for business. Tell them to take notes.

Skills activity: Students should complete Skills activity 1 on page 379 of the Student's Book as a whole class. They will prepare a visual montage and analyse the extent of globalisation. If possible, give students a world map and bring to the lesson examples of goods made in a variety of countries.

Tip: This is a useful (and interactive) exercise to do on the board as a whole class. Draw, pin or project a world map onto the board. Ask students to draw or stick printed images of products in the locations in which they are made. Use the map to draw out themes related to globalisation.

Student activity: Students should form small groups and complete Skills activity 2 on page 381 of the Student's Book. This is preparation for Activity 6.3.1 and an introduction to/reinforcement of the benefits and drawbacks of globalisation,

Tip: If students will be doing Activity 6.3.1, keep this activity brief. Use it as preparation for the main debate (and to introduce students to the rules of debating).

Protect it: Without introducing the concept of protectionism, ask students, in small groups, to imagine they are the government of a country suffering the harmful effects of globalisation. Tell them to list and describe all the measures they might take to protect their country. Use their responses to formally introduce methods of protectionism.

Extension: Ask students to imagine they are a foreign firm wanting to trade in the country. What would be the implications of protectionism for this firm?

Knowledge check: Students should answer the Knowledge check questions on page 382 of the Student's Book.

Tip: This exercise could be given as a homework task.

Plenary suggestion

Student activity: Activity 6.3.1 is a debate on the opportunities and threats of globalisation, designed as a synoptic activity for this topic. Running the debate properly is likely to take a full lesson (plus preparation time) and so will ideally be the last lesson in a series delivered on this topic.

Answers to Student's Book activities

Skills activities: possible outcomes

Skills activity 1 (page 379)

Use students' visual montage to draw out the following points:

- an increase in international trade between countries
- the sale of homogeneous (similar) products by multinational companies (MNCs) across many countries
- the adoption of a common language (often English, but increasingly Mandarin)
- the movement of production from developed countries to less economically developed countries
- increasing exposure to global media that affects tastes and fashion (making them more similar).

Skills activity 2 (page 381)

In their arguments for and against globalisation, students may draw from the advantages and disadvantages in the table on page 380 of the Student's Book.

Knowledge check (page 382)

1 **Define** the term globalisation.

   The increasing trend for businesses to trade across international boundaries and for people to live in or travel to countries that are not their own. In the process countries (and the people within them) become more similar and their livelihoods more integrated.

2 **Identify** three reasons why globalisation is occurring.

   Any three from: improved communication and transport systems; increased labour migration and cultural integration; increased number of economic trading blocs; recession in developing countries combined with rapid economic growth in many developing and emerging economies, encouraging businesses to set up new branches in these growing countries; MNCs seeking the benefits of lower labour costs in developing/emerging countries.

3. **Explain** the differences and similarities between tariffs and quotas.
   - Tariff: a specific form of tax imposed (charged) on imported goods.
   - Quota: a limit on the quantity (amount) of a particular good that can be imported into a country.
4. **Identify** three advantages and three disadvantages of globalisation.

   Any three from each column:

Advantages	Disadvantages
• Globalisation allows countries to specialise and therefore increase GDP.	• The benefits of globalisation favour rich countries.
• Consumers get much wider variety of products to choose from.	• Globalisation does not benefit everyone equally.
• It promotes understanding and goodwill among different countries.	• Globalisation leads to financial problems that affect not just one country but many.
• Inward investment by MNCs helps countries by providing employment for local people.	• There are no guarantees that the wealth from MNC investment will benefit the local community.
• Globalisation makes people more aware of, and more likely to find solutions to, global issues such as deforestation and global warming.	• It can be argued that globalisation has led to an increase in environmental and ethical problems.
	• Some people view globalisation as a threat to global diversity.

6.3.1 The importance of globalisation: Activity

Activity type

Class debate

Time

80 minutes (over two lessons)

Content

Globalisation and international trade

Key terms

communication; developing economies; economic growth; economic trading blocs; emerging economies; export; fair trade agreement; globalisation; homogeneous; import; interdependent; international trade; labour migration; protectionism

Aims

To understand the opportunities and threats of globalisation for countries and businesses (6.3.1)

Skills practised

AO1: Knowledge and understanding	✓
AO2: Application	✓
AO3: Analysis	✓
AO4: Evaluation	✓

Preparation

Make one copy of Activity sheets 6.3.1A and 6.3.1B for each pair of students.

Procedure

1. Tell students that they are going to use their knowledge to participate in a debate on globalisation and international trade.

2. Divide the class into two groups, A and B. Give a copy of Activity sheet 6.3.1A to each student in group A and a copy of Activity sheet 6.3.1B to each student in group B.

3. Write the motion on the board: *'Globalisation and international trade benefit everyone and should be encouraged.'* Students in group A are the affirmative team and will be arguing for the motion while students in group B are the negative team and will be arguing against the motion.

4. Within either Team A or Team B, students will be working in groups of three and will have time to research and prepare their arguments.

5. Refer students to the activity sheet and explain that each student in the group will be allowed to speak for one minute uninterrupted. Each team member should present a different argument and back it up with any evidence they are able to find in the Student's Book or online.

6. Students will decide the winning team democratically. Each spectator will cast one vote for the team they think has the most persuasive arguments. They may abstain from voting if they are undecided.

7. Arrange students within each team into groups of three and allow them 20 minutes to prepare their arguments. Then give them a further 10 minutes to practise their arguments within their group. Move around the different groups offering advice on how to present their ideas more effectively.

8. Begin the debate. Nominate a timekeeper and instruct them to indicate when speakers have 10 seconds remaining, perhaps by tapping on the desk.

9. Follow the structure on the activity sheet (with each debating 'team' taking turns to present their arguments). Give the audience time to ask questions once all team members have spoken. If practical, invite students from other classes to watch the debate.

10. Students should vote for the team they think had the most persuasive arguments. They should try to remain objective and not be influenced by their personal views on the topic.

11. Depending on class size, some groups may have to present their debates in the next lesson.

Extension: In groups of three, students could consider the opportunities and threats of globalisation mentioned in the debate and discuss how these might impact businesses specifically. They could present their ideas in the form of a concept map to share with the class.

Teacher tip: Because of the language demands of this kind of speaking task, it is important to allow students time to practise presenting their arguments in the safety of small groups before asking them to present their ideas in front of the class.

Note: *Do not allow more competent or advanced English speakers to dominate the debate. Encourage support for all speakers, regardless of their English ability. If possible, assign roles (team leader, debate chair, note-taker, and so on) according to English ability. Assign easier roles to those who may find the exercise more difficult.*

6.3.2 The importance and growth of multinational companies (MNCs)

Aims (6.3.2)

Knowledge

By the end of this section, students will understand:

- the benefits to a business of becoming a multinational and the impact on its stakeholders
- the potential benefits to a country and/or economy where a MNC is located, for example, jobs, exports, increased choice, investment
- the potential drawbacks to a country and/or economy where a MNC is located, for example, reduced sales of local businesses, repatriation of profits.

Resources

- Student's Book pages 383–386
- Activity sheet 6.3.2
- Websites with information about MNCs operating in the students' countries

Key business terms

economies of scale; exchange rates; fossil fuels; free trade agreements; multinational company (MNC); raw materials; repatriation of products; subsidies; transnational corporation

Lesson ideas

You should aim to cover the materials in 6.3.2 in a single one-hour lesson, plus, as appropriate, a homework assignment. To achieve the Aims for this topic, we recommend doing some of the following activities over the course of the lesson.

Starter suggestion

Context: First define the concept of a multinational company (MNC), then ask students to list as many MNCs operating in the country as they can. If there are many, it may be necessary to set a short time frame for this exercise. Students should list at least three reasons why the MNCs are located in the country.

Main lesson activities

Discussion and note-taking (whole class): Use student responses to the starter activity as a basis for discussing the reasons for the growth of MNCs.

Student activity: Students should complete Activity 6.3.2. They will use the Student's Book to find out about the benefits and drawbacks for a business of becoming an MNC and the benefits and drawbacks for a country of having MNCs located there.

Skills activity: Students should do the Skills activity on page 386 of the Student's Book, examining the implications of MNCs operating in their own country. If possible, first direct students to suitable websites and other information sources or brainstorm local MNCs onto the board.

Tip: This exercise could be given as homework.

Plenary suggestion

Knowledge check: Students should answer the Knowledge check questions on page 386 of the Student's Book.

Answers to Student's Book activities

Skills activity (page 386): possible outcomes

Encourage students to take the viewpoint of an employee working for the company, applying the advantages/disadvantages appropriately. Anticipate 200–300 words for the blog, written in an informal style.

Possible areas of response might include:

- Advantages: See the suggested answers for Question 4 of the Knowledge check.
- Disadvantages: See the suggested answers for Question 3 of the Knowledge check.

Knowledge check (page 386)

1 **Outline** the term multinational company.

   A firm that has operational bases in a number of different countries.

2 **Identify** two reasons why a business may wish to become a multinational.

   Any two from: increased sales potential; spreading the risk of operating in only one country; cost of advertising campaigns can be shared across countries; global brands potentially more desirable; economies of scale can be gained in production; economic downturn in one country (and a fall in sales) might be offset by economic growth (and rising sales) in other countries; benefiting from lower (labour) costs in host countries; accessing raw materials (particularly fossil fuels) not available in own country; locating branches/factories within a country to avoid protectionist barriers; localising products and reducing transport costs and delivery times.

3 **Explain**, using suitable examples, two ways in which multinationals might damage the countries in which they operate.

   Any two from: MNC may offer low wages and poor working conditions for employees; jobs created are often low-skilled manual jobs that offer little opportunity for long-term development and future economic growth; profits from MNC may go back to the MNC's own country and may not be spent in the host country; increased competition for local businesses (potentially forcing closure); MNCs use up a country's resources and may contribute to environmental issues; MNCs often use complex accounting rules to avoid paying tax in the host country; MNCs often have significant power with local governments and may be able to affect decision making in their favour (possibly disadvantaging local firms).

4 **Identify** three advantages for a country of attracting multinationals to locate there.

   Any three from: increased job opportunities; increased exports from a country (helping to strengthen its currency); increased consumer choice; investment by the MNCs in infrastructure (roads, rail links, and so on) and in training/education; MNCs will pay (at least some) tax in the host countries, increasing funds available to the government.

6.3.2 The importance and growth of multinational companies (MNCs): Activity

Activity type

Jigsaw reading activity

Time

40 minutes

Content

Multinational companies

Key terms

economies of scale; exchange rates; fossil fuels; free trade agreements; multinational company (MNC); raw materials; repatriation of products; subsidies; transnational corporation

Skills practised

AO1: Knowledge and understanding	✓
AO2: Application	
AO3: Analysis	
AO4: Evaluation	

Preparation

Make one copy of Activity Sheet 6.3.2 for each student in the class.

Aims

To understand the reasons for the importance and growth of multinational companies (MNCs) (6.3.2)

Procedure

1 Tell students that they are going to read about the benefits and drawbacks of MNCs, make notes and discuss their points with other students in the class.

2 Divide the class into two equal groups, A and B, and give a copy of Activity sheet 6.3.2 to each student.

3 Students in group A will read about the benefits and drawbacks to a business of becoming an MNC in the Student's Book (pages 383–384), while students in group B will read about the benefits and drawbacks to the host country in which an MNC is located (pages 385–386). Students should make notes in the relevant sections of Activity sheet 6.3.2 (see the Teacher tip below).

4 To speed things up, tell students in each group to read and make notes on the benefits, while the others should make notes on the drawbacks. They should then work together, sharing their information to complete their sections of the activity sheet. Remind students that they should only complete their assigned sections and should leave the others blank.

5 Next pair each student from group A with a student from group B and ask them to share the information they learned from the Student's Book. Emphasise that this is intended as a speaking activity so students should not simply hand their completed table to their partner to copy – they should listen to each other's points and make brief notes on their activity sheet as they listen. They should only note down key words as they will have the chance to develop the points in more detail later. Encourage students to ask each other if they do not understand a particular point.

6 Move around the room, making sure students are completing the activity correctly.

7 As a homework task, you could ask students to complete their tables in more detail, using what they learned from their partner as well as the information in the Student's Book.

8 To round off the activity, nominate a few students in the class to outline one or two of the benefits and drawbacks they discussed with their partner. Offer examples of MNCs to provide context to the points made.

Extension: Students should carry out the Skills activity (Evaluation) on page 386 of the Student's Book, investigating an MNC operating in their home country.

Teacher tip: *Before students start this activity, you may need to tell them how to take notes effectively. Read aloud the first two paragraphs of Topic 6.3.2 on page 383 of the Student's Book and ask students to make notes. Explain that they will not have time to write down every word and should concentrate on noting the content words (the words that contain meaning) in each sentence. Read the paragraphs aloud to the class at a natural pace. Then analyse the paragraphs with the class and identify the content words they should have noted down. For example, in the first paragraph, the content words are:*

- *MNC*
- *operate*
- *production*
- *sales*
- *in more than one country.*

Students should compare the notes they made with the content words identified in the text.

6.3.3 The impact of exchange rate changes

Aims (6.3.3)

Knowledge
By the end of this section, students will understand:

- depreciation and appreciation of an exchange rate
- how exchange rate changes can affect businesses as importers and exporters of products, for example, prices, competitiveness, profitability.

Resources
- Student's Book pages 387–392
- Activity sheet 6.3.3
- Websites with information about imports to and exports from different countries
- Maps of students' chosen countries
- Images of import and export products

Key business terms
appreciation; balance of payments; competitive; depreciation; exchange rate; export; favourable exchange rates; free trade agreements; import; price inelastic; profitability; price inelastic; repatriation of profits; stable exchange rate; subsidies

Lesson ideas

You should aim to cover the materials in 6.3.3 in two one-hour lessons, plus, as appropriate, a homework assignment. To achieve the Aims for this topic, we recommend doing some of the following activities over the course of the lessons

Note: This topic is relatively technical so is likely to need more teacher input than other topics. You may need to focus on teacher-led exposition to start with. Once students are comfortable with the concepts, use activities (such as those in the Student's Book and the suggestions below) to reinforce knowledge and understanding.

Starter suggestion

Context: Introduce students to the concepts of international trade, imports and exports. Then ask them to investigate imports and exports within a country of their choice. Guide them towards a suitable website if necessary. Ask them to consider the following:

- What are the top three imports?
- What are the top three exports?
- Does the country import more (in total) than it exports, or vice versa?

Students should present their findings as a spider diagram, perhaps with a map of their chosen country in the centre surrounded by images of the imports and exports supported by written explanation. They should give only basic detail. Use this activity to introduce definitions of imports/exports and link to exchange rate issues.

Tip: You could give students this exercise as a pre-topic homework and then discuss the results as a lesson starter.

Main lesson activities

Discussion and note-taking (whole class): Talk students through exchange rates and, in particular, how exchange rate changes can affect businesses. Tell them to take notes.

Group discussions: Students should sit in small groups and discuss their experiences of exchange rate changes. They should share:

- examples of how exchange rate changes have made holidays cheaper or more expensive
- knowledge of products that have been made more or less expensive by exchange rate changes.

Different groups should report back on their experiences and use the discussions to introduce formal topic language such as appreciation and depreciation.

Student activity: Students should complete Activity 6.3.3. They will consider the impact of exchange rate changes.

Practice: Ask students to write an exam-style question (and mark scheme) on the impact of exchange rate changes on a business. Give different groups within the class different topics on which to focus (profitability, price, and so on). If possible, give students an example question, but tell them they must create their own version and not simply copy.

Plenary suggestion

Knowledge check: Students should answer the Knowledge check questions on page 392 of the Student's Book.

Tip: This exercise could be given as homework.

Answers to Student's Book activities

Skills activity (page 392): possible outcomes

Guide students to a suitable website and, depending on ability level, give hints about government action to 'protect' the currency. If possible, use the recording software on tablet computers or smartphones to record students' short news reports. Offer them feedback and clear up any misunderstandings.

Knowledge check (page 392)

1 **Define** the term exchange rate.

   The value of one currency expressed in another.

2 **Identify** one impact on an exporter of an appreciation of their country's currency.

   Any one from: goods seem relatively more expensive overseas (possible fall in sales); any imported goods used in manufacture cost less to buy (increasing profit margin or enabling prices to be lowered).

3 **Identify** one impact on an importer of a depreciation of their country's currency.

   Any one from: goods are relatively cheaper overseas (possible increase in sales); any imported goods used in manufacture cost more to buy (reducing profit margin or increasing prices and potentially harming competitiveness).

4 **Explain** one way in which exchange rate changes might affect a firm's profitability.

   Assuming a fixed price in location of sale profitability may increase or decrease depending on direction of exchange rate shift. An appreciation may make imported raw materials cheaper but profit margins overseas lower; a depreciation may make profit margins overseas higher but raw material imports more expensive.

5 **Explain** how exchange rate changes might affect competitiveness.

   Exchange rate changes may force a firm to raise the price of its goods, or may enable them to be lowered. The extent of the price change depends on the price elasticity of demand for the firm's product and its exposure to overseas markets.

6.3.3 The impact of exchange rate changes: Activity

Activity type

Categorising activity

Time

30 minutes

Content

Exchange rates

Key terms

appreciation; competitive; depreciation; export; exchange rate; favourable exchange rates; import; profitability; stable exchange rate

Aims

To understand how exchange rate changes can affect businesses as importers and exporters of products (6.3.3)

Skills practised

AO1: Knowledge and understanding	✓
AO2: Application	✓
AO3: Analysis	✓
AO4: Evaluation	

Preparation

Photocopy and cut up one set of the cards on Activity sheet 6.3.3 for each group of three students.

Procedure

1. Tell students that they are going to complete a categorising activity about how exchange rate changes can affect businesses.
2. Divide the class into groups of three students and give a set of cards from Activity sheet 6.3.3 to each group.
3. Ask students to remove the category cards (black) and place them on the table in front of them (writing side up). They should place the remaining cards in a pile face down on the table.
4. Students take turns to draw one card from the pile and read it aloud to their group. They must then collectively agree on the category to which the card belongs.

    For example, if a student picks up 'The business's product becomes more expensive overseas', the correct categorisation would be 'Effect of an exchange rate appreciation on exporters'.

5. If students cannot agree or are unsure about where to place the card, they can put it to one side and move on to the next card.
6. Get the correct answers from students during the class feedback stage of the activity so students can check their answers.
7. Students should discuss how exchange rate fluctuations can affect the total revenue that exporters and importers receive from sales. Use this as a lead-in to a class discussion on the effects of price elasticity of demand on a firm's total revenue (revision from Topic 3.3.2).

Teacher tip: Emphasise to students that this is not a competitive activity and the objective is not to be the first group to finish. Rather, they should take their time to consider each card and make sure they can justify where they have placed it. Move around the class, making sure students are doing the activity correctly and asking groups to justify how they have placed and sequenced their cards.

Extension: If they have not done so already, ask students to sequence the cards for exporters and importers in order of cause and effect.

For example, first 'The business's product becomes more expensive overseas' (cause) and then 'The firm becomes less competitive in overseas markets' (effect).

Then ask students to answer the following exam-style question:

Thai Style is a business that imports handmade furniture from northern Thailand for sale in the United Kingdom. Discuss the effect of an appreciation in the British pound on Thai Style's business.

6 External influences on business activity: Key terms revision

Define each term and provide an example or explanation. There are 2 marks per definition.

Term	Description/Definition
boom	
business ethics	
central bank	
corporation tax	
emerging economies	
exchange rate appreciation	
globalisation	
import	
interest rate	
multinational company (MNC)	
positive externality	
sustainable development	
tariff	
unemployment	

Scheme of work

CIE CODES: IGCSE 0450; O LEVEL 7115

Timings are based on an approximate allocation of 2 hours teaching time per section. This Scheme of work is provided as an aid to planning, it is not intended to be prescriptive, nor complete. Availability of resource, time and individual school calendars will all impact on what is practical and achievable; the Scheme of work as offered here is presented to provide ideas on which teachers can build. Timings are indicative only and the activities a suggested list from which teachers may choose as appropriate to local conditions.

1 Understanding business activity

Core topic(s)	Aims	Students will understand:	Resources	Key themes
1.1 Business activity	1.1.1 Understand the purpose and nature of business activity plus: **Course overview** Broadly understand what your Business Studies course entails in terms of the content, skills required and assessment.	• the concepts of needs, wants, scarcity and opportunity cost • the importance of specialisation • the purpose of business activity • the concept of adding value and how added value can be increased.	**Student's Book** pp. 8–16 **Teacher's Guide Activities** Activity 1.1.1A: Sorting task of needs, wants and scarcity Activity 1.1.1B: Matching game on opportunity costs and business decisions Activity 1.1.1C: Voting task on added value	the economic problem scarcity needs/wants product goods services opportunity cost factors of production (land, labour, capital, enterprise) consumer/producer raw materials value added division of labour specialisation profit

Core topic(s)	Aims	Students will understand:	Resources	Key themes
1.2 Classification of businesses 1.4 Types of business organisation	1.2.1 Understand business activity in terms or primary, secondary and tertiary sectors 1.2.2 Classify business enterprises between private sector and public sector in a mixed economy 1.4.1 Understand the main features of different forms of business organisation	• the basis of business classification, using examples to illustrate the classification • the reasons for the changing importance of business classification, for example, in more and less industrialised countries • how to classify business enterprises between private sector and public sector in a mixed economy • the key features of sole traders, partnerships, private and public limited companies, franchises and joint ventures • the differences between unincorporated businesses and limited companies • the concepts of risk, ownership and limited liability • how to recommend and justify a suitable form of business organisation to owners/management in a given situation • business organisations in the public sector, for example, public corporations.	Student's Book pp.17–23; 41–54 **Teacher's Guide Activities** Activity 1.2.1: Primary, secondary and tertiary sectors – Linking activity on business classifications Activity 1.2.2: Case study on public and private sector businesses Activity 1.4. 1A–D: Worksheets on types of business ownership	sole trader partnership private limited company public limited company co-operative limited liability unlimited liability partnership agreement unincorporated business shareholders dividends franchise joint venture public sector private sector privatisation primary sector public corporations secondary sector tertiary sector mixed economy developed economies developing economies

Core topic(s)	Aims	Students will understand:	Resources	Key themes
1.5 Business objectives and stakeholder objectives	1.5.1 Understand that businesses can have several objectives – and that the importance of these can change 1.5.3 Demonstrate an awareness of the differences in the objectives of private sector and public sector enterprises 1.3.3 Understand why some businesses grow and others remain small 1.5.2 Understand the role of stakeholder groups involved in business activity	• the need for business objectives and the importance of them • how to outline different business objectives, for example, survival, growth, profit and market share • the differences in the aims and objectives of private sector and public sector enterprises • the objectives of social enterprises • why the owners of a business may want to expand it • different ways in which businesses can grow • problems that are linked to business growth and how these might be overcome • why some businesses remain small • how to describe the main internal and external stakeholder groups • the objectives of different stakeholder groups • how to explain how these objectives might conflict with each other, using examples.	**Student's Book** pp.55–66; 33–37 **Teacher's Guide Activities** Activity 1.5.1A: Linking activity on business objectives Activity 1.5.1B: Case study on a social enterprise Activity 1.5.3: Case studies on aims of social enterprise and public/private enterprises Activity 1.3.3A: Case studies and sorting activity on business growth Activity 1.5.2: Sorting task examining stakeholders	business objectives survival growth profitability market share stakeholder consumers employees managers owners shareholders government local community pressure groups

Core topic(s)	Aims	Students will understand:	Resources	Key themes
1.3 Enterprise, business growth and size	1.3.2 Understand the methods and problems of measuring business size 1.3.4 Understand why some (new or established) businesses fail 1.3.1 Understand enterprise and entrepreneurship	• the methods of measuring business size, for example, number of people employed, value of output, capital employed (NB - profit is *not* a valid method of measuring business size) • the limitations of methods of measuring business size • the causes of business failure, for example, lack of management skills, changes in the business environment, liquidity problems • why new businesses are at a greater risk of failing • the characteristics of successful entrepreneurs • the contents of a business plan and how business plans assist entrepreneurs • the reasons why and how governments support business start-ups, for example, grants, training schemes.	**Student's Book** pp.24–40 **Teacher's Guide Activities** Activity 1.3.2A: Case study examining measures of business size Activity 1.3.2B: Limitations of each measure Extension activity: Benefits and limitations of each measure in relation to case study Activity 1.3.1D: Case study on business failure Activity 1.3.1A: Concept map on entrepreneurship Activity 1.3.1B, C: Worksheets on business plans	entrepreneurs capital employed output management liquidity business plan grants

2 People in business

Core topic(s)	Aims	Students will understand:	Resources	Key themes
2.1 Motivating employees	2.1.1 Understand the importance of a well-motivated workforce 2.1.2 Understand methods of motivation	• why people work and what motivation means • concept of human needs, for example, Maslow's hierarchy • key motivational theories: Taylor and Herzberg • financial rewards, for example, wage, salary, bonus, commission and profit sharing • non-financial methods, for example, job enrichment, job rotation, teamworking, training, opportunities for promotion • how to recommend and justify appropriate method(s) of motivation in given circumstances.	**Student's Book** pp.78–94 **Teacher's Guide Activities** Activity 2.1.1A, B: Categorisation exercise examining motivational theories. Activity 2.1.2A, B: Jigsaw reading activity on motivation methods.	motivation F.W. Taylor Maslow's Hierarchy of Needs Herzberg job enlargement job enrichment job rotation autocratic leadership democratic leadership laissez-faire leadership wage time rate piece-rate salary commission profit sharing bonus performance-related pay share ownership fringe benefits

Core topic(s)	Aims	Students will understand:	Resources	Key themes
2.2 Organisation and management	2.2.1 Draw, interpret and understand simple organisational charts 2.2.2 The role of management 2.2.3 Leadership styles 2.2.4 Trade unions	• simple hierarchical structures: span of control, levels of hierarchy, chain of command and delegation • the roles and responsibilities of directors, managers, supervisors, other employees in an organisation and inter-relationships between them • the functions of management, for example, planning, organising, co-ordinating, commanding and controlling • the importance of delegation; trust versus control • the features of the main leadership styles, for example, autocratic, democratic and laissez faire • how to recommend and justify an appropriate leadership style in given circumstances • what a trade union is and the effects of employees being union members.	**Student's Book** pp.95–109 **Teacher's Guide Activities** Activity 2.2.1: Worksheet on organisation structure Activity 2.2.2A, B, C, D, E: Group work activity on the role of management Activity 2.2.3: Categorisation exercise examining types of leadership Activity 2.2.4A, B: Role play activity on trade unions	organisational structure levels of hierarchy job description delegation chain of command span of control line managers subordinates functional departments decentralised/centralised management structure management/leadership autocratic, democratic and laissez-faire trade union collective bargaining negotiation compromise industrial action strike picketing work to rule go slow over-time ban non-cooperation lock-out

Core topic(s)	Aims	Students will understand:	Resources	Key themes
2.3 Recruitment, selection and training of employees	2.3.1 The methods of recruiting and selecting workers 2.3.2 The importance of training and the methods of training 2.3.3 Why reducing the size of the workforce might be necessary 2.3.4 Legal controls over employment issues and their impact on employers and employees	• methods of recruitment and selecting • the difference between internal recruitment and external recruitment • the main stages in recruitment and selection of employees • how to recommend and justify who to employ in given circumstances • the benefits and limitations of part-time employees and full-time employees • the importance of training to a business and employees • the benefits and limitations of induction training, on-the-job training and off-the-job training • the difference between dismissal and redundancy with examples to illustrate the difference • situations in which downsizing the workforce might be necessary, for example, automation or reduced demand for products • how to recommend and justify which employees to make redundant in given circumstances • legal controls over employment contracts, unfair dismissal, discrimination, health and safety, legal minimum wage.	**Student's Book** pp.110–131 **Teacher's Guide Activities** Activity 2.3.1 A, B, C: Role-play activity on recruitment Activity 2.3.2: Group discussion on methods of training Activity 2.3.3A, B: Pair-work crossword on workforce size reduction Activity 2.3.4A, B: Case study discussion exercise on legal controls	job analysis job description job specification internal recruitment external recruitment CV appraisal contract of employment induction training on-the-job training off-the-job training workforce planning dismissal redundancy legislation

Core topic(s)	Aims	Students will understand:	Resources	Key themes
2.4 Internal and external communication	2.4.1 Why effective communication is important and the methods used to achieve it 2.4.2 Demonstrate an awareness of communication barriers	• effective communication and its importance to business • the benefits and limitations of different communication methods including those based on information technology (IT) • how to recommend and justify which communication method to use in given circumstances • how communication barriers arise and problems of ineffective communication; how communication barriers can be reduced or removed.	**Student's Book** pp.132–148 **Teacher's Guide Activities** Activity 2.4.1: Memory/ matching game examining communication methods Activity 2.4.2: Listening activity on communication barriers	internal communication external communication verbal communication written communication visual communication message sender receiver medium of communication feedback one-way communication two-way communication

3 Marketing

Core topic(s)	Aims	Students will understand:	Resources	Key themes
3.1 Marketing, competition and the customer	3.1.1 The role of marketing 3.1.2 Market changes	• the role of marketing in identifying customer needs • the role of marketing in satisfying customer needs • the role of marketing in maintaining customer loyalty • the role of marketing in building customer relationships • why customer/consumer spending patterns may change • the importance of changing customer needs • why some markets have become more competitive • how business can respond to changing spending patterns and increased competition.	**Student's Book** pp.160–167 **Teacher's Guide Activities** Activity 3.1.1: Pair-work gap-fill exercise on the role of marketing Activity 3.1.2: Investigation activity on market changes	market marketing market orientated product orientated
	3.1.3 Concepts of niche marketing and mass marketing 3.1.4 How and why market segmentation is undertaken	• the benefits and limitations of niche and mass marketing • how markets can be segmented, for example, according to age, socio-economic grouping, location, gender • the potential benefits of segmentation to business • how to recommend and justify an appropriate method of segmentation in given circumstances.	**Student's Book** pp.168–173 **Teacher's Guide Activities** Activity 3.1.3A, B: Investigation activity on niche and mass marketing Activity 3.1.4: Jigsaw discussion activity on market segmentation	segmentation target market target audience mass market niche market

Core topic(s)	Aims	Students will understand:	Resources	Key themes
3.2 Market research	3.2.1 The role of market research and methods used 3.2.2 Presentation and use of market research results	• market-oriented businesses (uses of market research information to a business) • the benefits and limitations of primary research and secondary research • different methods of primary research, for example, postal questionnaire, online survey, interviews, focus groups • the need for sampling • the methods of secondary research, for example, online, accessing government sources, paying for commercial market research reports • the factors influencing the accuracy of market research data • how to analyse market research data shown in the form of graphs, charts and diagrams: draw simple conclusions from such data.	**Student's Book pp.174–183** **Teacher's Guide Activities** Activity 3.2.1: Focus group activity on the role of market research Activity 3.2.2: Data gathering and analysis task on presentation of results	primary research secondary research questionnaire consumer panels focus group random sample quota sample bar chart pictogram pie chart
3.3 Marketing mix	3.3.1 Product	• the costs and benefits of developing new products • brand image; impact on sales and customer loyalty • the role of packaging • the product life cycle: main stages and extension strategies; draw and interpret a product life cycle diagram • how stages of the product life cycle can influence marketing decisions, for example, promotion and pricing decisions.	**Student's Book pp.184–191** **Teacher's Guide Activities** Activity 3.3.1: Categorisation activity on product life cycle	packaging brand name brand loyalty brand image unique selling point (USP) product life cycle development introduction growth maturity saturation decline extension strategies

Core topic(s)	Aims	Students will understand:	Resources	Key themes
	3.3.2 Price	- pricing methods, for example, cost plus, competitive, penetration, skimming and promotional; their benefits and limitations - how to recommend and justify an appropriate pricing method in given circumstances - the benefits and limitations of different pricing strategies - the significance of price elasticity: difference between price elastic demand and price inelastic demand; importance of the concept in pricing decisions (knowledge of the formula and calculations of PED will *not* be assessed).	**Student's Book** pp.192–198 **Teacher's Guide Activities** Activity 3.3.2: Categorisation activity on pricing strategies	demand supply market price substitute products complementary products elasticity of demand price inelastic demand price elastic demand cost of production taxes subsidies pricing strategies cost-plus pricing penetration pricing market skimming competitive pricing promotional pricing loss leader pricing
	3.3.3 Place	- the advantages and disadvantages of different channels, for example, use of wholesalers, retailers or direct to consumers - how to recommend and justify an appropriate distribution channel in given circumstances.	**Student's Book** pp.199–204 **Teacher's Guide Activities** Activity 3.3.3: Jigsaw reading activity examining distribution strategy	channel of distribution retailer wholesaler agent

Core topic(s)	Aims	Students will understand:	Resources	Key themes
	3.3.4 Promotion	• the aims of promotion • the different forms of promotion and how they influence sales, for example, advertising, sales promotion • the need for cost effectiveness in spending the marketing budget on promotion.	**Student's Book** pp.205–213 **Teacher's Guide Activities** Activity 3.3.4: Investigation activity examining methods of promotion	informative advertising persuasive advertising advertising budget advertising campaign advertising media promotional methods point-of-sale personal selling public relations social-media marketing
	3.3.5 Technology and the marketing mix	• how to define and explain the concept of e-commerce • the opportunities and threats of e-commerce to business and consumers • the use of the internet and social media networks for promotion.	**Student's Book** pp.214–220 **Teacher's Guide Activities** Activity 3.3.5: Evaluation activity on technology use in marketing	internet relationship marketing social-media marketing
3.4 Marketing strategy	3.4.2 The nature and impact of legal controls related to marketing	• the impact of legal controls on marketing strategy, for example, misleading promotion, faulty and dangerous goods.	**Student's Book** pp.225–226 **Teacher's Guide Activities** Activity 3.4.2: Evaluation activity examining legal controls on marketing	marketing legislation consumer protection legislation
	3.4.3 The opportunities and problems of entering new foreign markets 3.4.1 Justify marketing strategies appropriate to a given situation	• the growth potential of new markets in other countries • the problems of entering foreign markets, for example, cultural differences and lack of knowledge • the benefits and limitations of methods to overcome such problems, for example, joint ventures, licensing • the importance of different elements of the marketing mix in influencing consumer decisions in given circumstances • how to recommend and justify an appropriate marketing strategy in given circumstances.	**Student's Book** pp.227–232; 221–224 **Teacher's Guide Activities** Activity 3.4.3: Snakes and ladders game examining the problems and opportunities of entering markets abroad Activity 3.4.1: Investigation activity requiring justification of a marketing strategy	language barriers cultural barriers legislation protectionism joint ventures

4 Operations management

Core topic(s)	Aims	Students will understand:	Resources	Key themes
4.1 Production of goods and services	4.1.1 The meaning of production 4.1.2 The main methods of production 4.1.3 How technology has changed production methods	• how to manage resources effectively to produce goods and services • the difference between production and productivity • the benefits of increasing efficiency and how to increase it, for example, increasing productivity by automation and technology, improved labour skills • why businesses hold inventories • the concept of lean production: how to achieve it, for example, just-in-time inventory control and Kaizen; benefits of lean production • the features, benefits and limitations of job, batch and flow production • how to recommend and justify an appropriate production method for a given situation • how technology has changed production methods, for example, using computers in design and manufacturing.	**Student's Book** pp.244–55 **Teacher's Guide Activities** Activity 4.1.1: Dominoes activity on the meaning of production Activity 4.1.2A, B: Discussion activity on types of production Activity 4.1.3: Gap-fill reading activity on technology and production	production productivity efficiency stock management lean production kaizen flow production job production batch production CAD/CAM JIT

Core topic(s)	Aims	Students will understand:	Resources	Key themes
4.2 Costs, scale of production and break-even analysis	4.2.1 Identify and classify costs	• how to classify costs using examples fixed, variable, average, total • how to use cost data to help make simple cost-based decisions, for example, to stop production or continue	**Student's Book** pp.256–263 **Teacher's Guide Activities** Activity 4.2.1: Group activity on classification of costs Activity 4.2.2: Pair-work discussion task on economies and diseconomies of scale	fixed/direct costs variable/indirect costs overhead costs total costs unit costs economies of scale average cost/unit cost purchasing economies marketing economies financial economies managerial economies technical economies risk-bearing economies diseconomies of scale
	4.2.2 Economies and diseconomies of scale	• the concepts of economies of scale with examples, for example, purchasing, marketing, financial, managerial, technical • the concepts of diseconomies of scale with examples, for example, poor communication, lack of commitment from employees, weak coordination.		
	4.2.3 Break-even analysis	• the concept of break-even • how to construct, complete or amend a simple break-even chart • how to interpret a given chart and use it to analyse a situation • how to calculate break-even output from given data • how to define, calculate and interpret the margin of safety • how to use break-even analysis to help make simple decisions, for example, impact of higher price • the limitations of break-even analysis.	**Student's Book** pp.264–270 **Teacher's Guide Activities** Activity 4.2.3A, B, C: Information sharing activity in break-even charts	break-even point break-even chart sales revenue/sales turnover total revenue profit loss margin of safety

Core topic(s)	Aims	Students will understand:	Resources	Key themes
4.3 Achieving quality production	4.3.1 Why quality is important and how quality production might be achieved	• what quality means; why it is important for all businesses • the concept of quality control and how businesses implement quality control • the concept of quality assurance.	**Student's Book** pp.271–273 **Teacher's Guide Activities** Activity 4.3.1A, B: Role-play activity examining quality	quality control quality assurance total quality management (TQM)
4.4 Location decisions	4.4.1 The main factors influencing the location and relocation decisions of a business	• factors relevant to the location decision of manufacturing businesses and service businesses • factors that a business could consider when deciding which country to locate operations in • the role of legal controls on location decisions • how to recommend and justify an appropriate location for a business in given circumstances.	**Student's Book** pp.274–278 **Teacher's Guide Activities** Activity 4.4.1A, B: Ranking activity on location decisions	external economies of scale legislation government subsidies tariff barriers

5 Financial information and decision making

Core topic(s)	Aims	Students will understand:	Resources	Key themes
5.1 Business finance: needs and sources	5.1.1 The need for business finance 5.1.2 The main sources of finance	• the main reasons why businesses need finance, for example, start-up capital, capital for expansion and additional working capital • the difference between short-term and long-term finance needs • internal sources and external sources with examples • short-term and long-term sources with examples, for example, overdraft for short-term finance and debt or equity for long-term finance • the importance of alternative sources of capital, for example, micro-finance, crowd-funding • the main factors considered in making the financial choice, for example, size and legal form of business, amount required, length of time, existing loans • how to recommend and justify appropriate source(s) of finance in given circumstances.	**Student's Book** pp.292–307 **Teacher's Guide Activities** Activity 5.1.1A: Jigsaw reading activity on why businesses needs funds Activity 5.1.1B: Memory game on short-term, long-term sources of finance Activity 5.1.2A: Dominoes activity on main sources of capital Activity 5.1.2B: Ranking sources of finance on a continuum	internal finance external finance debt start-up capital capital expenditure revenue expenditure equity retained profit share issue bank loan debentures debt factoring subsidies grants overdraft trade credit hire purchase leasing
5.2 Cash flow forecasting and working capital	5.2.1 The importance of cash and of cash flow forecasting 5.2.2 Working capital	• why cash is important to a business • how to explain what a cash flow forecast is, how a simple one is constructed and the importance of it • how to amend or complete a simple cash flow forecast • how to interpret a simple cash flow forecast • how short-term cash flow problems might be overcome, for example, increasing loans, delaying payments, asking debtors to pay more quickly • the concept and importance of working capital.	**Student's Book** pp.308–316 **Teacher's Guide Activities** Activity 5.2.1A, B: Simulation exercise on cash flow forecasting Activity 5.2.2: Worksheet on working capital	cash flow profit cash inflows cash outflows cash flow cycle cash flow forecast opening cash balance net cash flow closing cash balance sources of finance solving cash flow crisis

Core topic(s)	Aims	Students will understand:	Resources	Key themes
5.3 Income statements	5.3.1 What profit is and why it is important 5.3.2 Income statements	• how a profit is made • the importance of profit to private sector businesses, for example, reward for risk taking/enterprise, source of finance • how to explain the difference between profit and cash • the main features of an income statement, for example, revenue, cost of sales, gross profit, profit and retained profit • how to use simple income statements in decision making based on profit calculations (*construction of income statements will **not** be assessed*).	**Student's Book** pp.317–324 **Teacher's Guide Activities** Activity 5.3.1A, B, C: Worksheets on profit calculations, understanding how profit is made and difference between cash and profit Activity 5.3.2A, B, C: Worksheets on the purpose, components and features of income statements	profit accounts financial statements cost of sales revenue raw materials gross profit income statement finance costs
5.4 Statement of financial position	5.4.1 The main elements of a statement of financial position 5.4.2 Interpret a simple statement of financial position and make deductions from it	• the main classifications of assets and liabilities, using examples • how to interpret a simple statement of financial position and make deductions from it, for example, how a business is financing its activities and what assets it owns, sale of inventories to raise finance (*constructing statements of financial position will **not** be assessed*).	**Student's Book** pp.325–330 **Teacher's Guide Activities** Activity 5.4.1A: Matching exercise on liabilities/assets Activity 5.4.1B: Worksheet on construction of balance sheets Activity 5.4.2: Interpreting a balance sheet	statement of financial position assets liabilities current assets current liabilities non-current assets non-current liabilities trade receivables trade payables share capital inventory

Core topic(s)	Aims	Students will understand:	Resources	Key themes
5.5 Analysis of accounts	5.5.1 Profitability 5.5.3 How to interpret the financial performance of a business by calculating and analysing profitability ratios and liquidity ratios	• the concept and importance of profitability • how to interpret the financial performance of a business by calculating and analysing profitability ratios and liquidity ratios: gross profit margin, profit margin, return on capital employed, current ratio, acid test ratio.	Student's Book pp.331–336 Teacher's Guide Activities Activity 5.5.1A, B, C: Case study on accounting ratios	performance/profitability ROCE gross profit margin (GPM) net profit margin (NPM) capital employed sales turnover/sales revenue
	5.5.2 Liquidity 5.5.4 Why and how accounts are used	• the concept and importance of liquidity • the needs of different users of accounts and ratio analysis • how to explain how users of accounts and ratio results might use information to help make decisions, for example, whether to lend to or invest in the business.	Student's Book pp.314–316; 337–340 Teacher's Guide Activities Activity 5.2.2: Worksheet on liquidity Activity 5.5.3A, B, C: Worksheet on users of accounts	liquidity working capital current ratio acid test ratio stakeholders

6 External influences on business activity

Core topic(s)	Aims	Students will understand:	Resources	Key themes
6.1 Economic issues	6.1.1 Business cycle 6.1.2 How government control over the economy affects business activity	• the main stages of the business cycle, for example, growth, boom, recession, slump • the impact on businesses of changes in employment levels, inflation and Gross Domestic Product (GDP) • how to identify government economic objectives, for example, increasing Gross Domestic Product (GDP) • the impact of changes in taxes and government spending • the impact of changes in interest rates.	**Student's Book** pp.354–366 **Teacher's Guide Activities** Activity 6.1.1A, B: Definitions and examples Activity 6.1.2A, B: Board game activity reinforcing how government control affects business activity	inflation unemployment economic growth the balance of payments real income Gross Domestic Product (GDP) fiscal policy direct taxes indirect taxes monetary policy interest rates
6.2 Environmental and ethical concerns	6.2.1 Environmental concerns and ethical issues as both opportunities and constraints for businesses	• how business activity can impact on the environment, for example, global warming • the concept of externalities: possible external costs and external benefits of business decisions • sustainable development; how business activity can contribute to this • how and why business might respond to environmental pressures and opportunities, for example, pressure groups • the role of legal controls over business activity affecting the environment, for example, pollution controls • the ethical issues a business might face: conflicts between profits and ethics • how business might react and respond to ethical issues, for example, child labour.	**Student's Book** pp.367–377 **Teacher's Guide Activities** Activity 6.2.1: Dominoes activity on environmental issues and ethical concerns	ethics sustainable development legislation fines pollution controls regulations externalities negative externalities positive externalities corporate social responsibility (CSR) pressure groups stakeholder conflicts

Core topic(s)	Aims	Students will understand:	Resources	Key themes
6.3 Business and the international economy	6.3.1 The importance of globalisation 6.3.2 Reasons for the importance and growth of multinational companies (MNCs)	• the concept of globalisation and the reasons for it • the opportunities and threats of globalisation for businesses • why some governments might introduce import tariffs and quotas • the benefits to a business of becoming a multinational and the impact on its stakeholders • the potential benefits to a country and/or economy where a MNC is located, for example, jobs, exports, increased choice, investment • the potential drawbacks to a country and/or economy where a MNC is located, for example, reduced sales of local businesses, repatriation of profits.	**Student's Book** pp.378–386 **Teacher's Guide Activities** Activity 6.3.1A, B: Class debate on globalisation Activity 6.3.2: Jigsaw reading activity on growth of multinational companies	multinational corporation globalisation tariffs quotas protectionism
	6.3.3 The impact of exchange rate changes	• depreciation and appreciation of an exchange rate • how exchange rate changes can affect businesses as importers and exporters of products, for example, prices, competitiveness, profitability (*exchange rate calculations will not be assessed*).	**Student's Book** pp.387–392 **Teacher's Guide Activities** Activity 6.3.3: Categorising activity on exchange rates	exchange rate appreciation depreciation trade barriers protectionism imports exports balance of payments trading bloc common currency